This book is the first to be devoted to the music of Stravinsky's last compositional period. In the early 1950s, Stravinsky's compositional style began to change and evolve with astonishing rapidity. He abandoned the musical neo-classicism to which he had been committed for the preceding three decades and, with the stimulus provided by his newly gained knowledge of the music of Schoenberg and Webern, launched himself on a remarkable voyage of compositional discovery. The book focuses on five historical, analytical, and interpretive issues: Stravinsky's relationship to his serial predecessors and contemporaries; his compositional process; the problem of creating formal continuity in a repertoire so obviously discontinuous in so many ways; the problem of writing serial harmony; and the problem of expression and meaning. Challenging conventional interpretations, the book shows that Stravinsky's serial music is not only of great historical significance, but also of astonishing structural originality and emotional power.

JOSEPH N. STRAUS is Professor of Music at Queens College and Graduate Center, City University of New York. He has written widely on topics in twentieth-century music and is the author of *Remaking the Past* (1990), *The Music of Ruth Crawford Seeger* (Cambridge University Press, 1995), and *Introduction to Post-Tonal Theory* (second edition, 2000).

CAMBRIDGE STUDIES IN MUSIC THEORY AND ANALYSIS

GENERAL EDITOR: IAN BENT

This series is designed for those absorbed by the theoretical and intellectual issues of music, whether as historians of ideas, as practical analysts, or as theoreticians. It includes full-length analyses of works; scholarly translations of major theoretical texts, with editorial commentary; studies in the history of theory; and newly formulated theoretical constructs.

Published titles

1 Haydn's "Farewell" Symphony and the Idea of Classical Style
Through Composition and Cyclic Integration in His Instrumental Music
James Webster

2 Ernst Kurth: Selected Writings
ed. and trans. Lee A. Rothfarb

3 The Musical Dilettante
A Treatise on Composition by J. F. Daube
ed. and trans. Susan Snook Luther

4 Rameau and Musical Thought in the Enlightenment
Thomas Christensen

5 The Masterwork in Music
Volume I (1925)
Heinrich Schenker
ed. William Drabkin

6 Mahler's Sixth Symphony
A Study in Musical Semiotics
Robert Samuels

7 Aesthetics and the Art of Musical Composition in the German Enlightenment
Selected Writings of Johann Georg Sulzer and Heinrich Christoph Koch
ed. and trans. Nancy Kovaleff Baker and Thomas Christensen

8 The Masterwork in Music
Volume II (1926)
Heinrich Schenker
ed. William Drabkin

9 Schenker's Argument and the Claims of Music Theory
Leslie David Blasius

10 The Masterwork in Music
Volume III (1930)
Heinrich Schenker
ed. William Drabkin

11 Schenker's Interpretive Practice
    Robert Snarrenberg

12 Musical Form in the Age of Beethoven
    A. B. Marx
    ed. and trans. Scott Burnham

13 Franz Schubert: Sexuality, Subjectivity, Song
    Lawrence Kramer

14 Reading Renaissance Music Theory
    Hearing with the Eyes
    Cristle Collins Judd

15 Gendering Musical Modernism
    The Music of Ruth Crawford, Marion Bauer, and Miriam Gideon
    Ellie M. Hisama

16 Stravinsky's Late Music
    Joseph N. Straus

STRAVINSKY'S
LATE MUSIC

JOSEPH N. STRAUS

CAMBRIDGE
UNIVERSITY PRESS

PUBLISHED BY THE PRESS SYNDICATE OF THE UNIVERSITY OF CAMBRIDGE
The Pitt Building, Trumpington Street, Cambridge, United Kingdom

CAMBRIDGE UNIVERSITY PRESS
The Edinburgh Building, Cambridge CB2 2RU, UK
40 West 20th Street, New York, NY 10011-4211, USA
10 Stamford Road, Oakleigh, VIC 3166, Australia
Ruiz de Alarcón 13, 28014 Madrid, Spain
Dock House, The Waterfront, Cape Town 8001, South Africa

http://www.cambridge.org

First published 2001

Printed in the United Kingdom at the University Press, Cambridge

Typeface Monotype Bembo 11/13 pt.   *System* QuarkXPress™ [SE]

A catalogue record for this book is available from the British Library

Library of Congress Cataloguing in Publication data
Straus, Joseph Nathan.
Stravinsky's late music / Joseph N. Straus.
p.   cm. – (Cambridge studies in music theory and analysis ; 16)
Includes bibliographical references (p.) and index.
ISBN 0 521 80220 2 (hardback)
1. Stravinsky, Igor, 1882–1971 – Criticism and interpretation.   I. Title.   II. Series.
ML410.S932 S72 2001
780′.02–dc21   00–046733

ISBN 0 521 80220 2 hardback

for Michael and Adam

CONTENTS

Foreword by Ian Bent   *page* xi
Preface   xiii
List of abbreviations   xvii

1 Stravinsky and the serialists   1

2 Compositional process   42

3 Form   81

4 Harmony   141

5 Expression and meaning   183

List of Stravinsky's late works   249
Bibliography   250
Index   259

FOREWORD BY IAN BENT

Theory and analysis are in one sense reciprocals: if analysis opens up a musical structure or style to inspection, inventorying its components, identifying its connective forces, providing a description adequate to some live experience, then theory generalizes from such data, predicting what the analyst will find in other cases within a given structural or stylistic orbit, devising systems by which other works – as yet unwritten – might be generated. Conversely, if theory intuits how musical systems operate, then analysis furnishes feedback to such imaginative intuitions, rendering them more insightful. In this sense, they are like two hemispheres that fit together to form a globe (or cerebrum!), functioning deductively as investigation and abstraction, inductively as hypothesis and verification, and in practice forming a chain of alternating activities.

Professionally, on the other hand, "theory" now denotes a whole subdiscipline of the general field of musicology. Analysis often appears to be a subordinate category within the larger activity of theory. After all, there is theory that does not require analysis. Theorists may engage in building systems or formulating strategies for use by composers; and these almost by definition have no use for analysis. Others may conduct experimental research into the sound-materials of music or the cognitive processes of the human mind, to which analysis may be wholly inappropriate. And on the other hand, historians habitually use analysis as a tool for understanding the classes of compositions – repertories, "outputs," "periods," works, versions, sketches, and so forth – that they study. Professionally, then, our ideal image of twin hemispheres is replaced by an intersection: an area that exists in common between two subdisciplines. Seen from this viewpoint, analysis reciprocates in two directions: with certain kinds of theoretical enquiry, and with certain kinds of historical enquiry. In the former case, analysis has tended to be used in rather orthodox modes, in the latter in a more eclectic fashion; but that does not mean that analysis in the service of theory is necessarily more exact, more "scientific," than analysis in the service of history.

The above epistemological excursion is by no means irrelevant to the present series. Cambridge Studies in Music Theory and Analysis is intended to present the work of theorists and of analysts. It has been designed to include "pure" theory – that is, theoretical formulation with a minimum of analytical exemplification; "pure" analysis – that is, practical analysis with a minimum of theoretical underpinning; and writings that fall at points along the spectrum between the two extremes. In these capacities, it aims to illuminate music, as work and as process.

However, theory and analysis are not the exclusive preserves of the present day. As subjects in their own right, they are diachronic. The former is coeval with the very study of music itself, and extends far beyond the confines of Western culture; the latter, defined broadly, has several centuries of past practice. Moreover, they have been dynamic, not static fields throughout their histories. Consequently, studying earlier music through the eyes of its own contemporary theory helps us to escape (when we need to, not that we should make a dogma out if it) from the pre-conceptions of our own age. Studying earlier analyses does this too, and in a particularly sharply focused way; at the same time it gives us the opportunity to re-evaluate past analytical methods for present purposes, such as is happening currently, for example, with the long-despised methods of hermeneutic analysis of the late nineteenth century. The series thus includes editions and translations of major works of past theory, and also studies in the history of theory.

In the present volume, Joseph Straus brings Stravinsky's late works out from the shadow of the Second Viennese School. He enables us finally and definitively to view these works – stretching from 1952 to 1968, three years before the composer's death – in their own right, as a separate strain of musical modernism that is only now coming to full recognition and appreciation. These are works of great warmth and immediacy: brilliant, vivid, and at the same time deeply expressive. At their best – for example, in the ballet *Agon* (1957), and the choral *Requiem Canticles* (1966) – they stand among the greatest artistic products of the twentieth century.

Straus offers a radical challenge to the received wisdom about these late works, confronting in particular the relationship of their musical language to that of Stravinsky's earlier works; their intrinsic aesthetic; and the supposed subservience of their serial method to the methods of Schoenberg, Webern, Krenek, and others. Straus's account is unfailingly approachable. He first takes us through the final period of Stravinsky's life and the musical personalities with whom the composer was associated. He then initiates us into Stravinsky's methods of working, and his engagement with the texts that he set to music. His accounts of the technicalities of composition are never dry or abstruse. In his final chapter, he takes on issues of expression and meaning in this music, dealing fascinatingly with musical symbolism, historical reference, and musical topoi. In so doing, he overturns the accepted view of Stravinsky as an "anti-expressive" composer, and reveals his music to be, on the contrary, rich in expressive gesture and filled with latent meaning. Indeed, he shows that in these late works Stravinsky developed a new musical language, powerfully expressive and at times movingly emotional. As a result, he offers us a new way in which to hear such glorious works as the *Cantata* on late-medieval English verse (1952), *Canticum sacrum* (1955), and the magnificent set of Lamentations of Jeremiah entitled *Threni* (1958).

PREFACE

In the early 1950s, Stravinsky's compositional style began to change and evolve with astonishing rapidity. He abandoned the musical neoclassicism to which he had been committed for the preceding three decades and, with the stimulus provided by his newly gained knowledge of the music of Schoenberg and Webern, launched himself on a remarkable voyage of compositional discovery. The last sixteen years of his active compositional life, from the *Cantata* of 1952 to the *Requiem Canticles* of 1966, comprised a surprising second spring, a late flowering of compositional activity. During that period, Stravinsky wrote twenty new compositions, of which twelve may be considered major by virtue of their length and scope. Their quality varies, but among them are works that rival anything he ever wrote in originality, vitality, structural richness, and expressive power. This book is the first to be devoted to Stravinsky's late music.

My approach is not chronological and the coverage is not comprehensive. Rather, I have chosen to focus on five historical, analytical, and interpretive issues that strike me as particularly interesting or pressing. In the process of addressing these issues, however, I do discuss all of the works from Stravinsky's late period, many in considerable detail.

In Chapter 1, I place Stravinsky in the context of music by his twelve-tone predecessors (Schoenberg and Webern) and contemporaries (Krenek, Boulez, and Babbitt) in order to evaluate the extent of their influence on him. I also consider the influence on his late music of his own earlier music. In Chapter 2, I describe Stravinsky's compositional process during this late period. In the course of this discussion, I make extensive use of compositional sketches and manuscripts, only recently available to scholars and, for the most part, not previously discussed in print. In Chapter 3, I address the question of formal combination in Stravinsky's late music, the problem of combining musical units to create coherent wholes. Chapter 4 deals with the vexing question of writing meaningful harmonies in a musical style that is essentially contrapuntal. Finally, Chapter 5 takes up perhaps the most difficult question in musical interpretation, and particularly in the interpretation of apparently autonomous instrumental works, namely the question of expression and meaning.

Although they focus on different aspects of Stravinsky's late work, the five chapters of this book share a commitment to six overarching ideas, each of which challenges conventional interpretations:

1 STRAVINSKY IN RELATION TO HIS SERIAL PREDECESSORS

In the conventional view, Stravinsky's serial music is weakly derivative of the music of other composers, Webern in particular. I will demonstrate, on the contrary, its striking originality, emphasizing what distinguishes Stravinsky's works from those of Schoenberg and Webern. In the process, I will show that Stravinsky's serial music provides a critique of Schoenberg's and Webern's. Even as he adopts their serial point of departure, he writes music that implicitly satirizes theirs.

2 STRAVINSKY IN RELATION TO HIS OWN EARLIER MUSIC

In the conventional view, Stravinsky's late music, despite its serialism, is not all that different from his earlier music, particularly by virtue of its continuing interest in harmonies derived from the octatonic scale. While there is some truth in the cliché that Stravinsky always sounds like Stravinsky, nonetheless the late works differ radically from the earlier ones at every level, from their deep modes of musical formation to the rhythmic and intervallic details of the musical surface. In the face of this radical change, I will show that the links between Stravinsky's early and late music are both less and more significant than previously thought: less, because the late music does not, in fact, make much use of Stravinsky's traditional harmonic vocabulary, and what references there are diminish over the course of the period; more, because Stravinsky's late music does connect with his earlier music in demonstrable ways, and far more extensively than previously recognized, but these connections are largely beneath the surface. The connection to the earlier music involves a process of sublimation, attenuation, abstraction, and concealment. Musical gestures that had been overt move underground into the very substructures of the music. Everything is compressed, miniaturized, rarefied.

3 STRAVINSKY'S REASON FOR COMPOSING SERIALLY

Stravinsky had many reasons for so radically altering his compositional approach. Among these, the conventional view emphasizes the pressure he felt from the younger generation of avant-garde serial composers (including Babbitt and Boulez) and his own desire to appear *au courant*. In this view, Stravinsky's turn to serialism is a sign of his weakness and susceptibility. I will show, however, that whatever his initial impulse, Stravinsky's commitment to the serial approach had deep musical and psychological roots in his life-long interest in imposing severe limitations on the compositional enterprise.

Throughout his career, but particularly in the late period, Stravinsky sought various kinds of limitations on his field of activity, strictures and rules to give the musical enterprise shape and definition. Most of the late works are musical settings of written texts, which impose welcome musical restrictions at all levels, from the larger forms to the surface rhythms. The serialization of pitch played a similar role, providing a starting point and a framework for free compositional play. Stravinsky adopted the serial approach not in spite of the limitations it imposed on the nature and flow of musical ideas but rather precisely because of those limitations.

4 EXPRESSIVE POWER

In the conventional view, Stravinsky's music tends to be arid and anti-expressive, and this is particularly true of the late works, with their elaborate serial schemes. I will show, however, that his late works, like his earlier ones, are richly expressive of a variety of dramatic situations and human emotions. Indeed, many of Stravinsky's most striking technical innovations during this period, particularly in the realm of serial harmony, emerged in response to particular expressive needs.

5 CONTINUITY AND DISCONTINUITY

A familiar modernist critique holds that Stravinsky's music is too disjointed, too discontinuous, too inorganic in its construction to achieve the structural depth and integration of great musical masterworks. The independence of its constituent parts, their high degree of self-insulation and self-enclosure, seems to preclude the possibility of cohering into meaningful larger wholes. More recently, critics with a post-modernist leaning have celebrated the same discontinuities, linking this aspect of Stravinsky's music to developments in post-war music, including "moment form." But both the modernist critique and the post-modernist celebration are fundamentally unbalanced, and for the same reason: they unfairly downplay the musical connections among the musical "moments," the powerful ties that bind the disparate sections.

It is beyond debate that Stravinsky's music, including his late music, is highly sectionalized, built up from discrete, static blocks. Indeed, that sectionalization is one of the most distinctive features of his music, one of the defining elements of the distinctive Stravinskian sound. The music deploys strong centripetal forces, with each of the formal units asserting its own independence and integrity. But the centrifugal forces are equally strong, holding the sections together. The result in Stravinsky's music is not the gentle harmonious reconciliation of opposing tendencies, but rather a furious tension, at all levels, between the forces of integration and disintegration. What emerges is a kind of inorganic musical coherence. Stravinsky's music gives no sense of spontaneous growth from a single seed, of a seamless fabric, a single improvisatory sweep. Its jagged edges are everywhere apparent but, as I shall argue, the forces of abruption are everywhere balanced by equally strong forces that bind the music together.

6 MUSICAL QUALITY

The serial music of Stravinsky's final compositional period is a repertoire worth studying and celebrating. For its historical significance (as a manifestation of post-

war compositional trends), its biographical interest (as an astonishing stylistic reorientation by the dominant composer of the twentieth century), and its intrinsic
power, this music demands and rewards close study. Scholars and performers have
tended to ignore or slight it in favor of the early ballets and well-known neoclassical
works. I will show, however, that Stravinsky's late music includes works as structurally challenging and rich, and as expressively powerful and moving, as any he
ever wrote.

In writing this book, I had the benefit of guidance and criticism from a number of
friends and colleagues. Two eminent Stravinskians, Lynne Rogers and David
Smyth, read the entire manuscript and made numerous valuable suggestions for
revision, generously sharing unpublished results of their current research. I am
deeply grateful to them. Wayne Alpern also read the entire manuscript and, in
matters of both style and content, helped shape it very much for the better.
Christoph Neidhofer generously shared information about Stravinsky's compositional sketches. I also received useful advice from my fellow members of the
Princeton Theory Group: Kofi Agawu, Scott Burnham, and Chris Hasty. Jeffrey
Kresky offered valuable guidance at an early stage, while Ian Bent offered welcome
polish as it neared completion. Students in seminars at Harvard University and the
Graduate Center of the City University of New York also helped to shape this
book, as did the students and faculty who attended colloquia and presentations on
Stravinsky's late music at Indiana University, The Hartt School, Rutgers University,
Pennsylvania State University, and the University of Kentucky-Lexington. I did
much of the work during a leave supported by a Presidential Research Award at
Queens College. The musical examples were expertly prepared by David Smey,
supported by a research award from the Research Foundation of the City
University of New York. At Cambridge University Press, Penny Souster supported
the project from its inception while Lucy Carolan refined and guided it into print.
As always, my deepest gratitude goes to Sally Goldfarb, peerless advisor and companion.

Excerpts from Stravinsky's compositional sketches reprinted by permission of the
Paul Sacher Foundation (Igor Stravinsky Collection) where the source material is
preserved. Excerpts from Arnold Schoenberg, Suite, Op. 29 and Wind Quintet
used by permission of Belmont Music Publishers. Excerpts from Anton Webern,
Quartet for Violin, Clarinet, Saxophone, and Piano, Op. 22 and Variations for
Orchestra, Op. 30 used by permission of European-American Music Distributors
Corporation, sole US and Canadian agent for Universal Edition A. G., Vienna.
Excerpts from Igor Stravinsky, *Anthem, Cantata, Canticum Sacrum, Double Canon,
Elegy for J. F. K., Epitaphium, Fanfare for a New Theater, The Flood, In Memoraim Dylan
Thomas, Introitus, Movements, Orpheus, The Rake's Progress, Requiem Canticles, Septet,
A Sermon, a Narrative, and a Prayer, Three Shakespeare Songs, Threni, Variations*
reprinted by permission of Boosey & Hawkes, Inc.

ABBREVIATIONS

Avec Stravinsky	Robert Craft, *Avec Stravinsky* (Monaco: Editions du Rocher, 1958)
Bravo Stravinsky	Robert Craft, *Bravo Stravinsky*, photographed by Arnold Newman, text by Robert Craft (Cleveland: World Publishing Corp, 1967)
Chronicle	Robert Craft, *Stravinsky: Chronicle of a Friendship 1948–1971* (New York: Knopf, 1972; revised and expanded edn. Nashville: Vanderbilt University Press, 1994)
Conversations	Igor Stravinsky and Robert Craft, *Conversations with Igor Stravinsky* (New York: Doubleday, 1959; reprint edn. Berkeley: University of California Press, 1980)
Dialogues	Igor Stravinsky and Robert Craft, *Dialogues* (London: Faber and Faber, 1982; Berkeley: University of California Press, 1982)
Dialogues and a Diary	Igor Stravinsky and Robert Craft, *Dialogues and a Diary* (New York: Doubleday, 1963)
Expositions and Developments	Igor Stravinsky and Robert Craft, *Expositions and Developments* (New York: Doubleday, 1962; reprint edn. Berkeley: University of California Press, 1982)
Glimpses of a Life	Robert Craft, *Stravinsky: Glimpses of a Life* (New York: St. Martin's Press, 1992)
Memories and Commentaries	Igor Stravinsky and Robert Craft, *Memories and Commentaries* (New York: Doubleday, 1960, reprint edn. Berkeley: University of California Press, 1981)
Pictures and Documents	Robert Craft and Vera Stravinsky, *Stravinsky in Pictures and Documents* (New York: Simon and Schuster, 1978)
Poetics	Igor Stravinsky, *Poetics of Music in the Form of Six Lessons*, trans. Arthur Knodel and Ingolf Dahl

	(Cambridge, Mass.: Harvard University Press, 1970)
Present Perspectives	Robert Craft, *Present Perspectives: Critical Writings* (New York: Alfred A. Knopf, 1984)
Selected Correspondence	*Stravinsky: Selected Correspondence*, ed. Robert Craft, 3 vols. (New York: Alfred A. Knopf, 1982–85)
Themes and Conclusions	Igor Stravinsky and Robert Craft, *Themes and Conclusions* (Berkeley: University of California Press, 1982)
Themes and Episodes	Igor Stravinsky and Robert Craft, *Themes and Episodes* (New York: Alfred A. Knopf, 1966)

1

STRAVINSKY AND THE SERIALISTS

STRAVINSKY IN AMERICA

Stravinsky came to America in September 1939, one step ahead of the conflagration that was to engulf Europe, with the limited intention of fulfilling some concert engagements and delivering the Norton Lectures at Harvard University. But, apart from extensive travels abroad after the war, he remained in America until his death in 1971. His emigration, with its attendant cultural and linguistic dislocation, led eventually to a radical reorientation of his music.

At the time of his arrival in America, Stravinsky was undoubtedly the most famous and successful composer of the day, but the war sharply reduced the scope of his musical activities, both as a composer and conductor. This was a difficult period for Stravinsky, both financially and artistically. He supported himself primarily by conducting, and by accepting a series of artistically inconsequential commissions:

During the Second World War, when his European royalties were nonexistent and his [American royalties] were in three figures, Stravinsky was better known in America as a conductor than as a composer. During the forties, too, the kind of commission that Stravinsky sought and often accepted reflects these straitened financial circumstances. In pursuit of a popular, paying success, or an acceptable film, for which he would write a do-it-once-and-retire score, he was forever chasing wild geese, among them Paul Whiteman, Billy Rose, Woody Herman, and Sam Goldwyn. His most spectacular flops in this sense . . . were in fact openly aimed at the commercial market. As a result, the Stravinsky *Köchelverzeichnis* contains too many tiny, if genial, masterpieces-for-money – the Preludium, Circus Polka, Norwegian Moods, Scherzo à la russe, Babel – and too few larger works, or works born purely of inner necessity.[1]

This was also a period of relative social isolation for Stravinsky. He had not yet become an active participant in the cultural or social life of his adopted country.

---

[1] "The Relevance and Problems of Biography," in *Glimpses of a Life*, 278. *Scherzo à la Russe* (1944) was commissioned by Paul Whiteman for his band. *Scènes de Ballet* was commissioned by Billy Rose for a Broadway show he produced called *Seven Lively Arts*, which ran at the Ziegfeld Theater in New York from December 7, 1944 to May 12, 1945. *Ebony Concerto* (1946) was written for and premiered by Woody Herman and his band. The middle movement of *Ode* (1943) had originally been intended as music for the hunting scene in the Orson Welles film *Jane Eyre* – this was one of several inconclusive engagements with the film industry. For an account of the genesis of these works, see *Pictures and Documents*, 356–77.

Rather, after he settled in Los Angeles, he was immersed in a large circle of European émigrés, speaking Russian and French almost exclusively – his English was still poor. He was isolated from Europe by living in America, and isolated from America by living within a small European émigré community.

The isolation extended as well to Stravinsky's musical horizons. During his early American years he remained, as he had in the inter-war years in France, wilfully ignorant of the music of Schoenberg, Webern, and Berg and their musical descendants. Even as interest in these composers grew in the musical world, both among his contemporaries and among younger composers, and even though he lived a few miles away from his fellow émigré, Schoenberg, Stravinsky maintained an attitude of haughty distaste. His artistic cocoon later ruptured with surprising, almost violent, suddenness.

Stravinsky's definitive emergence from the isolation of the war and post-war years came with the composition of *The Rake's Progress*. This brilliant, Mozartean opera was Stravinsky's first setting of a text in English – an extraordinarily beautiful libretto by W. H. Auden and Chester Kallman. The opera had its premiere in Venice in 1951 and was performed at major opera houses throughout the world in the years that followed. It was warmly received (except among young composers of the musical avant-garde) and returned Stravinsky to a position of international prominence, which he maintained for the rest of his life. *The Rake's* brilliant evocation and transformation of eighteenth-century operatic conventions mark it as the masterpiece and culmination of Stravinsky's brand of musical neoclassicism. It also marked a decisive turning point in Stravinsky's career, and provoked a personal and artistic crisis.

By the spring of 1952, Stravinsky had reached the end of the neoclassical road he had traveled since *Pulcinella* in 1920. He came to consider *The Rake's Progress*, for all of its brilliance and success, an artistic dead end, and lost interest in composing another in the same vein.[2] He had become aware of the low value placed on his music by outspoken members of the younger generation of avant-garde composers, and he had begun, for the first time, to acquaint himself with the music of Schoenberg and Webern, to whom younger composers were unfavorably comparing him. Craft describes the growing sense of strain, the crisis, and its immediate aftermath:

The Rake's Progress was regarded by most critics as the work of a master but also a throwback, the last flowering of a genre. After the premiere, conducting concerts in Italy and Germany,

---

[2] After the success of *The Rake's Progress*, Stravinsky discussed with Auden the possibility of another operatic collaboration. In January 1952, Stravinsky described the early stages of the proposed collaboration: "I had time before leaving New York to fix with Auden the main lines of an opera in one act . . . Auden is 'blue-printing' the libretto, and he will complete it with Kallman when the latter (whose collaboration is very valuable) will be back. The theme is. . . a celebration of Wisdom in a manner comparable to Ben Jonson's Masques. Nevertheless, we will not stick to any set style musically or otherwise. The opera will require about six characters; a small chorus, a chamber ensemble of about 18; several tableaux" (letter to Boosey & Hawkes, January 8, 1952; reprinted in *Pictures and Documents*, 204). The libretto was completed and titled *Delia*, but Stravinsky never wrote a note of music for it.

Stravinsky found that he and Schoenberg were everywhere categorized as the reactionary and the progressive. What was worse, Stravinsky was acutely aware that the new generation was not interested in the *Rake*. While in Cologne, he heard tapes of Schoenberg's Violin Concerto (played by Tibor Varga) and of the Darmstadt performance of "The Golden Calf" (from *Moses and Aaron*); he listened attentively to both, expressing no reaction . . . In contrast, a few days later, in Baden-Baden, when a recording of Webern's orchestra Variations was played for him, he asked to hear it three times in succession and showed more enthusiasm than I had ever seen from him about any contemporary music . . . Then, on February 24, 1952, at the University of Southern California, I conducted a performance of Schoenberg's *Septet-Suite* (in a program with Webern's Quartet, Opus 22), with Stravinsky present at all the rehearsals as well as the concert. This event was the turning point in his later musical evolution . . . On March 8, he asked to go for a drive to Palmdale, at that time a small Mojave Desert town . . . On the way home he startled us, saying that he was afraid he could no longer compose and did not know what to do. For a moment, he broke down and actually wept . . . He referred obliquely to the powerful impression that the Schoenberg piece [Septet-Suite, Op. 29] had made on him, and when he said that he wanted to learn more, I knew that the crisis was over; so far from being defeated, Stravinsky would emerge a new composer.[3]

Craft gave a slightly different version of the story in 1994, omitting the actual shedding of tears and emphasizing even more emphatically the impact on Stravinsky of Schoenberg's music:

We drove to Palmdale for lunch, spareribs in a cowboy-style restaurant, Bordeaux from I. S.'s thermos. A powdering of snow is in the air, and, at higher altitudes, on the ground. Angelenos stop their cars and go out to touch it. During the return, I. S. startles us, saying he fears he can no longer compose; for a moment he actually seems ready to weep. V[era] gently, expertly, assures him that whatever the difficulties, they will soon pass. He refers obliquely to the Schoenberg Septet and the powerful impression it has made on him. After 40 years of dismissing Schoenberg as "experimental," "theoretical," "démodé," he is suffering the shock of recognition that Schoenberg's music is richer in substance than his own.[4]

The discrepancy between the accounts inevitably raises the question of Craft's reliability as a reporter. His intimate involvement in all aspects of Stravinsky's life makes him an extraordinarily valuable source of information. He was there, and possessed the musical skills and keen intelligence to make sense of all that was happening around him. At the same time, he is not an unbiased reporter. His own personal interests seem to intrude from time to time, and I will try to take note when this happens. In the accounts of Stravinsky's near-breakdown in Palmdale, however, the essence of the story is the same in both cases, and I see no reason to question its fundamental accuracy.

Stravinsky himself described the episode several years later in more dispassionate terms:

---

[3] "Influence or Assistance?," in *Present Perspectives*, 251–53.

[4] *Chronicle* (revised and expanded edn. Nashville: Vanderbilt University Press, 1994). Strangely, the original edition of the *Chronicle* (New York: Knopf, 1972) had no entry for this date.

I have had to survive two crises as a composer, though as I continued to move from work to work I was not aware of either of them as such, or, indeed, of any momentous change. The first – the loss of Russia and its language of words as well as of music – affected every circumstance of my personal no less than my artistic life, which made recovery more difficult . . . Crisis number two was brought on by the natural outgrowing of the special incubator in which I wrote *The Rake's Progress* (which is why I did not use Auden's beautiful *Delia* libretto; I could not continue in the same strain, could not compose a sequel to *The Rake*, as I would have had to do).[5]

The crisis led Stravinsky to a dramatic stylistic reorientation. From this point forward, his music engaged, tentatively at first and then with growing individuality and confidence, the serial and twelve-tone thinking of Schoenberg and Webern. From a technical, music-constructivist point of view, his works after *The Rake's Progress* describe a remarkable succession of firsts, including his first works to use a series (*Cantata* [1952], Septet [1953], *Three Songs from William Shakespeare* [1954]); his first fully serial work (*In Memoriam Dylan Thomas* [1954]); his first work to use a twelve-tone series (*Agon* [1954–7]); his first work to include a complete twelve-tone movement ("Surge, aquilo," from *Canticum Sacrum* [1956]); his first completely twelve-tone work (*Threni* [1958]); his first work to make use of twelve-tone arrays based on hexachordal rotation (*Movements* [1959]); his first work to use the verticals of his rotational arrays (*A Sermon, a Narrative, and a Prayer* [1961]); his first work to rotate the series as a whole (*Variations* [1965]); his first work to rotate the tetrachords of the series (*Introitus* [1965]); and his first work to use two different series in conjunction (*Requiem Canticles* [1966] – his last major work). And, even apart from the technicalities of their pitch construction, the works of this period are strikingly original in their sheer impact, by virtue of their unusual forms and rhythms and their striking timbral juxtapositions.

The pattern of innovation is remarkable, persistent, and unprecedented. No other major composer, at a comparably advanced age and pinnacle of recognition

---

[5] *Themes and Episodes*, 23. The authenticity of the Stravinsky–Craft dialogues is open to question. It is not always entirely clear that the words attributed to Stravinsky are, in fact, his own. Craft himself has been somewhat ambiguous on this subject. In some accounts, he claims that Stravinsky does speak in his own words in the dialogues, as opposed to earlier works like the *Poetics* and the *Autobiography*: "Apart from programme notes and 'open' letters, the 'conversation books' are the only published writings attributed to Stravinsky that are very largely by him. Unlike the entirely ghosted *Poétique musicale* and *Chroniques de ma vie*, the pamphlet on Pushkin and the essay on Diaghilev, most of the 'conversations' – for which many of the manuscript and typescript drafts survive – were in fact written or dictated by the composer" ("Conversations with Stravinsky," in *Glimpses of a Life*, 61). In others, he acknowledges a more active role: "I would lean over [Stravinsky's] shoulder as he wrote, each of us acting as the other's intercessory, contributing words or phrases, suggesting changes, beginning sentences which the other would finish . . . In short, and presumptuous as it is for me to say so . . . a merger (exchange, symbiosis) *has* taken place between the senior and the junior, the creative and imitative components of our firm" (*Chronicle*, 374). For a thorough and highly critical assessment of Craft's role, see Kathryn Bailey, "The Craft/Stravinsky Conversation Books: Bibliography and Commentary," *Studies in Music (Ontario)* 3 (1978), 48–71. Bailey argues that, whatever the nature of the collaboration in the earlier dialogues (*Conversations*, *Memories and Commentaries*, and *Expositions and Developments*), "very little of the material attributed to Stravinsky after 1962 was written by him" (49). While I do plan to make use of the Craft–Stravinsky dialogues, I think it wise to do so with some reasonable skepticism about their ultimate authenticity.

and success, so thoroughly altered his compositional approach, or created late works that differ so greatly from his earlier ones. Furthermore, Stravinsky's late works are not only radically different from the earlier ones, but are highly individuated from each other as well. There is no major work in this period in which Stravinsky did not explore something new.

The result was an astonishing outpouring of music, remarkable for its sheer quantity as well as its ceaseless innovation, and all the more remarkable as the product of a man who was seventy years old at the time of the *Cantata* and eighty-four at the time of the *Requiem Canticles*. And, while the quality is uneven in certain respects, the late works include some of the finest that Stravinsky ever wrote. *Agon*, *Movements*, and *Requiem Canticles* are towering artistic achievements. *Abraham and Isaac*, *Introitus*, *Variations*, and *The Flood*, while less powerful, are nonetheless vivid and evocative. Even the comparably minor compositions of the period, such as the *Three Shakespeare Songs*, *In Memoriam Dylan Thomas*, and *Epitaphium*, are small compositional gems.

Yet, with the possible exception of *Agon*, now permanently in the repertory of the New York City Ballet, the works of Stravinsky's late period are rarely performed and little known. There are several reasons for the apparent neglect. First, these works pose intrinsic difficulties for both performers and listeners, owing both to their serial idiom and their striking originality. They are structurally complex and hermetic in some ways, and thus create the problems of comprehensibility and accessibility shared by many of the products of musical modernism. Second, most of the works in the late period are written for unusual combinations of instruments, and none for soloists or established ensembles like piano trio or string quartet. As a result, there have been few performer-advocates for this music, which is as awkward to program as it is challenging to perform. Finally, Stravinsky's late music has run afoul of changes in musical fashion. When it was written, serialism was at the cutting edge of musical taste, at least within a small community of interested composers, performers, and listeners. Even in its heyday, however, serialism was never more than a marginal phenomenon in American or European musical life. Serial works rarely penetrated the repertoires of established performers or ensembles, hardly attracted notice in the mass media, and scarcely entered the consciousness of most musical audiences.[6] So while Stravinsky's music fell, at the time, into an established niche, it was a niche very much at the periphery of the musical world. More recently, of course, serialism's star, never very high, has fallen into almost total eclipse, and Stravinsky's late music has suffered the same neglect as other serial works from the 1950s and 1960s. As a result, to paraphrase Milton Babbitt's quip about Schoenberg, Stravinsky's late music was never in fashion, and now it is neglected as old-fashioned.[7]

---

[6] For a discussion of the position of serialism in American musical life of this period, see Joseph N. Straus, "The Serial 'Tyranny' of the 1950's and 1960's," *The Musical Quarterly* 83/3 (1999), 301–43.

[7] Milton Babbitt, *Words About Music*, ed. Stephen Dembski and Joseph N. Straus (Madison: University of Wisconsin Press, 1987), 165.

The irony is that, even as Stravinsky began to write music that did not attract, and has not yet attracted, a broad audience, he was becoming an international celebrity, the first and still the only composer of classical music to become a media superstar. Apart from composing and performing his music, his life was consumed with endless interviews and television documentaries, attending parties and dinners, receiving honors and awards from presidents and monarchs. Amid the adulation, however, the musical path he had chosen was increasingly a lonely one.

To understand why Stravinsky abandoned the idiom that had made him so famous and successful, why he embarked on an arduous voyage of compositional discovery, never settling into a new pattern, and why he persisted in this voyage in the face of musical, social, and financial obstacles, it is necessary to understand him in relationship to other figures whose musical thinking bore directly on his own. Among these, the first and most important is Robert Craft.

CRAFT

In the summer of 1947, Robert Craft, then a 23-year-old aspiring composer and conductor, wrote to Stravinsky asking to borrow a copy of the score of the *Symphonies of Wind Instruments* for a concert he was planning.[8] Stravinsky's response, generously offering to participate in the concert himself, led to a close association that profoundly shaped the remainder of his personal and artistic life. From 1948 until the end of Stravinsky's life, Craft was a member of the household, living and traveling with Stravinsky and his wife. In one sense, Craft was simply a glorified "gofer," the last in a long line of musicians engaged by Stravinsky to help handle the complex logistics of his career.[9] But Craft was also an active and influential collaborator in all of Stravinsky's musical endeavors. He gradually took over more and more of Stravinsky's conducting duties. Craft shared concert programs with Stravinsky and led rehearsals for works Stravinsky conducted in concert or in recording sessions.[10] He also was Stravinsky's principal link to the English-speaking world and selected, or helped to select, the many English-language texts that Stravinsky set during the last decades of his life.

Craft's most important contribution, however, was to introduce Stravinsky to the music of Schoenberg and Webern. Until Craft arrived on the scene, Stravinsky had

[8] For Craft's own account of the origins and nature of his relationship with Stravinsky, see *Chronicle*, "A Personal Preface," *The Score* 20 (1957), 7–13; and "On a Misunderstood Collaboration: Assisting Stravinsky," *The Atlantic Monthly* (December 1982), 68; reprinted as "Influence or Assistance?" in *Present Perspectives*, 246–64; reprinted again in *Glimpses of a Life,* 33–51.

[9] Arthur Lourié and Nadia Boulanger are Craft's two best-known predecessors in this role. See *Selected Correspondence*, vol. I, 237–61, for letters to Boulanger requesting assistance with proofreading and similar relatively menial musical chores. In Chapter 2, I discuss the role of Claudio Spies in proofreading Stravinsky's final works for departures from his serial intentions.

[10] "Almost all their performances, both in concert and in the studio, through the 1950's and '60's were an inextricable blend of both their influences. Craft generally took the players through their first reading of the score when Stravinsky was due to conduct and the composer was normally on hand when it was Craft's turn to wield the baton" (Philip Stuart, *Igor Stravinsky – The Composer in the Recording Studio: A Comprehensive Discography* [New York: Greenwood, 1991], 16).

known virtually nothing of their music, although he was increasingly aware of their reputation among the younger generation of composers in Europe and America. According to Craft, "When I met Stravinsky, he did not know a single measure of music by Schoenberg, Berg, or Webern, had no copy in his library of any of their pieces, and did not understand the meaning of the word tone-row." [11]

Craft was one of the earliest and most effective performer-advocates of the music of Schoenberg and Webern in the United States.[12] As a result, Stravinsky was placed in close contact with music of extraordinary interest and power of which he had been almost entirely ignorant. The shock propelled him along the compositional path he followed for the rest of his life. As a conduit and exponent of this music, Craft's influence was of central importance for Stravinsky's development:

When I met Stravinsky, in the spring of 1948, his fortunes were at a low ebb. Most of his music was not in print, he was not recording, and concert organizations wanted him to conduct only *Firebird* and *Petrushka*. More important, he was becoming increasingly isolated from the developments that extended from Arnold Schoenberg and had attracted the young generation. Stravinsky was aware of this despite the acclaim for *Orpheus*, his latest composition, and if he wanted to understand the other music, he did not know how to go about it. I say in all candor that I provided the path and that I do not believe Stravinsky would ever have taken the direction he did without me. The music that he would otherwise have written is impossible to imagine.[13]

[Stravinsky] quickly saw that a member of a much younger generation, and a native American at that, could react in fresh and possibly stimulating ways. What must be admitted is that Stravinsky *wanted* to be influenced . . . In truth, every Stravinsky opus, after and including *Three Songs from William Shakespeare* (1953), was undertaken as a result of discussions between us. The texts of *A Sermon, a Narrative and a Prayer* were entirely my choice . . . Apart from subject matter, I sometimes went so far as to suggest forms that new pieces might take . . . Without me, Stravinsky would not have taken the path he did after *The Rake's Progress*. Those music lovers preferring another opera (Auden's *Delia*, perhaps), more pas de deux, and some additional concertos will feel that they have been cheated; others, admirers of *Abraham and Isaac*, of the *Variations* and *Requiem Canticles*, will thank me.[14]

Stravinsky was always generous in acknowledging the extent of his indebtedness to Craft, as in the following comment made near the end of his life:

---

[11] "Influence or Assistance?," in *Present Perspectives*, 261.

[12] Craft directed the first recordings of the complete works of Webern and most of Schoenberg's music, and also conducted music by Berg, Varèse, and Boulez. See Patrick J. Smith, "Robert Craft," in *The New Grove Dictionary of Music and Musicians*, ed. Stanley Sadie (London: Macmillan, 1980), vol. V, 17–18.

[13] "A Centenary View, Plus Ten," in *Glimpses of a Life*, 16–17.

[14] "Influence or Assistance?," in *Present Perspectives*, 259–60. Craft's claim that the texts for *A Sermon, a Narrative, and a Prayer* were entirely his choice should go some way toward exculpating Stravinsky from claims regarding their anti-Semitic content. See Robert Craft, "Jews and Geniuses," *New York Review of Books*, February 16, 1989, 35–37; reprinted in *Small Craft Advisories* (New York: Thames & Hudson, 1989), 274–81; Richard Taruskin and Robert Craft, "Jews and Geniuses: An Exchange," *New York Review of Books*, June 15, 1989, 57–58; and Richard Taruskin, "Stravinsky and the Subhuman," in *Defining Russia Musically: Historical and Hermeneutical Essays* (Princeton: Princeton University Press, 1997), 360–467. For a balanced assessment of Stravinsky's attitude toward Jews, see Stephen Walsh, *Stravinsky, A Creative Spring: Russia and France, 1882–1934* (New York: Alfred A. Knopf, 1999), 517–22 and passim.

We have been working together for twenty-three years . . . [Craft] introduced me to almost all of the new music I have heard in the past two decades . . . and not only to the new music but to the new everything else . . . The plain truth is that anyone who admires my *Agon*, my *Variations*, my *Requiem Canticles*, owes some gratitude to the man who has sustained my creative life these last years.[15]

It was obviously not in Craft's power to force Stravinsky to do anything. Stravinsky chose his own new compositional path and followed it with persistence, integrity, and astonishing originality for the remainder of his life. But it was certainly Craft who helped to reorient Stravinsky at the beginning of the new journey and assist his steps along the way.

I am thought of as a plenipotentiary, rather than a famulus, which is more often the case – along with satellite, court jester, and gray eminence who "operates" I. S. and is responsible for shanghaiing him into the "12-tone system" (as if anyone could even lead *that* horse to water, if it didn't want to go, let alone make it drink).[16]

Furthermore, Craft's own intellectual limitations restricted his ability to act as Stravinsky's guide beyond the initial introduction. Craft was a passionate and skilled performer of music by Schoenberg, Webern, and Boulez at a time when their music was virtually unknown to audiences and composers in America, very much including Stravinsky. Craft was in a position to introduce Stravinsky to this music, to impart some of his own enthusiasm, and to explain, in a rudimentary way, how it was put together. But Craft had no particular interest in theoretical abstractions. He apparently understood little of twelve-tone composition and twelve-tone theory beyond the basic facts of writing and manipulating a series. When Stravinsky entered the serial world, therefore, he did it essentially on his own, making things up as he went. And when he came to the point of creating his own distinctive and highly original twelve-tone structures, the rotational arrays of the 1960s, Craft had only a vague idea of what he was up to.[17] So Craft's role was crucial, particularly in the early stages, but limited. When Stravinsky began to write serial music, and especially when he began to write his own distinctive brand of twelve-tone serial music based on rotational arrays, he did so on his own, without significant guidance from Craft or anyone else.

SCHOENBERG

Prior to Stravinsky's awakening interest in Schoenberg's music in 1952, there had been a long history of animosity between the two composers. Stravinsky made some pointed and widely distributed remarks to journalists in the early 1920s,

---

[15] Letter to the Music Editor of the *Los Angeles Times*, June 23, 1970; reprinted in *Themes and Conclusions*, 216.

[16] *Chronicle*, 64.

[17] Craft rarely refers to the technical aspect of Stravinsky's serial music, and when he does, he often betrays a surprising lack of understanding. See, for example, his description of *Introitus* (*Pictures and Documents*, 474–76), which shows complete unawareness of the rotational arrays on which it is based. Stravinsky's habitual secrecy about his composing methods (see Chapter 2) would also have contributed to Craft's lack of understanding.

expressing his disdain for self-described "modernist" composers, "the gentlemen who work with formulas instead of ideas."[18] Schoenberg responded with his scathing essay, "Igor Stravinsky: *Der Restaurateur*" (1926) and the even more cutting *Three Satires*, Op. 28 (1925), a work whose music and text both mock Stravinsky's neoclassical orientation, although without explicitly naming him. Schoenberg's second *Satire* asks: "Why who could be drumming away there? If it isn't little Modernsky! He's had his pigtails cut. Looks pretty good! What authentic false hair! Like a peruke! Quite (as little Modernsky conceives of him), quite the Papa Bach!"[19] There could have been no doubt in Stravinsky's mind that he was the "little Modernsky" Schoenberg had in mind. The resulting bitterness, intensified by polemics from supporters on both sides, seemed to divide the musical world into two hostile camps.

This division persisted even when Schoenberg and Stravinsky became near-neighbors in Hollywood. Despite their physical proximity over a period of eleven years, from Stravinsky's arrival in Los Angeles in 1940 until Schoenberg's death in 1951, they never once met or spoke to each other. According to Craft,

When I first moved there Los Angeles was divided, like the rest of the musical world, into twin hegemonies of Stravinsky and Schoenberg . . .They were kept separate and isolated. Paris and Vienna had crossed the world with them, re-establishing small and exceedingly provincial Viennas and Parises separated by only ten miles of Hollywood's no-man's land, but as far apart as ever. Musicians came from all over the world to visit them, not mentioning to one composer their meetings with the other one.[20]

Leonard Stein, Schoenberg's close associate, describes a similar unbridgeable gulf between the two composers:

In 1934, Schoenberg came to Los Angeles. Two years later. . . he settled down in Brentwood Park, West Los Angeles, just north of Sunset Boulevard. Stravinsky arrived in Los Angeles around 1940 and found residence the following year in a house one block north of Sunset Boulevard – but ten miles east of Schoenberg's. However, they might as well have lived a thousand miles apart as far as social contacts were concerned. I believe they glimpsed each other on only a few occasions . . . What kept them apart was more a matter of cultural background, one that divided the community along national lines – the German-speaking Central Europeans on one side, the French and Russians on the other.[21]

---

[18] "I detest modern music . . . My music is not modern music nor is it music of the future. It is the music of today. One can't live in yesterday nor tomorrow . . . [The modernists are] the gentlemen who work with formulas instead of ideas. They have done that so much they have badly compromised that word 'modern.'" Cited in Scott Messing, *Neoclassicism in Music: From the Genesis of the Concept Through the Schoenberg/Stravinsky Polemic* (Ann Arbor: UMI Research Press, 1988), 141. Walsh, *Stravinsky, A Creative Spring*, 400 and 421–22, also offers a useful account of Stravinsky's remarks about "modern music" and Schoenberg's response.

[19] The text of the second *Satire* is reprinted and translated in Leonard Stein, "Schoenberg and 'Kleine Modernsky,'" in *Confronting Stravinsky: Man, Musician, and Modernist*, ed. Jann Pasler (Berkeley: University of California Press, 1986), 312. Schoenberg's essay, "Igor Stravinsky: *Der Restaurateur*," is reprinted in *Style and Idea*, ed. Leonard Stein, trans. Leo Black (Berkeley: University of California Press, 1984), 481–82. For full accounts of the Stravinsky–Schoenberg polemic and its musical consequences, see Stein, "Schoenberg and 'Kleine Modernsky'" and Messing, *Neoclassicism in Music*.

[20] Craft, "A Personal Preface," 12. See also "Influence or Assistance?," in *Present Perspectives*, 248–49.

[21] Stein, "Schoenberg and 'Kleine Modernsky,'" 314–15.

Stravinsky's sudden burst of interest in Schoenberg's music followed almost immediately upon Schoenberg's death. This has given rise to various psychologically oriented explanations, that Stravinsky had been fearful of engaging Schoenberg's music in his living presence, or that Stravinsky's interest in Schoenberg's music represented a sublimated expression of either grief or survivor-guilt upon Schoenberg's death.[22]

But there is a simpler, practical explanation: until the time of Schoenberg's death, his music was virtually unavailable in America. There were no recordings, extremely few performances, and even the scores themselves were difficult to obtain. This situation began to change in the early 1950s, in part through the efforts of Robert Craft.[23] When Schoenberg's music became available, and when there was someone around who could assist him in making sense of it, Stravinsky was willing to take a look, and became intrigued with what he found.

It is important to understand what Stravinsky learned, and did not learn, from Schoenberg. Stravinsky began almost immediately to adopt the essential Schoenbergian principle of serial ordering. That is, in the absence of the traditional organizing power of tonality (with its major and minor scales, its orientation toward a key, and its commitment to resolution of dissonance), music may be organized instead with respect to a predetermined arrangement of notes, that is, a series. Serial works draw their motivic, melodic, and harmonic substance from a series, which may vary in length. Stravinsky's early serial works employed series that consist of either fewer than twelve notes (*Cantata*, Septet [first movement], "Musick to heare" and "Full fadom five" from *Three Shakespeare Songs*, *In Memoriam Dylan Thomas*, *Agon* Pas-de-Quatre) or, allowing for repetitions, more than twelve (the second and third movements of the Septet). Only in portions of *Canticum Sacrum* (1956) and *Agon* (1957), and then in the entire vast expanse of *Threni* (1958), did Stravinsky begin to rely exclusively on twelve-tone series.

Whatever the length of the series, Stravinsky also began immediately to adopt another Schoenbergian principle, that the series, when presented in transposition, inversion, retrograde, or retrograde-inversion, retains its basic intervallic identity, and that series related by these transformations can be understood to constitute a homogeneous class. For Stravinsky, as for Schoenberg, the series–class, or row–class, provides the basic pitch material for a composition. More specifically, Stravinsky accepted from the outset the Schoenbergian idea that four members of the series–class, bound together by some particular musical relationship, might function as a referential norm, somewhat in the manner of a tonic region in a tonal composition. So not only the idea of a series, and a series–class, but also the

---

[22] See Mikhail Druskin, *Igor Stravinsky: His Personality, Works, and Views*, trans. Martin Cooper (Cambridge: Cambridge University Press, 1983). Druskin asks, "Had Schoenberg's death had such a deep effect on him? Had he in fact wished to study dodecaphonic methods earlier and had been embarrassed by the existence of a rival whose death alone could liberate him from this inhibition?" (141).

[23] "Perhaps Schoenberg's death did 'liberate' Stravinsky, but not in Druskin's 'psychological' sense. What really happened is that Schoenberg's music began to be performed only after his death – in those first few years, more of it by me, I am proud to say, than by anyone else" ("Influence or Assistance?," in *Present Perspectives*, 257).

possibility of establishing a kind of tonic area within the series-class, came directly from Schoenberg.

But while Stravinsky adopted Schoenberg's points of departure, he moved immediately in very different musical directions. In doing so, he simultaneously developed his own, highly original serial style and offered a strong, if implicit, critique of Schoenbergian serialism. From the very outset, Stravinsky simultaneously invokes and remakes Schoenberg.[24]

The *Cantata* and the Septet, Stravinsky's first post-*Rake* compositions, are also the first to bear the imprint of Stravinsky's new interest in Schoenbergian serialism, and of his vigorous compositional response:

"To-morrow Shall Be My Dancing Day" [from the *Cantata*] marks the first effect on Stravinsky of Schoenberg's serial principle, for, although cancrizans of the kind found in this Ricercar were employed centuries before, Stravinsky came to them here by way of his contemporary, having heard some of the Viennese master's music, as well as much discussion about it, in Europe in the autumn of 1951 . . . While composing "To-morrow Shall Be My Dancing Day," Stravinsky attended rehearsals, conducted by this writer, of Schoenberg's Septet-Suite. After the first of these, on February 12 [1952], Stravinsky asked numerous questions about the construction of the piece, as he did after rehearsals on the 17th, 20th, 21st, and 24th.[25]

The first notation for the second movement [of the Septet], the Passacaglia, is found on a sheet of eight-stave music paper, on one side of which is the series of Schoenberg's wind Quintet, in the hand of the present writer, together with a demonstration of the way in which Schoenberg deployed the twelve pitches harmonically; on the other side, Stravinsky has drawn the series of his Passacaglia, clearly using the Schoenberg as a model.[26]

Comparisons of these two pairs of compositions – Stravinsky's "Tomorrow Shall Be My Dancing Day" from the *Cantata* and Schoenberg's Septet-Suite, Op. 29; Schoenberg's Wind Quintet and Stravinsky's Septet – exemplifies Stravinsky's response to the challenge of Schoenberg's music. Example 1.1a contains a passage from Schoenberg's Septet-Suite Op. 29. The original, or "prime" ordering of the series on which the passage is based – consisting of all twelve tones with one statement of each – is shown in Example 1.1b. It is arranged so that its last six notes are the unordered inversion of its first six around the inversional axis that balances E♭ in the first hexachord against G♯ in the second, G in the first hexachord against E in the second, and so on.[27] As a result, when the series as a whole is inverted around

---

[24] My sense of Schoenberg's impact on Stravinsky is informed by Harold Bloom's well-known theory of poetic influence. For an adaptation of this theory for twentieth-century music, see Joseph N. Straus, *Remaking the Past: Musical Modernism and the Influence of the Tonal Tradition* (Cambridge, Mass.: Harvard University Press, 1990). See also Kevin Korsyn, "Towards a New Poetics of Musical Influence," *Music Analysis* 10/1–2 (1991), 3–72; Kevin Korsyn, "Directional Tonality and Intertextuality: Brahms's Quintet op. 88 and Chopin's Ballade op. 38," in *The Second Practice of Nineteenth-Century Tonality*, ed. William Kinderman and Harald Krebs (Lincoln: University of Nebraska Press, 1996), 45–83; and Wayne Petty, "Chopin and the Ghost of Beethoven," *19th-Century Music* 22/3 (1999), 281–99.   [25] *Pictures and Documents*, 422.   [26] Ibid.

[27] Inversional symmetry of this kind has been widely discussed in the theoretical literature. For an introduction to the subject, including "pitch-class clockfaces" like the one in Example 1.1b, see Joseph N. Straus, *Introduction to Post-Tonal Theory* (2nd edn., Upper Saddle River, NJ: Prentice-Hall, 2000), 39–47, 78–79, and 127–33.

Example 1.1   Schoenberg, Suite Op. 29: (a) mm. 1–4, with series-forms identified; (b) P-form of series, with inversional symmetry around B/C, B♭/D♭, A/D, G♯/E♭, G/E, and F♯/F; (c) P and I, with hexachords exchanged and tetrachords retained

the same axis, producing the I-form beginning on G♯, the two hexachords switch places (see Example 1.1c).[28] In addition, in this particular case, the three discrete segmental tetrachords of the series remain intact. The P-form starting on E♭, the I-form starting on G♯, and their retrogrades, comprise the basic, "tonic" twelve-tone area for this piece, and make up the entire substance of this passage.[29]

The beginning of Stravinsky's "Tomorrow Shall Be My Dancing Day" is shown in Example 1.2a. There are significant similarities and differences between the two passages. As in Schoenberg's Septet-Suite, Op. 29, Stravinsky's melodic line is also based on a series and consists entirely of four basic forms: a P-form that begins on E; its retrograde (labeled R); its inversion beginning on C (this is the inversion that exchanges C and E, and balances around D); and the retrograde of the inversion (labeled RI). As in the Schoenberg, the series is also marked by significant internal inversional symmetry. In this case, it is nearly symmetrical around D – only the E♭ lacks its inversional partner (see Example 1.2b). And, again as in the Schoenberg, that internal symmetry is the basis for the creation of a "tonic" area. The inversion of the entire series around D creates an almost complete duplication of content: five of the six different notes of the series are present also in its inversion (see Example 1.2c). In each of these ways – reliance on a series and exploitation of inversional symmetry as a basis for combining series forms – Stravinsky has apparently borrowed from Schoenberg.

But the differences are far more telling than the similarities. First, whereas Schoenberg's series is twelve notes long and contains one statement of each of the twelve pitch-classes, Stravinsky's series is only eleven notes long and, because of repetitions, contains only six different notes: B, C, D, E♭, E, and F. Because it has fewer than twelve different notes, its pitch content changes when it is transposed or inverted, unlike a Schoenbergian twelve-tone series where only the order of the notes changes with transposition or inversion. When Stravinsky's series is inverted around D, five of the notes stay the same, while C♯ replaces E♭. As a result, the entire melody, which combines all four forms of the series, involves only seven different notes: B–C–C♯–D–E♭–E–F. There is a great deal of repetition in the melody. One has the sense of a static incantation within a narrow compass rather than, as in the Schoenberg, an endless, open-ended flow of developing variation.

Furthermore, Stravinsky's melody maintains a strong key feeling of C major. It centers on the interval C–E, within which the E♭ is felt as a minor inflection of the E and the C♯ as a chromatic passing note. The principal melodic framework

---

[28] This property is known as "hexachordal inversional combinatoriality" and is a defining characteristic of Schoenberg's mature twelve-tone style. There is an extensive theoretical literature on this subject. For an account of its evolution in Schoenberg's music and thought, see Ethan Haimo, *Schoenberg's Serial Odyssey: The Evolution of His Twelve-Tone Method, 1914–1928* (London: Oxford University Press, 1990).

[29] On Schoenberg's twelve-tone "areas," see David Lewin, "Inversional Balance as an Organizing Force in Schoenberg's Music and Thought," *Perspectives of New Music* 6/2 (1968), 1–21; "*Moses und Aron*: Some General Remarks, and Analytic Notes for Act I, Scene 1," *Perspectives of New Music* 6/1 (1967), 1–17; and "A Study of Hexachord Levels in Schoenberg's Violin Fantasy," *Perspectives of New Music* 6/1 (1967), 18–32.

Example 1.2 Stravinsky, *Cantata*, Ricercar II, "Tomorrow Shall Be My Dancing Day"
(a) mm. 1–8, with series-forms identified

(a)

Example 1.2 (*cont.*)
(b) P-form of the series, with inversional symmetry around D
(c) P- and I-forms related by inversion around D

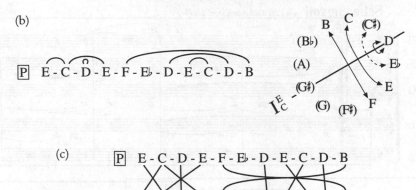

involves the notes of a C major scale: B–C–D–E–F. This diatonic, "C majorish" feel
is further reinforced by the non-serial accompanying chords, which contain only
four notes: C, D, E, and G. Schoenberg's harmony, like his melody, is based on a
twelve-tone series; both harmony and melody project a dense chromaticism.
Stravinsky's harmony, in contrast, is simply a non-serial, diatonic chord which
underscores the diatonic qualities of his serial melody.

The Schoenbergian aggregate itself thus becomes a subject of Stravinsky's
implicit critique. Schoenberg's twelve-tone music treats the aggregate, the total collection of the twelve notes, as a basic structural unit. It creates aggregates within the
series, between series forms (the first hexachord of P combines with the first hexachord of I to create an aggregate, as does the second hexachord of P and the second
hexachord of I), and across wider musical spans. Stravinsky's early serial music and
even his later twelve-tone music, in contrast, are generally unconcerned with the
aggregate.[30] Indeed, Stravinsky employs a variety of compositional strategies to
ensure intensive repetition of some notes and exclusion of others at all levels of
structure.

Equally striking, Stravinsky persistently identifies his series with a theme – he
gives it a distinctive melodic shape and keeps it in a single instrumental voice.
Schoenberg, in contrast, makes use of sophisticated partitioning schemes in which
the series is often divided up among the instrumental voices.[31] Stravinsky's
approach represents a significant simplification.

---

[30] The apparent paradox of a twelve-tone music that is not concerned with twelve-note aggregates will be resolved
   in Chapter 2. In brief, Stravinsky's late twelve-tone music begins with a twelve-note series, but manipulates its
   hexachords independently to create frequent doublings and repetitions.
[31] For a general description of partitioning in Schoenberg's music, see Ethan Haimo, *Schoenberg's Serial Odyssey*,
   17–26.

Example 1.3 Schoenberg, Wind Quintet, first movement
(a) mm. 1–15, with series forms indicated

Example 1.3 (*cont.*)
(b) P-form of the series, with inversional symmetry around E♭
(c) P- and I-forms related by inversion around E♭

(b)

P⃞ E♭ - G - A - B - C♯ - C - B♭ - D - E - F♯ - A♭ - F   I⃞ $^{E♭}_{E♭}$

(c) P⃞ E♭ - G - A - B - C♯ - C - B♭ - D - E - F♯ - A♭ - F

I⃞ E♭ - B - A - G - F - F♯ - G♯ - E - D - C - B♭ - C♯

Stravinsky thus begins with the Schoenbergian premises of row, row transformation, and row-class, but quickly swerves in a different direction. Mobile Schoenbergian chromaticism becomes static Stravinskian diatonicism; the protean Schoenbergian aggregate becomes the focused Stravinskian referential collection; complex Schoenbergian partitioning schemes become a simple thematicism. In the process, the rapid, ceaseless flow of developing variation in Schoenberg's music becomes static, timeless, and ritualistic in Stravinsky's music. In the course of this transformation, Stravinsky implies that Schoenberg's music is wildly excessive both in its endless chromaticism and its comparatively overwrought emotional character. It is as though Stravinsky has taken Schoenberg's music and emptied it of all its excesses in order to create his own.

A similar transformation, in which Schoenbergian material is emptied of structural and emotional excess by being rendered static, repetitive, diatonic, and tonally focused is apparent in a comparison of Schoenberg's Wind Quintet with Stravinsky's Septet.[32] The first movement of Schoenberg's Wind Quintet begins with four basic series forms (P, the I-form that begins on the same note, and their retrogrades), defining a "tonic area" for the movement (see Example 1.3a).[33] The series is oriented toward whole-tone harmonies and embeds a strong sense of inversion around its first note, E♭ (see Example 1.3b). As a result, the inversion of the series around E♭ produces many invariant segments (see Example 1.3c). For example, the first four notes of the series, E♭–G–A–B, return in a slightly different order as the first four notes of the inversion, E♭–B–A–G.

---

[32] As noted above, Craft used Schoenberg's Wind Quintet to demonstrate serial principles to Stravinsky, and Stravinsky responded by composing the second movement of his Septet.

[33] The Wind Quintet was written before Schoenberg's discovery of hexachordal inversional combinatoriality and the hexachords of its series are not related by inversion. Schoenberg still combines the P-form with a preferred I-form, but here the preferred I-form is the one that begins on the same note, E♭. This combination, of a P-form and an I-form that begin on the same note, was Stravinsky's preference throughout his serial career.

Example 1.4   Stravinsky, Septet, second movement
(a) series and its inversion around E

The second movement of Stravinsky's Septet, written as a critical response to Schoenberg, is based on a series that is sixteen notes long, but contains only eight different pitch-classes (see Example 1.4a). Stravinsky's series maintains a strong sense of pitch-class redundancy, diatonicism, and tonal orientation, initially toward E minor and then toward A minor. Schoenberg's first four notes were E♭–G–A–B, and these were retained in the inversion around E♭, as E♭–B–A–G. Stravinsky's first four notes are E–B–A–G, and the first three of these are retained in the inversion around E, as E–A–B. Like Schoenberg in his Wind Quintet, Stravinsky combines a series with its inversion starting on the same first note, but by substituting E for E♭ at the beginning of the series, renders both the series and its inversion diatonic and tonally focused.[34]

In the eighth variation of the second movement, Stravinsky layers four series forms (P, its inversion starting on the same first note, and their retrogrades) in a nearly-homophonic chorale (see Example 1.4b).[35] The middle of the passage is a somewhat chromatic, contrapuntal wash, but the first harmony (A–B–C–E) and the last one (E–G♯–A–B) are clearly diatonic, and are related to each other by inversion around E. This tonal clarity works in conjunction with the stately chorale texture to create an impression that is simple, direct, emotionally reserved, and quietly devotional. If one imagines Schoenberg's Wind Quintet as a starting point and distant reference for this passage, the dramatic effect is to empty Schoenberg's music of what Stravinsky would have perceived as its rhetorical and expressive excesses.

Even as Stravinsky adopted Schoenberg's serialism as a point of compositional departure, he never compromised the radically distinct aesthetic orientations of the two composers. When Craft, in one of the conversation books, asked Stravinsky to "comment on the popular notion of Schoenberg and Stravinsky as thesis and antithesis," Stravinsky responded by constructing a revealing set of contrasts, including the following:[36]

---

[34] There may be some symbolic use of musical ciphers here. Schoenberg frequently used the note E♭ as a musical self-reference (E♭ = Es = Schoenberg). Stravinsky renders the opening motive diatonic precisely by supplanting the Schoenbergian E♭. Of course, Stravinsky's own name also begins with S, so, although Stravinsky did not, to my knowledge, refer to himself musically by using E♭, it is difficult to draw any definitive conclusions.

[35] The layering of four series forms to create a chorale texture is a consistent procedure throughout Stravinsky's late period (see Chapter 4 for an extended discussion).   [36] *Dialogues*, 107–08.

Example 1.4 (*cont.*)
(b) mm. 64–72, Variation 8

STRAVINSKY:	SCHOENBERG:
Reaction against "German music" or "German romanticism." No "*Sehnsucht*," no "*ausdrucksvoll*."	"Today I have discovered something which will assure the supremacy of German music for the next hundred years." Schoenberg, July 1921.
"Music is powerless to express anything at all."	"Music expresses all that dwells in us . . ."
Metronomic strictness, no *rubato*. Ideal is of mechanical regularity (*Octuor*, Piano Concerto, etc.).	Much use of *rubato*.
Secco. Scores contain minimum of expression marks. Prefers spare, two–part counterpoint.	*Espressivo*. Scores full of expression marks. Preferred dense eight–part counterpoint (the choruses, op. 35; the Genesis Prelude canon).

Despite his interest in Schoenberg's music, Stravinsky never warmed to what he considered its emotional bombast and self-indulgent excess:

Schoenberg's work has too many inequalities for us to embrace it as a whole. For example, nearly all of his texts are appallingly bad, some of them so bad as to discourage performance of the music. Then, too, his orchestrations of Bach, Handel, Monn, Loewe, Brahms differ from the type of commercial orchestration only in the superiority of craftsmanship: his intentions are no better . . . His expressionism is of the naivest sort . . . His late tonal works are as dull as the Reger they resemble or the César Franck.[37]

It is this aesthetic distaste that in part motivates the simplicity of Stravinsky's early serial style. Although Stravinsky's early serial music may seem primitive in comparison to Schoenberg's, it is better understood as a deliberate and effective critique of Schoenberg rather than as a compositional failure of Stravinsky's. By emptying his own music of structural and emotional excess, Stravinsky makes Schoenberg sound overinflated and self-indulgent in comparison. The relative simplicity of Stravinsky's serial music comes as a willed self-abnegation. He neither imitates Schoenberg nor yields to him. Rather, he strips away all that seems self-indulgent, bombastic, or hyper-expressive in the Schoenbergian edifice, and attempts to build something new, and better, on the foundation that remains.

    Stravinsky's early serial music engages Schoenberg in direct and demonstrable ways. As Stravinsky's style coalesced into what became, for him, a standard serial practice, Schoenberg's presence receded and eventually disappeared. Stravinsky never made use of, or gave any particular indication of knowing about, many of the hallmarks of Schoenberg's mature twelve-tone style, including its "hexachordal inversional combinatoriality."[38] This property, which became a compositional

---

[37] *Conversations*, 78–9.   [38] See footnote no. 28, p. 13 above.

trademark of Schoenberg's mature twelve-tone music, is present only in a nascent state in his earlier twelve-tone works – the Serenade, Wind Quintet, and Septet-Suite – which were the first with which Stravinsky became familiar.[39] Even as Stravinsky became acquainted with Schoenberg's later works, however, he never adopted this central Schoenbergian tenet, if indeed he was even aware of its existence.[40]

It is hard to know how well, or in precisely what sense, Stravinsky knew Schoenberg's music. He was familiar with certain works through repeated hearing at rehearsals and concerts. As for their technical, structural bases, however, it is not obvious how far his understanding extended beyond the basic features of row presentation and transformation. Stravinsky was not much inclined toward music-theoretical speculation or analytical close reading. Nonetheless, it is clear that Schoenberg provided him with a vital challenge and compositional stimulus, a starting point and a useful framework for musical inquiry. Stravinsky's initial compositional response, in his early serial works, engaged Schoenberg directly, employing basic Schoenbergian ideas, but deflecting and transforming them. Later, as Stravinsky's style coalesced into what became a standard operating procedure for him, the sense of engagement with Schoenberg diminished to the vanishing point.

WEBERN

Compared with Schoenberg, the shock of Stravinsky's initial contact with Webern was at least as profound, and its effects longer lasting. He ultimately achieved the same artistic independence from Webern, although the stylistic affinities and structural debts are deeper.[41]

---

[39] The series for the Septet-Suite is combinatorial, as noted above, but this property is not thoroughly or consistently exploited in the work. As Haimo points out: "The Suite, Op. 29, with its all-combinatorial set, makes a perceptible step towards the systematic exploitation of combinatoriality. In numerous passages in the composition Schoenberg states combinatorially related set forms opposite one another and in the process creates aggregates. However, although Schoenberg does exploit combinatoriality to a limited degree, he is still far from the mature style . . . In sum, hexachordal combinatoriality is an isolated procedure in the Suite, and therefore has none of the profound implications of the later works: there is no impact on the form, no control of the harmony, no systematic creation of aggregates" (Haimo, *Schoenberg's Serial Odyssey*, 133–34).

[40] The central, third movement of *Canticum Sacrum* is an apparent exception. Its series is built from an all-combinatorial hexachord, and there are several passages in which hexachords from different series forms are combined to create aggregates (this was first pointed out by Milton Babbitt in "Remarks on the Recent Stravinsky," *Perspectives of New Music* 2/2 (1964), 35–55; reprinted in *Perspectives on Schoenberg and Stravinsky*, ed. Benjamin Boretz and Edward Cone (Princeton: Princeton University Press, 1968; reprint edn. New York: Norton, 1972), 165–85). But the formation of aggregates is probably fortuitous and certainly isolated, both within this piece and Stravinsky's serial music more generally.

[41] The Stravinsky–Webern relationship has been extensively discussed in the literature. See, among many, Carl Wiens, "Igor Stravinsky and 'Agon'" (Ph.D. dissertation, University of Michigan, 1997); Henri Pousseur, "Stravinsky by Way of Webern," *Perspectives of New Music* 10/2 (1972), 13–51 and 11/1 (1972), 112–45; Pieter van den Toorn, *The Music of Igor Stravinsky* (New Haven: Yale University Press, 1983); and Susannah Tucker, "Stravinsky and His Sketches: The Composing of *Agon* and Other Serial Works of the 1950s" (D.Phil. dissertation, Oxford University, 1992).

In the years between 1952 and 1955 no composer can have lived in closer contact with the music of Webern. Stravinsky was familiar with the sound of the Webern Cantatas and of the instrumental songs at a time when some of these works had not yet been performed in Europe. The challenge of Webern has been the strongest in his entire life. It has gradually brought him to the belief that serial technique is a possible means of musical composition.[42]

Laudatory, almost reverential, comments about Webern permeate Stravinsky's writings and interviews throughout the 1950s and 1960s.

Webern is for me the *juste de la musique*, and I do not hesitate to shelter myself by the beneficent protection of his not yet canonized art.[43]

[Webern] is the discoverer of a new distance between the musical object and ourselves and, therefore, of a new measure of musical time; as such he is supremely important . . . The desperate contrivance of most of the music now being charged to his name can neither diminish his strength nor stale his perfection. He is a perpetual Pentecost for all who believe in music.[44]

Webern's pointillistic textures are rarely duplicated in Stravinsky, but his spareness, his transparency, his relative contrapuntal simplicity often are. And three of the most characteristic features of Webern's musical structure find vivid, if distorted, reflections in Stravinsky's music.

The first of these is canon. Like Webern, Stravinsky initially identified the series with a canonic subject, and its serial transformations (transposition, inversion, retrograde, retrograde-inversion) as canonic imitations. Stravinsky's early serial music is usually contrapuntal/imitative in texture. Later, the canons go underground, absorbed into the special kind of arrays on which Stravinsky based his later twelve-tone music.

A second shared feature involves a common interest in inversional balance and symmetry. In Webern's twelve-tone music, a series and its inversion are often poised against each other. At the beginning of the Quartet, Op. 22, for example, P_1 and I_{11} are heard in inversional canon (see Example 1.5). The two interwoven parts balance symmetrically around C (and F$\sharp$). In measure 6, the canon continues, now with P_7 against I_5 (an independent melodic line in the saxophone does not participate). Each of the parts has been transposed by tritone, so the axis of inversion remains the same: the two lines still balance symmetrically around C (and F$\sharp$).

The Quartet, Op. 22, was one of the first pieces by Webern which Stravinsky encountered, and it had a powerful impact on him.[45] The impact of this "close contact" with Webern is felt in virtually all of Stravinsky's early serial music, including the largely diatonic *Cantata* (see Example 1.6). In the first passage, shown in Example 1.6a, a rhythmically free inversional canon between flute and English horn

[42] "A Personal Preface," 13.   [43] *Conversations*, 127.   [44] *Memories and Commentaries*, 103–05.
[45] "Stravinsky's first deep impression of [serial] music came from the Quartet opus 22 by Webern which he heard several times in January and February, 1952" (Craft, "A Personal Preface," 12).

balances two diatonic melodies symmetrically around C. Later in the movement, the passage in Example 1.6b transposes the flute melody down five semitones and the English horn melody up by five semitones. As a result, the second pair, like the first, and like Webern's melodies, still balances around C. In Webern's music, the inversional balance involved all twelve notes of the chromatic scale. In Stravinsky's revisionary response, however, only the diatonic seven are involved, and the canonic imitations are tonal (with interval qualities adjusted), not real. The idea of selecting transpositions so as to preserve a fixed axis of inversional symmetry is a distinctively Webernian idea, which Stravinsky transforms in striking fashion. Webern's entangled, opaque chromaticism, with its insistence on the primacy of the twelve-tone aggregate, is washed away in favor of a crystalline, transparent diatonicism, replete with constant pitch repetitions.

The comparison of Webern and the serial Stravinsky in the analytical literature often centers on Webern's Orchestral Variations in relation to Stravinsky's *Agon*.[46] Representative, and strikingly similar, passages are illustrated in Examples 1.7 and 1.8. Webern's twelve-note series (Example 1.7b) begins with the four-note fragment A–Bb–Db–C. This can be thought of as two minor thirds (A–C and Bb–Db) a semitone apart. It represents tetrachord-type (0134), and three additional forms of it, related by either transposition or inversion, are also embedded in the series (indicated with brackets). The passage begins with the first four notes of the series (P_9) in the solo violin with the first four notes of R_9 (the same as the last four of P_9) as an accompanimental chord in the brass. Both melody and chord represent (0134), and Webern has arranged them to feature their constituent minor thirds. The melody presents A–C in its lower register with Bb–Db above, while the accompanying chord has F–Ab in its lower register with E–G above. This integration of musical space, with the same musical idea projected simultaneously as a melody and a harmony, is typical of Webern's practice. The passage continues with the first four notes of RI_9 in the violins (again a statement of (0134) disposed to feature its minor thirds) accompanied by a different kind of four-note chord which can, however, also be thought of as two minor thirds (B–D and Eb–F#). All series forms continue and conclude as the music continues beyond the excerpt in Example 1.7.

The passage from *Agon* is strikingly similar. Its melodic line is based on the same four-note fragment A–Bb–Db–C (heard in retrograde in the highest part) and its derivative forms, often represented by a three-note subset. The melodic minor thirds are very much in evidence. As in the Webern, the melody is also accompanied

[46] See again sources cited above in note 34. Tucker, "Stravinsky and His Sketches," 203–12, provides detailed documentation of the extent of Stravinsky's knowledge of Webern, including particularly the *Variations for Orchestra*. According to Craft, during a visit to Baden-Baden in 1951, Stravinsky was "stunned by Webern's Orchestra Variations, asking to hear the tape three times in succession and again the next day . . . before then Stravinsky had neither heard nor seen any music by Webern" ("Influence or Assistance?," in *Present Perspectives*, 252).

Example 1.5   Webern, Quartet for Violin, Clarinet, Saxophone, and Piano, Op. 22, first
movement
(a) mm. 1–15 with series forms indicated

(a)

Example 1.5 (*cont.*)
(b) two pairs of inversionally related series-forms

(b)

$$I_C^C$$

| P₁ | Db - Bb - A -⌈C⌉- B - Eb - E - F - F♯ - G♯ - D - G |
| I₁₁ | B - D - Eb -⌊C⌋- C♯ - A - Ab - G - F♯ - E - Bb - F |

| P₇ | G - E - Eb - Gb - F - A - Bb - B -⌈C⌉- D - Ab - C♯ |
| I₅ | F - Ab - A - F♯ - G - Eb - D - C♯ -⌊C⌋- Bb - E - B |

by a four-note chord that can be partitioned into minor thirds: A–C from bass to soprano and G–Bb from alto to tenor.

But it is here, in the accompanying chord, that Stravinsky's different aesthetic and stylistic orientation becomes apparent. First, the chord is structurally different from the melodic fragments: a vertical (0235) in contrast to the linear (0134). As a result, the passage is intervallically more heterogeneous than Webern's. Second, the chord is a diatonic scale segment (equivalent to the first four notes of a G minor scale). Third, the chord contains notes in common with the melody it harmonizes, most obviously the shared A and C. Finally, the chord is simply repeated throughout the passage whereas Webern's chord changes, moving onto its transpositionally or inversionally equivalent forms. Compared to Webern, then, Stravinsky's music is heterogeneous rather than intervallically uniform, diatonic rather than chromatic, duplicative of the melody rather than exclusive of it, and static rather than mobile. In each of these ways, Stravinsky has begun with Webernian premises, then swerved in a different, and distinctively Stravinskian, direction. Webern's pervasive aggregate-based chromaticism and his restless developing variation have been stripped away, and the resulting music seems clarified and simplified and immobilized.

Stravinsky's musical critique of Webern is much less pointed, however, than his critique of Schoenberg. His music evinces a deep and sincere engagement with Webern rather than the more distant, ironic treatment of Schoenberg. Nonetheless, even in his early serial period, when Stravinsky borrowed most overtly and extensively from Webern, there is always a strong sense of transformation. Webern's mannerisms are sometimes present, but recontextualized and filtered through Stravinsky's distinctive sensibility. Later, as Stravinsky's music became thoroughly twelve-tone and abandoned entirely the persistent diatonic references of the early serial music, it paradoxically became less rather than more Webernian. As with the influence of Schoenberg, the principal impact of Webern was to shake Stravinsky

Example 1.6   Stravinsky, Cantata, Ricercar I, "The Maidens Came"
(a) mm. 1–5

free of many old compositional habits, and to suggest a new way of thinking about basic musical materials. Schoenberg and Webern provided a new framework for the compositional enterprise, new rules for the game, and had an immense initial impact. But as Stravinsky increasingly found his own way, and created his own distinctive musical world, their presence gradually diminished and, finally, seemed to vanish almost entirely.

KRENEK

Although overshadowed by Schoenberg and Webern, both in Stravinsky's imagination and in public reputation, Ernst Krenek was an important source of twelve-tone information for Stravinsky. Stravinsky acknowledged Krenek's treatise, *Studies in Counterpoint* (1940) – a beginner's manual of twelve-tone composition – as "the first work I read on that subject."[47] He also attended Krenek's lecture at the Princeton Seminar in Advanced Musical Studies (Summer 1959), which was later published as "The Extents and Limits of Serial Techniques."[48] In addition to whatever general information about serialism Stravinsky gained from these

---

[47] *Dialogues*, 103. "At the age of seventy, [Stravinsky] was deeply influenced by Krenek's *Studies in Counterpoint*" ("The Relevance and Problems of Biography," in *Glimpses of a Life*, 285).

[48] Ernst Krenek, "Extents and Limits of Serial Techniques," *Musical Quarterly* 46/2 (1960), 210–32; reprinted in *Problems of Modern Music*, ed. Paul Henry Lang (New York: W. W. Norton & Co., 1960), 72–94. This article contains a clear account of Krenek's rotational arrays, later adopted wholesale by Stravinsky, including complete serial charts from Krenek's *Lamentatio Jeremiae Prophetae*. For additional published discussions of rotational arrays by Krenek see "Is the Twelve-Tone Technique on the Decline?," *Musical Quarterly* 39 (1953), 513–27; and "New Developments of Twelve-Tone Technique," *The Music Review* 4 (1943), 81–97.

Example 1.6 (cont.)
(b) mm. 43–49
(c) two pairs of inversionally related series

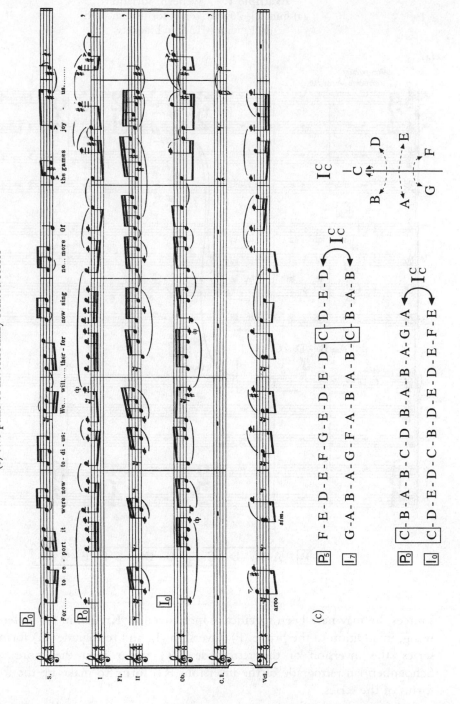

Example 1.7   Webern, Variations
(a) mm. 21–26 with series forms indicated
(b) P_9 with (0134) in brackets

(a)

(b) $\boxed{P_9}$ A - B♭ - D♭ - C - B - D - D♯ - F♯ - F - E - G - A♭

sources, he may have been specifically influenced by Krenek in his preference for using, in addition to the prime (P), inversion (I), and retrograde (R) forms of the series, the inversion of the retrograde (IR) rather than the more common Schoenbergian retrograde of the inversion (RI) form, to make up the four basic forms of the series.[49]

Stravinsky was also familiar with several twelve-tone works by Krenek, including

---

[49] In Krenek, *Studies in Counterpoint Based on the Twelve-Tone Technique* (New York: G. Schirmer, 1940), 11, IR is introduced simultaneously with RI as possible associates with P, I, and R, the other principal series forms.

Example 1.8 Stravinsky, *Agon*, mm. 473–83 (two-piano reduction)

Parvula corona musicalis (given as a gift by the composer to Stravinsky and, according to Craft, "a considerable influence on Stravinsky"), *Sestina*, and *Lamentatio Jeremiae Prophetae*.[50] *Lamentatio* is the most important of these for two reasons. First, it appears to have inspired Stravinsky's own setting of texts from the Lamentations of Jeremiah in *Threni*, his first completely twelve-tone work. Second and more significantly, Krenek's system of rotations and transpositions of the hexachords of the series, which he used for the first time in that piece, became the basis for all of Stravinsky's major compositions from *Movements* on.[51] Although rotation is also used in Schoenberg's early twelve-tone music, including the works apparently best known to Stravinsky, Krenek is the unmistakable source for what became the distinctive Stravinskian rotational array, including its independent treatment of the hexachords of the series, their systematic rotation, and the transposition of each of the rotations to begin on the same first note.[52]

Example 1.9 reproduces Krenek's row chart for his *Lamentatio* with Stravinsky's

[50] *Selected Correspondence*, vol. II, 326.
[51] See Catherine Hogan, "Threni: Stravinsky's Debt to Krenek," *Tempo* 141 (1982), 22–25.
[52] To be discussed in detail in Chapter 4.

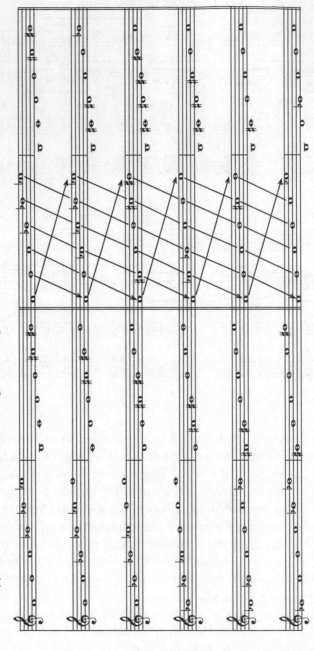

Example 1.9

(a) Krenek's row chart for *Lamentatio Jeremiae Prophetae*, with Stravinsky's analytical annotations

(a)

Example 1.9 (*cont.*)
(b) Stravinsky's own row chart for *Movements*

own analytical annotations.[53] For the sake of comparison, Stravinsky's row chart for his *Movements* is also provided. Krenek's chart is in two large halves, which he called "diatonic modes" and "chromatic modes" respectively. Across the top line of the "diatonic modes," he has written the two hexachords of a twelve-tone series. Each hexachord is simply rotated in the remaining rows of the chart, so that the first row begins on the first note, F, the second row begins on the second note, G, the third note begins on the third note, A, and so forth. Across the top line of the "chromatic modes," he again writes the hexachords of the series. Once again he rotates them as before, but now he also transposes each rotation to begin on the same first note, F. These "chromatic modes" evidently attracted Stravinsky's attention: he traced the transposed rotations in red pencil using diagonal lines and arrows.

Stravinsky's own charts for *Movements* are organized almost identically. First, he derives the "diatonic modes" from the two hexachords of a series (labeled, by him, α [alpha] and β [beta]). These are simple rotations, beginning on each successive note of the hexachord. Then he generates "chromatic modes" from the same two hexachords (now labeled γ [gamma] and δ [delta]), by rotation followed by transposition, again using diagonal lines to trace the transposed rotations. Stravinsky's debt to Krenek is self-evident.

Krenek was thus a crucial influence on Stravinsky, providing him with what would become the most distinctive and characteristic structure of his twelve-tone music: the rotational array. Like Stravinsky's borrowings from Schoenberg and Webern, however, his own use of these charts differs from Krenek's in profound ways. First, the series differ: Krenek's hexachords are nearly diatonic while Stravinsky's are based on the non-diatonic trichords (012) and (016).[54] Stravinsky had used a diatonic orientation to distinguish his music from Schoenberg and Webern's. By the time he began to use Krenek's rotational arrays, however, his language had evolved in more chromatic directions. He thus used Krenek's rotational arrays in such a way as to negate Krenek's diatonicism. Whereas Krenek used these charts to write music that sounds like imitative, Renaissance polyphony, Stravinsky used the same kind of charts to create a distinctive sound-world with no obvious antecedents. Second, Stravinsky made use of the six-note *verticals* or columns of these charts, whereas Krenek uses them only in their melodic, linear aspect.[55] Stravinsky, in short, conceived the charts in more abstract terms than Krenek. Krenek created them to write a pseudo-Renaissance modality. Stravinsky appropriated them more for their constructive possibilities than for any particular sound-realization they might suggest.[56]

---

[53] Krenek provided these row charts as part of the preface to the score of his *Lamentatio Jeremiae Prophetae*, a copy of which he gave to Stravinsky in December 1957. Stravinsky made his annotations, diagonal lines and arrows, in red pencil. The annotated score is in the Stravinsky Collection at the Paul Sacher Foundation. Stravinsky's row charts for *Movements* are Documents Nos. 110–0309 and Nos. 110–0310 in the Stravinsky Archive at the Paul Sacher Foundation.   [54] The generation of hexachords from smaller units is discussed at length in Chapter 3.

[55] These array verticals are discussed in Chapter 4.

[56] "For Krenek, the rotation technique was the solution to a self-imposed problem, namely, to integrate certain principles of the twelve-note technique with those of ancient modality. Once this had been solved, as far as he

It is obvious that Krenek's precompositional charts were enormously suggestive for Stravinsky, and his intellectual debt to Krenek correspondingly deep. At the same time, Stravinsky's music betrays not the slightest trace of influence from Krenek. Krenek's main function, then, was to help set Stravinsky in motion, to provide a starting point and a framework. Like Craft, Schoenberg, and Webern, he helped to provide an initial impetus, to indicate some possible directions to move in, to offer some useful guideposts for the journey. But it was a journey that Stravinsky persisted in alone.

BOULEZ

It is often asserted that Stravinsky's turn to serialism was, at least in part, an effort to ingratiate himself with a younger generation of composers, particularly Pierre Boulez. Comments by Ned Rorem, who likens Stravinsky to Copland in bowing to the dictates of fashion, are particularly blunt, but otherwise typical:

In the 60s, Copland had the world at his feet except for that small portion older composers most crave: young composers. The young at that moment were immersed in Bouleziana, a mode quite foreign to Copland's very nature (as to the nature of Stravinsky, who also sold out to the system) . . . It was poignant to see Copland and Stravinsky trying to please Boulez.[57]

Stravinsky became aware of Boulez's music in 1951 and there was close personal contact between the two composers during the brief period between 1956 and 1958.[58] In 1952, Stravinsky attended rehearsals of Boulez's *Polyphonie X* and, according to Craft, "made an analysis of the score."[59] Furthermore, the row for Boulez's *Structures 1A* appears among the compositional sketches for Stravinsky's *Threni*.[60] Both *Structures 1A* and *Polyphonie X* are among the early, "total" serial works of Boulez, in which his precompositional materials include series of twelve tones, twelve durations, twelve dynamics, and twelve modes of attack. It would not have been difficult for Stravinsky to figure out what Boulez had done in these works, but nothing remotely like it appears in his own music. Stravinsky also

---

was concerned, the technique could not be used in a similar way again without being repetitive. For Stravinsky the rotation method was a way of organizing and ensuring that which he was trying to achieve up to and including *Threni*, i.e. serial music in his own language" (Hogan, "Stravinsky's Debt to Krenek," 28). Krenek was aware of Stravinsky's use of his "chromatic modes" in *Movements*, writing "Of course, Stravinsky is as welcome as anyone to use an idea of rotation and transposition which to think up and to apply I perhaps happened to be the first" (Ernst Krenek, "Some Current Terms," *Perspectives of New Music* 4 [1966], 81–84).

[57] Ned Rorem, quoted in the *New York Times*, November 10, 1985 and January 16, 1994.

[58] The history of the Boulez–Stravinsky relationship is detailed by Robert Craft in "Boulez in the Lemon and Limelight," in *Prejudices in Disguise* (New York: Alfred A. Knopf, 1974), 207–13; and "Stravinsky: Letters to Pierre Boulez," *The Musical Times* 123 (1982), 396–402; revised and expanded in *Selected Correspondence*, vol. II, 347–63.   [59] Craft, "Boulez in the Lemon and Limelight," 209.

[60] This was recently discovered by David Smyth and reported in his unpublished article, "Stravinsky as Serialist: the Sketches for *Threni*." Boulez's series itself comes from Messiaen, *Mode de Valeurs et d'Intensités*. The relevance of this series to *Threni* is unclear to me, as it differs in every essential way from the series of *Threni*.

expressed admiration for *Le Marteau sans Maître*, Boulez's best-known work.[61] But the admiration certainly had more to do with the surface colors of the work than its serial structures, of which Stravinsky was entirely unaware.[62] Stravinsky's knowledge of Boulez's music was necessarily superficial and there is little sign in Stravinsky's music of a desire to emulate Boulez in any way. If Stravinsky did in fact want to please Boulez, he did not try to do so through perceptible imitation.

For his part, Boulez was generally contemptuous of Stravinsky's music after *Les Noces* and, apart from arranging a disastrous performance of *Threni* in Paris in 1958, expressed little interest in Stravinsky's serial music.[63] The following comment is typical of Boulez's condescending disapproval, expressed on many occasions:

The period in Stravinsky's output that I find most important is from 1911 to 1923. I think it was in 1923 that he finished the instrumentation of *Les Noces*. Afterwards there are a few points – a few oases – in his output: for instance, certain static passages in the third movement of the *Symphony of Psalms*. However, after an adventure that had taken him – like Schoenberg – such a long way, there came this regression, this fear of the unknown and the desire to organize the world in a reassuring way.[64]

It is striking that this judgment, made after Stravinsky's death, pointedly excludes all of his late music. Stravinsky knew Boulez's music only superficially, but generally liked what he heard. Boulez knew Stravinsky's most recent music somewhat better, and generally despised it.[65] In the aftermath of the *Threni* debacle, and once Stravinsky became aware of Boulez's attitude, he largely broke off contact.[66] In this poisonous personal environment, and in the absence of compelling musical evidence to the contrary, it is hard to credit Boulez as a significant influence on Stravinsky.

---

[61] Stravinsky and Craft, *Memories and Commentaries*, 123.

[62] Only in the past decade have theorists finally come to terms with the serial organization of *Le Marteau*. See Stephen Heinemann, "Pitch-Class Set Multiplication in Theory and Practice," *Music Theory Spectrum* 20/1 (1998), 72–96; and "Pitch-Class Set Multiplication in Boulez's *Le Marteau sans maître*" (D.M.A. diss., University of Washington, 1993); Lev Koblyakov, *Pierre Boulez: A World of Harmony* (London and New York: Harwood Academic Publishers, 1990).

[63] According to Craft, "Threni was so badly sung and played – at the Salle Pleyel, November 14, 1958 – that the audience received it with jeers, and when Boulez tried to maneuver Stravinsky into taking a bow, the humiliated composer curtly refused and swore that he would never again conduct in Paris, a vow that he kept . . . Stravinsky wrote in his diary that night: 'My concert (Threni) at Pleyel (unhappiest concert of my life!).' Back in California, Stravinsky attached a note to a packet of Boulez's letters: 'All this correspondence resulted in the scandalous concert in Paris on November 14, 1958'" (*Selected Correspondence*, vol. II, 353).

[64] *Pierre Boulez: Conversations with Célestin Deliège*, no translator named (London: Eulenburg Books, 1976), 107.

[65] Boulez's judgment on Stravinsky's *Variations* may be taken as typical: "I conducted *Variations* with the Berlin Philharmonic. It is admirable what Stravinsky has managed to achieve in his old age, although the quality of this work is questionable. There is nothing new there that Webern had not already done" (Jaroslav Buzga, "Interview mit Pierre Boulez in Prag," *Melos* 34 [1967], 162–64. My translation). According to Craft ("Letters to Boulez," *Selected Correspondence*, vol. II, 402), Stravinsky read this interview and was perturbed by it.

[66] A comment by Stravinsky in 1970 gives a sense of the situation: "I have not had any contact with M. Boulez myself since, shortly after visiting me in Hollywood three years ago, he talked about my latest compositions (in an interview) with unforgivable condescension, then went on to play them at a prestigious concert in Edinburgh. This was not the first proof of disingenuousness I had had of that arch-careerist, but it will be the last in which I have any personal connection" (Letter to the Music Editor of the *Los Angeles Times*, June 23, 1970; reprinted in Igor Stravinsky, *Themes and Conclusions* [London: Faber and Faber, 1972], 216).

If Stravinsky wrote twelve-tone music to impress Boulez, then he failed miser-
ably and knew that he had failed. Yet, even after conspicuously losing Boulez's
favor and attention, Stravinsky persisted in writing twelve-tone music. That alone
suggests that Stravinsky had other, more pressing motivations for composing as he
did.

BABBITT

Milton Babbitt would appear to be another possible influence on Stravinsky's late
music. Babbitt was, and remains, the dominant figure in American post-war serialism. Much of our common understanding of what twelve-tone music has been and
can be derives from Babbitt's influential theoretical writings and even more elo-
quent compositions. By the early 1950s, when Stravinsky began his serial turn,
Babbitt was already considered the leading serialist among the younger generation
of American composers.

What is more, he and Stravinsky were in frequent and friendly contact throughout this period.[67] Babbitt was an early and knowledgeable student of Stravinsky's
music; indeed, his analytical study from that period remains a standard source of
information.[68] Babbitt's knowledge of Stravinsky's music was profound, detailed,
and intimate, as the following anecdote suggests:

On the morning of 9 January 1960 Stravinsky conducted the final rehearsal for the first, so
to speak, performance of the *Movements*, after which he lunched with the pianist for whom
the work was commissioned, her husband, and others of us. Although or perhaps because
the luncheon wine had been ordinary neither in quality nor quantity, Stravinsky – at the
conclusion of lunch – insisted that Claudio Spies and I escort him from the Ambassador
Hotel – the luncheon scene – down the street to the Gladstone, and then up to his suite,
where he further insisted that we sit, surrounding him, while he produced and displayed all
of his copious notes, alphanumerical and musical, for the *Movements*, and then proceeded, as
if to restore for himself and convey to us his original, unsullied image of the work, to lead us
on a charted voyage of rediscovery. I do not know how long his exegesis lasted, but I do
recall that dusk arrived and we scarcely could follow visually the paths and patterns that his
finger fashioned from his arrays of pitch-class letters, but we dared not switch on the light
for fear it would disrupt the flow of his discourse and the train of his rethinking. But I doubt
that it would have, for he did not drop a syllable in whatever language he was speaking at
that moment when I, in a spontaneous burst of detente, observed that the hexachord of the
Movements was, in content, that of Schoenberg's *De Profundis*. If I do not recall when that

---

[67] Information about the Babbitt–Stravinsky relationship may be found in Milton Babbitt, "Order, Symmetry, and
   Centricity in Late Stravinsky," *Confronting Stravinsky*, ed. Jann Pasler (Berkeley: University of California Press,
   1986), 247–61; Milton Babbitt, "Stravinsky's Verticals and Schoenberg's Diagonals: A Twist of Fate," in
   Stravinsky Retrospectives, ed. Ethan Haimo and Paul Johnson (Lincoln, Nebr.: University of Nebraska Press,
   1987); and Babbitt, *Words About Music*. I have also received personal communications from Babbitt on the
   subject.
[68] Babbitt, "Remarks on the Recent Stravinsky." Babbitt has maintained an interest in Stravinsky's late music in
   more recent years. See his "Order, Symmetry, and Centricity in Late Stravinsky" and "Stravinsky's Verticals."

extraordinary exposition ended, I surely cannot recall how, but I do recall how Claudio Spies and I attempted immediately, collaboratively, and subsequently to reconstruct that grand tour.[69]

So Babbitt knew Stravinsky's music well, from its precompositional plans to the minute details of its compositional realization. The reverse, however, was not true. There is no evidence that Stravinsky was closely familiar with any of Babbitt's music. Stravinsky did praise a work of Babbitt's, *The Widow's Lament in Springtime*, but only in the most general terms.[70] He also expressed his lack of interest in or knowledge of Babbitt's theoretical writing about twelve-tone music.[71] Whatever composer's shop talk they shared moved in one direction only: Babbitt learned about Stravinsky, but not the other way around. Furthermore, and most conclusively, Stravinsky's twelve-tone music bears no significant relationship to Babbitt's.[72] If Babbitt influenced Stravinsky during this period, then, he did not do so by virtue of any musical ideas, as embodied either in his music or in his theorizing.

If the specific content of Babbitt's musical thought has no bearing on late Stravinsky, it is possible that Babbitt nonetheless exerted a more general kind of influence, in that his prestige may have been among the factors that led Stravinsky to write twelve-tone music. In this view, Stravinsky did what he did, at least in part, "to impress his friends at Princeton."[73] It has been argued that American academic serialists, with Babbitt at their forefront, played on Stravinsky's sense of his own intellectual inferiority to pressure him into writing a kind of music that would otherwise have been alien to him:

[69] Babbitt, "Order, Symmetry, and Centricity in Late Stravinsky," 248–49; similarly in "Stravinsky's Verticals," 16–17.

[70] Stravinsky referred in 1961 to "the many excellent smaller examples of – what seems to me anyway – a distinctly American and very lovely pastoral lyricism: Ruggles' *Angels and Lilacs*, Babbitt's *The Widow's Lament in Springtime*, Copland's Dickinson songs" (*Dialogues*, 100).

[71] See, for example, Stravinsky's "The New Terminology," in *Themes and Episodes*, 20–21, where he derides theoretical terms like "dyads,""simultaneities," and "pitch priorities," all of which are associated with Babbitt's theoretical work.

[72] The trichordal arrays that were the basis for Babbitt's music in this period bear suggestive similarities to Stravinsky's four-part arrays, to be discussed in Chapter 4. They similarly consist of four serial lines that unfold simultaneously, with the possibility of harmonies created as slices through the array. But on closer consideration, the profound differences outweigh the apparent similarities. Babbitt's arrays are concerned with trichordal derivation and with trichordal and hexachordal combinatoriality – these are considerations that play no role whatsoever in Stravinsky's music. One slight qualification is necessary. As mentioned above (footnote no. 40, p. 21), in the middle movement of *Canticum Sacrum*, "Ad Tres Virtutes Hortationes," Stravinsky uses a series based on the chromatic hexachord and occasionally exploits its combinatorial properties to create aggregates. But an interest in aggregates generally, and in hexachordal combinatoriality specifically, are not characteristic of Stravinsky's serial music. For Babbitt, the trichordal array was a theoretically fertile intersection of Schoenbergian combinatoriality and Webernian derivation, both suitably generalized, and susceptible of an astonishing variety of compositional realizations. For Stravinsky, the four-part array was something much simpler: it was a way of writing twelve-tone chorales, ultimately a local solution to a local problem. For an extended discussion of these matters, see Joseph Straus, "Babbitt and Stravinsky under the Serial 'Regime'," *Perspectives of New Music* 35/2 (1999), 17–32.

[73] Richard Taruskin, *Stravinsky and the Russian Traditions* (Berkeley: University of California Press, 1996), 1649n. The quoted phrase refers specifically to Stravinsky's serial setting of a tune from *The Firebird*, but seems to reflect more generally Taruskin's understanding of Stravinsky's interest in twelve-tone music.

Through *Mavra* Stravinsky approached the West as Russian music itself had done a century before. His stylistic renovations took the form of an accommodation between the irreducibly Eurasian elements of his style and the harmonic traditions and musical conventions of Italian opera . . . And alas [this accommodation] held the seeds of the inferiority complex vis-a-vis the West that overwhelmed the composer on completing another Italianate opera three decades later [i.e. *The Rake's Progress*], finishing off his neoclassicism and bringing on the one real creative crisis of his career.[74]

Like all Russian composers, Stravinsky envied the Germans their traditions. The mask fell when it became so terribly important for him to establish belated and retroactive connections with the New Vienna School. Typical of Stravinsky the serialist were self-pitying assertions like this one, from *Dialogues and a Diary*: "I am a double *émigré*, born to a minor musical tradition and twice transplanted to other minor ones." At a Stravinsky centennial symposium at Notre Dame in November 1982 I recalled this passage and asked, rhetorically, whether anyone could imagine calling the French tradition "minor." I can still hear Milton Babbitt's "Oh, I can!" – interjected only half in jest. I recalled that it was Babbitt who had shown Stravinsky Schenker's lofty dismissal of the Concerto for Piano and Winds in 1962, just when *Dialogues and a Diary* was being put together, and wondered how many such encounters with American academic serialists lay behind Stravinsky's confession.[75]

Stravinsky's desire to win the good opinion of Babbitt and other "American academic serialists," in an effort to mitigate his sense of his inferiority in relation to them and their Viennese forebears may have been a factor sparking his initial interest in serialism. He may well have been moved, at least in part, to find out and make use of what Schoenberg and Webern had done, by the intense interest in that music on the part of Babbitt and other younger composers. But beyond possibly motivating an initial contact, a desire to curry favor with the young and any sense of his own compositional limitations are wholly inadequate in accounting for the astonishing outpouring of original music that followed the completion of *The Rake*. Stravinsky was aware of new music around him, but in the world of twelve-tone composition, he was largely an autodidact. In its specific content, Stravinsky's twelve-tone music bears virtually no trace of influence from the younger generation of twelve-tone composers to whose system he is presumed, by some, to have capitulated.

Even in the case of Schoenberg and Webern, whose music he heard and studied, it is not at all clear exactly what Stravinsky learned, beyond the most obvious features of series construction and manipulation. He was never particularly interested

---

[74] Taruskin, *Stravinsky and the Russian Traditions*, 17.

[75] Ibid, 3n. Similarly: "Reconciliation with Wagner came after World War II, when it suddenly became important to Stravinsky to forge retrospective links with Wagner's self-styled heirs. He was responding to the panic he felt on returning to Europe and seeing that young composers, belatedly discovering the 12-tone music of Schoenberg and the New Vienna School, now thought his music passé. Not only did he take up 12-tone composition himself, Stravinsky also accepted, hook, line and sinker, the historiographical myths that supported the Schoenbergian claim to musical supremacy . . . The Wagnerian 'crisis of tonality' was not Wagnerian at all. It was read back into Wagner by Schoenberg's apologists, eventually including the intimidated Stravinsky" (*The New York Times*, June 6, 1999, *Arts and Leisure*, 26).

in theoretical abstraction and generalization. Rather, he had specific, concrete ideas of what kinds of sounds he wanted to write, and appropriated, discovered, or invented, ways of doing so.[76] Serialism presented itself to Stravinsky as an array of musical possibilities, some well understood, some only partly understood, and some creatively misunderstood. He took what he wanted, and invented the rest.

EARLY STRAVINSKY

Of all the earlier music Stravinsky had to come to terms with during his serial period, his own loomed largest. His change of style was in an obvious sense a repudiation and a rejection of what he had done before. The late music is really new, shockingly so, to Stravinsky and to the world. In ways to be explored in the subsequent chapters, neither he nor anyone else had written music like this before.

At the same time, of course, the stylistic break is far from complete, nor did Stravinsky seek to make a complete break. But as he matured as a serial composer, the links to his own earlier music became more and more tenuous. His familiar compositional habits – the harmonies, melodies, and rhythms that define his earlier style – gradually recede and almost disappear over the course of the late period.

Stravinsky's serial music does connect with and engage his earlier music, but not generally by reusing his traditional materials or subjecting them to his customary compositional routines. Instead, the connections lurk largely beneath the compositional surface. His familiar devices are sublimated, attenuated, abstracted, and concealed. Musical gestures that had previously been overt move underground into the very substructures of the music.

This process is exemplified in the rotational arrays that became the basis of all of Stravinsky's major works beginning with the *Movements* (refer again to Example 1.9). Despite their obvious differences from Stravinsky's earlier musical constructions, they nonetheless embody hidden affinities as well, having to do with centricity, ostinato, and canon. Stravinsky's neoclassical music had been deeply concerned with issues of musical centricity, of channeling and focusing the musical discourse around certain referential notes. In the rotational arrays, comparable centricity is assured, in part, by the simple fact that each row of the array begins on the same note. Stravinsky's neoclassical music, and his still earlier "Russian" music, made extensive use of ostinati – repeated patterns of notes and/or intervals. In the rotational arrays, an abstract kind of ostinato is embodied in the relations among the rows, all of which have the same intervals in the same order (although displaced by

---

[76] Although he was not so much interested in a high level of theoretical abstraction and generalization, Stravinsky did value precise and necessarily technical descriptions of music, including his own. Stravinsky's response to a lecture by Babbitt, later published as "Remarks on the Recent Stravinsky," is revealing: "Babbitt, in a highly technical exposition of Stravinsky's musical fabric, held him spellbound, and I heard him declare later in thanking Babbitt that 'there is only one possible way to discuss music, and that is in technically musical terms.' Any other approach – association of ideas, images, analogies – bored him to extremity, even if delivered in the most loving jargon by non-musicians" (Paul Horgan, *Encounters with Stravinsky* [New York: Farrar, Straus, Giroux, 1972], 216).

the rotations). In Stravinsky's neoclassical music, and in his early serial music, canons play an increasingly important role. Canons are also embedded in the rotational arrays, in the canonic relationships among the individual rows of the array.[77] In each of these respects – centricity, ostinato, canon – the overt compositional gestures of Stravinsky's earlier music are embodied in the precompositional substructure of his later practice. These same musical gestures are inevitably present when he composes with these arrays, but in a less overt or readily perceptible way.

In a certain sense, Stravinsky does to his own earlier music what he does to the music of Schoenberg, by emptying it of all apparent excesses – both expressive and structural. He begins with a certain set of compositional assumptions, materials, interests, then swerves sharply in a different direction. In the process, he places his own earlier music in a new, distant, and somewhat ironic light.

Accounts of the late music in recent Stravinsky scholarship have emphasized its connection with the earlier music. Such accounts have claimed that the octatonic collection, which both on its own and in interaction with the diatonic collection plays such a prominent role in Stravinsky's earlier music, persists also in the later music.[78] But close examination particularly of the last, fully twelve-tone works beginning with *Threni* shows, in fact, very little that can be meaningfully attributed to octatonicism or to octatonic/diatonic interaction. Indeed, octatonic and octatonic/diatonic effects would be more apparent in an entirely random distribution of the twelve tones than they are in Stravinsky's twelve-tone music.[79]

One of the side-effects of emphasizing musical continuities across the stylistic divide that separates early and middle Stravinsky from late Stravinsky has been to value the late music precisely for whatever qualities it shares with the earlier music, and thus to devalue its departures and innovations. Stravinsky scholarship has thus

[77] Each row of the array is a simple transposition of the row directly below it, but starting one position later. The result is a kind of six-voice canon with the sixth row as the leader, and the rows above it following at progressively later and later moments (and with all rows understood to wrap around the array in a continuous, circular motion).

[78] See particularly Taruskin, *Stravinsky and the Russian Traditions*, 1648–74 and van den Toorn, *The Music of Igor Stravinsky*, 378–455.

[79] An examination of the twelve-tone series used by Stravinsky in his thirteen fully twelve-tone works is revealing in this regard. In Stravinsky's twelve-tone series, octatonic and/or diatonic subsets actually occur somewhat less than would be predicted among random orderings of notes. Any twelve-tone series contains nine segmental tetrachords, or contiguous groupings of four notes. Given that thirteen of the twenty-nine tetrachord-types are subsets of the octatonic collection and a somewhat different thirteen are subsets of the diatonic collection, one would expect that in any random ordering of the twelve pitch-classes, roughly 13/29 (or nearly half) of the segmental tetrachords would be octatonic and a similar proportion would be diatonic. In Stravinsky's twelve-tone series, just under half of the segmental tetrachords are, in fact, diatonic subsets, suggesting that, while Stravinsky made no effort to enhance the diatonic content of his series beyond what can be taken as an ambient, neutral level, he made no effort to repress diatonic effects either. As for the octatonic effects, however, only one-third of the segmental tetrachords of Stravinsky's series are octatonic subsets, strikingly and significantly less than might have been expected under neutral conditions. In other words, in devising his twelve-tone series, Stravinsky creates a musical world that is less octatonic than the simple presence of the octatonic eight among the chromatic twelve might lead one to expect. And the series are a good proxy for the music based so directly and literally on them. Far from enhancing octatonic effects in his music, he seems to have taken some pains to repress them.

implicitly or explicitly criticized the late music for being insufficiently static, repetitive, rooted in a familiar blend of octatonic and diatonic harmonies and brief, easily grasped folk-like melodies – in short, insufficiently Stravinskian. From the opposite perspective, twelve-tone scholarship has occasionally viewed Stravinsky as a belated and derivative imitator of his Viennese forebears. Stravinsky's late music is devalued as insufficiently sophisticated, complex, and developmental – in short, insufficiently Schoenbergian.

I would like to counter both of these views by insisting on Stravinsky's independence of compositional models, including his own earlier music, an independence earned through considerable struggle. The late music is neither a falling away from an earlier greatness nor an inept, slavish capitulation to an alien power. Rather, it is a willed, adventurous voyage of compositional exploration.

The effect of serialism on Stravinsky was liberating. In a series of works, extending from the *Cantata* and Septet of 1952–53 through the *Requiem Canticles* of 1966, Stravinsky forged a distinctive way of composing under a very broad serial umbrella. There is hardly a work in the period in which he did not attempt something new – his music continually evolving in ways that were essentially independent of both previous and contemporary developments. Listening to and studying these works engenders a sense of courageous discovery. Here is an aging composer at the height of his eminence turning away from familiar habits to try something new, not just once, but again and again, searching restlessly, and creating works of unsurpassed beauty and power.

During the first phase of his life as a serial composer, Stravinsky was directly engaged with Schoenberg, Webern, Krenek and, to a lesser extent, younger composers like Boulez and Babbitt. He generally approached their music as, in an earlier period, he had approached the music of Bach and Mozart (not to mention Pergolesi, Tchaikovsky, and others). His stance is critical, and often ironic. He transforms his models in the process of borrowing from them.

In this first phase, much of the power and interest of the music comes from its tense engagement with its predecessors, particularly Schoenberg and Webern. Stravinsky's flippant comment about his propensity for compositional borrowing, made many years earlier, applies to his early serial phase as well:

My instinct is to recompose, and not only students' works, but old masters' as well. When composers show me their music for criticism all I can say is that I would have written it quite differently. Whatever interests me, whatever I love, I wish to make my own (I am probably describing a rare form of kleptomania).[80]

Stravinsky described himself, in contrast to Schoenberg, as one who "learns from others, [who has] a lifelong need for outside nourishment and a constant confluence with new influences."[81] And he maintained that openness to external influence throughout his life:

---

[80] *Memories and Commentaries*, 110.   [81] *Dialogues*, 107.

I have all around me the spectacle of composers who, after their generation has had its decade of influence and fashion, seal themselves off from further development and from the next generation (as I say this, exceptions come to mind, Krenek, for instance). Of course, it requires greater effort to learn from one's juniors, and their manners are not invariably good. But when you are seventy-five and your generation has overlapped with four younger ones, it behooves you not to decide in advance "how far composers can go," but to try to discover whatever new thing it is makes the new generation new.[82]

But in the second phase of his life as a serial composer, from *Movements* of 1960 to the *Requiem Canticles* of 1966, Stravinsky's engagement with the music of his predecessors gradually ceases. His compositional journey has taken him beyond them, beyond influence, into new and unexplored musical terrain.

[82] *Conversations*, 133.

2

COMPOSITIONAL PROCESS

THE PHYSICAL ENVIRONMENT

Within two years of his arrival in the United States, Stravinsky had become an American citizen and purchased the house at 1260 North Wetherly Drive in Hollywood, California where he and his wife lived for most of the following years. Stravinsky composed continuously, even while traveling, but his late works were composed primarily in the small studio in his modest house. Because it both shaped and reflected aspects of the music composed there, his studio merits a brief description. It was soundproofed with cork lining and physically separated from the rest of the house by thick double doors. Stravinsky did not like to be overheard as he composed, which he did largely at the piano.[1] Although he was extremely gregarious, his music was created in strict isolation.

Here is Nicolas Nabokov's colorful description of the studio, from December 1947:

His workroom is another example of the precision which orders his music and his language . . . In a space which is not larger than some twenty-five by forty feet [Craft notes that it was actually considerably smaller] stand two pianos (one grand, one upright) and two desks (a small, elegant writing desk and a draftsman's table). In two cupboards . . . are books, scores, and sheet music, arranged in alphabetical order. Between the two pianos, the cupboards and desks, are scattered a few small tables (one of which is a kind of "smoker's delight": it exhibits all sorts of cigarette boxes, lighters, holders, fluids, flints, and pipe cleaners) . . . chairs, and the couch Stravinsky uses for his afternoon naps . . . Besides the pianos and the furniture there are hundreds of gadgets, photographs, trinkets, and implements of every kind in and on the desks and tables and tacked on the back of the cupboards. [Stravinsky's] study [has] all the instruments needed for writing, copying, drawing, pasting, cutting, clipping, filing, sharpening, and gluing that the combined efforts of a stationery and hardware store can furnish (and yet he is always after new ones).[2]

The most poetic description of Stravinsky's gadget-laden worktable is that of C. F. Ramuz, his collaborator on *The Soldier's Tale*. Ramuz's memoir dates from

---

[1] "A cork lining and a double door keep the studio hermetically insulated from the outside world. They also keep the outer world from overhearing the pounding and tinkling process . . . Stravinsky cannot compose if he thinks anyone is listening to him. The double door . . . is the subject of a special rule. If one of the doors is left open, his wife may enter; if both doors are closed, no one may enter" (Robert Craft, quoted in *Life*, 23 March 1953; reprinted in *Pictures and Documents*, 649).   [2] Quoted in *Pictures and Documents*, 382.

1946, and the events it describes from twenty-five years earlier, but his observations remain pertinent to Stravinsky's physical work environment throughout his life:

Stravinsky's writing table resembled the shelf on which a surgeon places his instruments. The order in which a surgeon lays out his instruments is to increase his chances in his struggle against death. The artist also, in his manner, struggles against death. The bottles of ink in many colors, properly arranged, play their little part in a grand affirmation of a higher order. They rest next to erasers of various kinds and shapes and all kinds of shiny steel objects: rulers, erasing-knives, penknives, drawing-pens, without even mentioning a special roller for drawing five-line staves, of which Stravinsky was the inventor. One thinks here of the definition provided by Saint Thomas: beauty is the splendor of order. Order does not, in itself suffice; it must also illuminate. There was here an order which did illuminate, because it was but the reflection of an internal clarity.[3]

Vera Stravinsky's description from 1962 echoes that of Ramuz and shows how little Stravinsky's work environment had changed in the years between *The Soldier's Tale* and *Abraham and Isaac*:

Igor's studio is the most distant room from the kitchen. He cannot bear any odor while he is composing and he claims that pungent ones actually interfere with his hearing . . . He composes at a tacky-sounding and usually out-of-tune upright piano that has been muted and dampened with felt. Nevertheless, and though the studio is soundproofed and the door tightly closed, little noises as though from mice on the keyboard penetrate the next room. A plywood drawing board is fixed to the music rack and to it are clipped quarto-size strips of thick white paper. These are used for the pencil-sketch manuscript. A few smaller sheets of paper are pinned to the board around this central manuscript, like sputniks. They are the navigation charts of serial orders, the transportation [sic] tables, the calculations of permutations − "here the twelfth note becomes the second note . . . " − and so forth. A kind of surgeon's operating table stands to the side of the piano, the cutlery in this case being colored pencils, gums, stopwatches, electric pencil-sharpeners (they sound unpleasantly like lawn mowers), electric metronomes, and the styluses with which Igor draws the staves and of which he is the patented inventor.[4]

The varied writing implements and gadgetry, particularly related to cutting and pasting, play crucial roles in the construction of Stravinsky's music, assembled, as it so often appears to be, from discrete sonic blocks. The profound orderliness of his work space reflects a deep aspect of his creative personality:

Stravinsky perfectly fits Freud's description of the anal personality: the cataloguing; the thrift; the accumulating, hoarding (he picks up every piece of string and saves it), retaining; the exactness, tidiness, and neatness, for he cannot resist wiping the ring left on a table by the glass of a guest or dinner companion; the possessiveness, which extends to people (he demands absolute fealty from his friends and total subservience from servants); the exaggerated fears −

---

[3] C. F. Ramuz, *Souvenirs sur Igor Stravinsky* (Lausanne: Mermod, 1946), 77–78. My translation.

[4] Letter from Vera Stravinsky to Vladimir Ivanovitch Petrov, her cousin, December 10, 1962; reprinted in *Themes and Episodes*, 71. Vera Stravinsky's last reference is to the so-called "Stravigor," Stravinsky's ink-roller device for drawing a five-line staff onto a blank piece of paper.

of funerals, of illnesses (he will leave a room in which someone has coughed or sneezed), of being without money, of intestinal irregularities (especially oppilations).[5]

A LOVE OF RULES

The orderliness of Stravinsky's personality and his work space bears directly on his often expressed sense that musical composition, for him, involved "putting in order musical elements that have attracted my attention":[6]

The elements which the imagination receives must be passed through a sieve . . . and, like the sounds of nature, become music only after they have been organized, or controlled. The more controlled the art, the more free . . . And the composer must find unity in multiplicity, choose the reality of a limitation over the infinity of a division.[7]

Throughout his career, Stravinsky sought various kinds of limitations on his field of activity, strictures and rules to give the enterprise shape and definition:

The creator's function is to sift the elements he receives from [the imagination], for human activity must impose limits upon itself. The more art is controlled, limited, worked over, the more it is free . . .My freedom consists in my moving about within the narrow frame that I have assigned myself for each one of my undertakings. I shall go even further: my freedom will be so much the greater and more meaningful the more narrowly I limit my field of action and the more I surround myself with obstacles. Whatever diminishes constraint, diminishes strength. The more constraints one imposes, the more one frees one's self of the chains that shackle the spirit.[8]

Stravinsky approached musical composition as a game, one which made sense only in obedience to explicit, strict rules.[9] Unlike more familiar kinds of games, however, in this one the player is also the inventor of the rules. Indeed, devising appropriate constraints was, for Stravinsky, an integral part of the compositional or, more properly, precompositional process. Throughout his career, Stravinsky imposed many different kinds of constraints, obstacles, and limits upon his field of compositional action. In the late music, he chose two principal limitations: written texts to be sung and serial devices of various kinds. Indeed, the principal attraction of the serial enterprise for Stravinsky was its well-articulated ways of regulating the compositional flow:

---

[5] *Pictures and Documents*, 387.

[6] *Poetics*, 51. As with all of the documents that bear Stravinsky's name as author, there is serious question about the authenticity of the *Poetics*. According to Craft, the *Poetics* was almost entirely ghost written by Roland-Manuel and "not a single sentence by [Stravinsky] actually appears in the book of which he is the nominal author" ("Roland-Manuel and *La Poétique Musicale*," in *Selected Correspondence*, vol. II, 503). Nonetheless the sentiments, if not the actual language, can reasonably be attributed to Stravinsky.

[7] Interview in a newspaper called *Pour la Victoire*; reprinted in *Pictures and Documents*, 372.   [8] *Poetics*, 63–65.

[9] For a discussion of the relationship between Stravinsky's rule orientation and his early training in law, see Wayne Alpern, "Schenkerian Jurisprudence: The Impact of Schenker's Legal Education on his Musical Thought" (Ph.D. dissertation, City University of New York, in progress).

The rules and restrictions of serial writing differ little from the rigidity of the great contrapuntal schools of old. At the same time, they widen and enrich harmonic scope; one starts
to hear more things and differently than before. The serial technique I use impels me to
greater discipline than ever before.[10]

Stravinsky thus turned to serial composition not in spite of, but precisely because of
the strict discipline it promised.

POETIC AND LITERARY TEXTS

Stravinsky wrote a great deal of vocal music throughout his career, and his reliance
on written texts, particularly religious texts, to shape his compositions intensified as
he aged. Of twenty original compositions after the *Rake*, only five (Septet, *Agon*,
Movements, *Variations*, and the brief *Fanfare for a New Theater*) are purely instrumental. In the remaining works, the written texts, selected in advance, imposed
welcome musical restrictions at all levels, from the larger forms to the most immediate surface rhythms.

Stravinsky's texts during this period were either in Latin or in English (the
Hebrew *Abraham and Isaac* is the one exception) and were almost invariably religious or elegiac in tone, if not explicitly part of a mass or other religious observance
(see Table 2.1). The late period is dominated by sacred choral works and even the
secular texts often have a somber, religious aura. This orientation inflects many
aspects of Stravinsky's music, including its generally dark emotional impact, its generally slow tempi, and its recurring chorale or hymn-like textures.

The larger forms of the music inevitably follow the shape of the text. This is
most obvious in the way the works are divided into movements and large sections,
but is also evident at the level of the phrase. In Stravinsky's late music, a musical
phrase (often coextensive with a series statement) usually coincides with a phrase of
text.

In the opening of *Introitus*, for example, Stravinsky uses a single statement of the
twelve-tone series to set the first line of text, "Requiem aeternam dona ei,
Domine" (see Example 2.1).[11] In the initial sketch, Stravinsky sets each of the thirteen syllables of the text with a single note of his twelve notes of the series, repeat-
ing the last note (D$\sharp$) for the last syllable of "Domine" (Example 2.1a). The final,
fully rhythmicized vocal line is more complex, but still maintains the basic plan that
one series equals one musical phrase equals one line of written text (Example 2.1b).
In this way, the form of the text stays in intimate contact with the serial structure.

The final setting is notable also for its somewhat stilted speech rhythms. As is
Stravinsky's usual practice, the musical rhythms often cut against the natural stresses

[10] *Conversations*, 25.
[11] The sketch in Example 2.1a is reproduced in *Strawinsky: Sein Nachlass, Sein Bild*, ed. Hans Jörg Jans and Christian
Geelhaar (Basel: Kunstmuseum, 1984), 179. The sketch in Example 2.1b is reproduced as Plate 22 in *Pictures and
Documents*. The transcriptions, here and throughout this book, are mine unless otherwise noted.

Table 2.1 *Stravinsky's late music with text*

Date	Title	Language	Source
1952	*Cantata*	English	Late Medieval verse
1954	*Three Songs from William Shakespeare*	English	Shakespeare, Sonnet No. 8 ("Music to hear"), *The Tempest, Love's Labours Lost*
1954	*In Memoriam Dylan Thomas*	English	Dylan Thomas, "Do not go gentle"
1956	*Canticum Sacrum*	Latin	*Gospel according to Mark, Song of Solomon, Deuteronomy, First Epistle of John, Psalms*
1958	*Threni*	Latin	*Lamentations of Jeremiah*
1961	*A Sermon, A Narrative, and A Prayer*	English	*Epistle of Paul to the Romans, Hebrews, Acts of the Apostles*, Thomas Dekker, "Prayer"
1962	*Anthem*	English	T. S. Eliot, *Little Gidding*, part IV
1963	*The Flood*	English	*Genesis* and the York and Chester mystery plays (adapted by Craft)
1964	*Elegy for J.F.K.*	English	W. H. Auden, "When a Just Man Dies"
1965	*Abraham and Isaac*	Hebrew	*Genesis*
1965	*Introitus*	Latin	Requiem
1966	*Requiem Canticles*	Latin	Requiem
1967	*The Owl and the Pussycat*	English	Edward Lear, "The Owl and the Pussycat"

of the text.[12] In the first two measures, for example, the natural language stresses should be on the first syllable of "Requiem" and the second syllable of "aeternam," but Stravinsky supplies metric and/or agogic accents to all of the other syllables also. The result is a sung rhythm that denaturalizes the normal declamation and makes the words seem artificial. This is standard operating procedure for Stravinsky and reinforces his anti-expressive aesthetic: he wants his texts to serve more as independent phonemes to be manipulated in formal schemes than as semantic bearers of meaning. In this sense, the natural rhythms of the words become another compositional limitation to be worked within or, more commonly, against. The same is true of his English-language settings. Ironically, only in Hebrew, a language with which Stravinsky was entirely unfamiliar, do the musical rhythms reinforce the spoken rhythms in a naturalistic way.[13] When Stravinsky was linguistically at home, he employed his texts as a set of rhythmic givens to be consistently resisted or evaded.

---

[12] See Richard Taruskin, "Stravinsky's 'Rejoicing Discovery' and What it Meant: In Defense of His Notorious Text Setting," in *Stravinsky Retrospectives*, ed. Ethan Haimo and Paul Johnson (Lincoln, Nebr.: University of Nebraska Press, 1987), 162–99; and *Stravinsky and the Russian Traditions*, 1119–1236.

[13] Of *Abraham and Isaac*, Stravinsky writes, "No translation of the Hebrew should be attempted, the Hebrew syllables, both as accentuation and timbre, being a principal and fixed element of the music. I did not try to follow Hebrew cantillation, of course, as that would have imposed crippling restrictions, but the verbal and the musical accentuation are identical in this score, which fact I mention because it is rare in my music" (*Themes and Episodes*, 55).

Example 2.1 *Introitus*, mm. 3–7
(a) Stravinsky's first sketch of the vocal line, with his own analytical label
(b) Stravinsky's final sketch of the vocal line (identical to the published version), with his
analytical label retained

(a)

Ten.

Re - qui - em   ae - ter - nam   do - na   e - is   Do - mi - ne

(b)

Tenori

Re - qui - em   ae - ter - nam   do - na   e - i,   Do - mi - ne

If Stravinsky's chosen texts thus provided welcome external constraints on his music, the principal internal constraint involved serialism. Serialism was immediately attractive to Stravinsky as a way of organizing the flow of notes and intervals in the absence of traditional tonal constraints. Stravinsky had always composed with ostinati, or repeated groups of notes, and the series represents a kind of apotheosis of the ostinato. Stravinsky apparently described his music as "composing with intervals," and the series embodied a selection of chosen intervals, which would be repeated and varied in predictable ways as the series was transformed.[14] Stravinsky quickly recognized that the series could provide him with a useful point of departure, a way of regulating the musical flow, a set of rules and constraints to accept, struggle with, or evade as he saw fit. It thus opened a path into a new musical world. Like his hyper-organized studio and his carefully chosen texts, the serial idea gave shape to Stravinsky's creative impulses.

COMPOSITIONAL PROCESS

Once he had decided upon a text, Stravinsky's compositional process usually unfolded in five stages:

[14] Babbitt refers to the phrase "composing with intervals" in "Remarks on the Recent Stravinsky," in *Perspectives on Schoenberg and Stravinsky*, ed. Benjamin Boretz and Edward Cone (Princeton: Princeton University Press), 167. He offers a fuller account in *Words About Music*, 20: "One of the remarkable things that Stravinsky said, when people felt that he had committed a treasonable act by starting to write pieces where you could find successions of twelve [notes] at the beginning, was 'There's nothing to it; I've always composed with intervals.' Basically, of course, it was something of a witticism, but what it did show, much more than a witticism, was how profoundly this is an interval kind of syntax and not just a pitch-class syntax – fundamentally and centrally an interval syntax."

(1) Creating a central thematic idea, usually a one-line melody, often specific as to pitch, rhythm, and instrumentation. This might take place either at the piano or in Stravinsky's inner ear.

(2) Deriving an abstract series from the central thematic idea. In the early works of the period, the series might contain as few as four notes (*Musick to Heare*) or five (*In Memoriam Dylan Thomas*) or as many as sixteen (Septet, second movement). Beginning with *Canticum Sacrum* and *Agon*, the series tend to have – and from *Threni* on, always have – twelve notes.

(3) Writing charts and arrays derived from the series. These charts and arrays combine and manipulate the series in various ways to generate the basic pitch material for all of Stravinsky's late music. They comprise the boundaries for the compositional flow and delimit the field of action, simultaneously constraining and enabling. Stravinsky remains profoundly committed to them throughout his late period. Beginning with *Threni* in 1958, every single note has a demonstrable source in serial charts.

(4) Sketching and composing chunks or blocks of material. This stage of composition takes place at the piano, and includes extensive improvisation and testing of series- and array-derived materials. It also involves extensive self-analysis, with Stravinsky carefully notating the serial derivation of each note, particularly in passages where the derivation might not be readily apparent. The music is normally composed contrapuntally, with a principal melodic line composed in its entirety before accompanying lines, usually in canonic or other serial relationship, are added.

(5) Assembling the blocks into a continuous, finished composition. Stravinsky apparently assembled blocks into sections as he went along rather than doing an entire piece at once.[15] The blocks are often contrasting in character, but Stravinsky also forges subtle connections among them.[16]

At each of these stages, Stravinsky relied heavily on the piano, particularly at the first stage, when working toward a central, generating idea:

I begin work by relating intervals rhythmically. This exploration of possibilities is always conducted at the piano. Only after I have established my melodic or harmonic relationships do I pass to composition. Composition is a later expansion and organization of material . . . When my main theme has been decided I know on general lines what kind of musical material it will require. I start to look for this material, sometimes playing old masters (to put myself in motion), sometimes starting directly to improvise rhythmic units on a provisional row of notes (which can become a final row). I thus form my building material.[17]

Musical ideas were normally played immediately. The piano was thus used to verify ideas suggested in his inner ear. And the reverse process was even more important: Stravinsky's improvisations at the piano suggested ideas to be incorporated into his

---

[15] My thanks to Lynne Rogers for this observation.

[16] The tension between the self-insulation of the blocks and their propensity to be combined into larger wholes is a central theme of Chapter 3.   [17] *Conversations*, 15–16.

music. These improvisations, of course, took place within the narrow limits Stravinsky determined for any particular compositional endeavor. Even when the music seems most abstract, most reliant on intricate precompositional schemes, Stravinsky always worked out the details at the piano, in constant physical contact with the tactile and acoustical realities of the sounds he was writing.

WRITING A MELODY AND A SERIES

There is remarkable documentation of the first two stages of Stravinsky's compositional process in a series of twenty-four photographs taken by the photographer Arnold Newman during a visit to the composer's studio in 1967.[18] As Stravinsky began work on a new, and never-completed, composition, Newman stood behind him, shooting photographs over his shoulder, and produced a note-by-note record of Stravinsky at work. The first eleven photographs show Stravinsky using one of his gadgets, the so-called "Stravigor," to draw a single five-line staff on a blank piece of paper, and then gradually produce the musical idea shown in Example 2.2a. The alto clef suggests that this music is destined for the viola, but there is as yet no indication of rhythm or articulation. This initial five-note idea is designed as a wedge expanding outward from the initial B: first up one semitone to C and then (allowing for octave displacement) down one semitone to B♭; then up and down two semitones, to D♭ and A. The result is a five-note chromatic cluster, balanced around the initial tone.[19] Because of the registral dislocation of the B♭, however, the five-note idea has a dramatic contour, with its climax right in the middle – it is a satisfying, self-contained musical gesture.

In the thirteenth photograph, Stravinsky continues the viola line and adds a cello part, with each assigned a specific rhythm (see Example 2.2b). The two parts together create a balanced unit that begins B–C–D, an ascending semitone followed by a whole-tone, and ends A–B–C, in which the two intervals are reversed. The middle three notes of the viola line, C–B♭–D♭, present a differently ordered transposition of A–B–C.[20] The sense of balance around B is still present and, indeed, the cello's first note, D, is the next note in the wedge. A twelve-tone problem exists, however, in that the last two notes of the figure, B–C, repeat the first two. As Stravinsky massages the sketch into a twelve-tone row, this repetition will need to be eliminated.

In the fourteenth through twentieth photographs, Stravinsky extends the initial idea and slightly modifies its rhythm as in Example 2.2c. The second note in the viola has been changed from C to E♭, thus eliminating one of the problematic

---

[18] *Bravo Stravinsky.*

[19] The last four notes describe a tetrachord-type, (0134), that is familiar throughout Stravinsky's music, and the first note fills in the one gap in that tetrachord. The process is roughly the reverse of that of the series for *In Memoriam Dylan Thomas.* There the first four notes converge on the fifth and last.

[20] The generation of melodic ideas from the combination of motives via transposition or inversion is one of the themes of Chapter 3.

Example 2.2   The evolution of a musical idea, documented in photographs by Arnold
Newman
(a) a five–note idea, apparently for viola
(b) rhythm and cello part added
(c) duet expanded to twelve notes
(d) repetitions eliminated
(e) series

(a)

(b)

(c)

(d)

(e)

repetitions. The idea now contains twelve notes, six in the viola and six in the cello, and thus might initially have appeared to Stravinsky suitable as a basis for a twelve-tone row, and indeed, at this stage, he begins to write out a twelve-tone row on a separate staff. But as he does so, he apparently becomes aware that there are still undesirable repetitions: the B, which remained uncorrected from before, and the B♭, which was introduced at this stage. And two notes are missing: G and A♭.

In the final photographs, then, Stravinsky rewrites the musical idea as in Example 2.2d. Arrows indicate the notes that have been changed. Now all twelve pitch-classes are represented, once each. He then copies out the twelve notes of his musical idea (with the E♭ and E changing places) on a separate staff (see Example 2.2e), which he cuts out with scissors, and pastes onto the center of a new, blank page, to become, in Craft's words, "the incremental center of the composition":

Stravinsky has identified the sketch as "part of a string passage in the middle section of a symphonic piece," and the presence of instrumental indications (violas and cellos) in this initial stage argues that the springs of his invention are concrete. Nor does the scissoring out of a twelve-note series – which is the beginning of a formulating, not of an abstracting, process – contradict the claim. The composer's next step was to chart his fields of choice by drawing derivative serial forms. These he attached to the side of his piano writing-board, like dressmakers' patterns, pinning the sketch itself to the center, whence it became the incremental center of the composition. From this point, too, he worked exclusively at the piano, not having touched the instrument that morning but composing, as he said, in his inner ear. . . .He pretends to believe, incidentally, that coincidence is the only force at work, or play, when a line he composes contains twelve different pitches in succession, though if this phenomenon were reported of some other composer he would be the first to see that hearing and thinking in units of twelve is to some extent a matter of habit.[21]

In Stravinsky's initial stages of composition, then, there is constant interplay between the concrete and the abstract, in which the first two phases of the compositional process, theme-construction and series-creation, are melded into one. The initial sketches are extremely specific in their register, rhythm, and instrumentation, but they are forced to bend to the more abstract need for a twelve-tone series that contains no repetition. The series simultaneously emerges from and shapes the concrete musical idea. The musical ideas embodied in the initial sketches remain in the series, but in a more abstract form.[22] The cello's initial D–E returns as E–D in the second and third notes of the series and the viola's first three notes, B–C–B♭, return toward the end of the series. The combination of semitones and whole-tones that characterized the second sketch is also present in the series in its registral lines as

---

[21] *Bravo, Stravinsky*, 13; later reprinted and slightly revised in *Chronicle*, 303, 311.

[22] The final version of the series, derived from a highly individuated thematic idea, nonetheless bears striking resemblance to two earlier series: the segments that comprise its fifth through tenth notes, D♭–E♭ and A–B–C–B♭, are found also in the series for "Surge, aquilo" from *Canticum Sacrum*, the I-form of the series for the Coda in *Agon*, and *Anthem*. My thanks to David Smyth for pointing this out. It is striking that Stravinsky works so hard in 1966 to rediscover combinations he had already used in other works so many years earlier. Additional inter-opus references of this kind are discussed in Chapter 3.

Stravinsky has arranged them, most obviously E–D–D♭ and A♭–G♭–F. Even the
sense of inversional balance around B is still present in the series, in the proximity of
notes to their around–B partners, but in a subtle, attenuated way.[23] In moving from
initial sketch to series, Stravinsky moves from the concrete embodiment to the
abstract representation of a nexus of interconnected musical ideas.[24]

The same process, involving movement from a concrete musical theme to an
abstract series, shapes most of Stravinsky's late works, including his earliest efforts to
write in the serial idiom. Example 2.3 contains the initial compositional sketches
for "Full fadom five," a setting of verses from Shakespeare's *The Tempest*, published
as one of *Three Songs from William Shakespeare* (1954).[25] Stravinsky's first notated
sketch (Example 2.3a) is simply an ascending E♭ minor scale. It is not a specific
musical idea, as in Example 2.2, but it does establish a concrete starting point, providing material to be shaped into a series. The second sketch (Example 2.3b) takes
the seven notes of the scale and arranges them into an eight-note melody (the D♭
occurs twice) to set the first line of the poem:

> Full fadom five thy Father lies,
> Of his bones are corrall made:
> Those are pearles that were his eies,
> Nothing of him that doth fade,
> But doth suffer a Sea-change
> Into something rich and strange:
> Sea-Nimphs hourly ring his knell.
> Ding dong, ding dong
> Hearke now I heare them;
> Ding dong bell.

The widely spaced melody, with its exclusive use of perfect fourths, perfect fifths,
and minor sevenths, is designed to evoke the tolling of funeral bells, referred to at
the end of the poem.[26] In the third sketch (Example 2.3c), Stravinsky takes the
seven notes of the E♭ minor scale and presents them in a different ordering to set the

---

[23] The balancing dyadic pairs are B♭–C, A–D♭, A♭–D, G–E♭, and G♭–E. B and F balance themselves. An additional
striking idea becomes prominent only in the final series. Four of its segmental subsets are members of sc(026).
E–D–A♭ is the ordered inversion of D♭–E♭–A, which is overlapped with its retrograde-inversion, E♭–A–B. A
fourth segment, C–B♭–G♭, is related by unordered transposition or inversion to each of these. Motivic combinations of this kind are explored in Chapter 3.

[24] Stravinsky describes the same procedure in answer to an interviewer's question, "What were the origins of the
Requiem Canticles?" Stravinsky responds: "Intervallic designs which I expanded into contrapuntal forms and
from which, in turn, I conceived the larger shape of the work. The twofold series was also discovered early on,
in fact while I was completing the first musical sentence" (*Themes and Conclusions*, 98). And similarly with regard
to *Elegy for J. F. K.*: "The only light I can throw on the question of method is to say that I had already joined the
various melodic fragments before finding the possibilities of serial combination inherent in them" (*Themes and
Episodes*, 59).

[25] The sketches are transcribed from document No. 114–0737 in the Stravinsky Archive at the Paul Sacher
Foundation.

[26] Craft refers to this opening melody as the "bells motive" (*Avec Stravinsky*, 149). This and other evocations of
bells are discussed in Chapter 5. In the final version of the song, this melody is accompanied by canons in the
viola (in augmentation at the unison) and clarinet and viola (at the perfect fifth above).

Example 2.3   Compositional sketches for "Full fadom five"
(a) E♭ minor scale
(b) ordered as a melody for the first line of text
(c) reordered as a series

(a)

(b)

(c)

second line of text: "Of his bones are corrall made." This seven–note melody functions as the seven–note series on which most of the rest of the song is based. The
sketch reveals Stravinsky's intention to set the third line of text with the retrograde
of the series (which Stravinsky calls "Canon"), the fourth line of text with the
inversion (which Stravinsky calls "Inverse"), and the fifth line of text with the
inversion of the retrograde (or the "Inverse" of the "Canon").[27]

The same interest in inversional balance that shaped the sketches and resulting
series in Example 2.2 operates here as well. The series is arranged symmetrically
around A♭ and is designed as a wedge to converge on A♭. As a result, the IR–form,
which begins on A♭, wedges symmetrically outward from that note and contains
exactly the same seven notes as the P-form, namely the notes of the E♭ minor scale.
In this way, Stravinsky reveals his understanding of the inversional symmetry of any
diatonic scale and his commitment to inversional symmetry as a basic compositional
resource in his serial music.

Following these preliminary sketches, Stravinsky composes the entire melodic
line for the first half of the piece, maintaining the pitches and registers of the

[27] Stravinsky considered these four forms – referred to in this book as P (prime), I (for its inversion beginning on
the same note), R (retrograde), and IR (inversion of the retrograde) – as the basic forms of the series throughout
the remainder of his compositional life. Earlier, in the sketches for the second movement of the Septet (see Plate
14 of *Pictures and Documents*), Stravinsky wrote out IR, then crossed it out in favor of RI. In all subsequent
pieces, he made the opposite decision.

sketch, but adding rhythms (see Example 2.4).[28] The sequence of these sketches reveals that Stravinsky conceived and composed the vocal melody in its entirety before adding accompanying parts, which suggests his essentially contrapuntal conception of music in this period of his compositional life. The lines of a polyphonic fabric are understood as integral, self-sufficient, and musically comprehensible in themselves. Each line has its own serial and musical justification. The same melodic independence is evident also in the sketches for *Introitus* (see Example 2.1 above). Indeed, it is a hallmark of Stravinsky's compositional process throughout his late period.[29] The combination of lines into a polyphonic whole then becomes a separate compositional issue, one that is addressed later in the compositional process.

SELF-ANALYSIS

The presence of Stravinsky's own analytical markings is a striking feature of the sketch in Example 2.4. Despite the ready availability of his serial sketches and charts, normally directly in front of him at the piano, Stravinsky provides extensive analytical markings – brackets, arrows, and series labels – even though the music is already in virtually its final form. The second phrase is the retrograde of the first, and Stravinsky explicitly indicates this by brackets above the melody, linking the recurrent notes. Each of the first two phrases will be followed, eventually, by its "inverse" (inversion), as indicated by the labels and arrows beneath the staff. When those inversions arrive, they are also bracketed and labeled with backward-pointing arrows. A two-note overlap connects the fourth phrase to a bracketed but unlabeled repetition of the original form of the series. The melody concludes with a restatement of the I-form, which is neither bracketed nor labeled.

Serial self-analysis is a persistent feature of Stravinsky's compositional sketches throughout this period. It begins with the first serial passage Stravinsky ever wrote, the beginning of Ricercar II from the *Cantata* (see Example 2.5).[30] Stravinsky begins by writing out a series: E–C–D–E–F–E♭–D–E–C–D–B (Example 2.5a). It is eleven notes long, but because of repetitions, contains only six different pitch-classes. The series is followed by its retrograde (which Stravinsky calls "cancri-zans"), and the resulting retrograde symmetry is indicated by brackets connecting the corresponding notes. These two series forms are followed by the inversion (which Stravinsky here calls "riverse") and its retrograde (another "cancrizans"), and again the retrograde relationship is confirmed with brackets.

After completing the row chart, Stravinsky writes the opening melody in its

[28] Document No. 114–0738 in the Stravinsky Archive at the Paul Sacher Foundation. The sketch and the published score for this melody are identical in content.

[29] The same procedure – a layering of independent lines to create a polyphonic whole – underlies Stravinsky's arrangements of pre-existing compositions undertaken during this period, including Bach's Chorale Variations on *Vom himmel hoch*, *Greeting Prelude* (Stravinsky's arrangement of "Happy Birthday to You"), and *Canon (On a Russian Popular Tune)*, an arrangement of the main theme from the finale of *The Firebird*.

[30] This sketch is reproduced in *Strawinsky: Sein Nachlass, Sein Bild*, 157.

Example 2.4 "Full fadom five": final version of opening melody with Stravinsky's self-analytical markings

Example 2.5 Cantata, Ricercar II, "Tomorrow shall be my dancing day":
(a) Stravinsky's series chart

Example 2.5 (*cont.*)

(b) sketch for the initial melody with self-analytical brackets

(b)

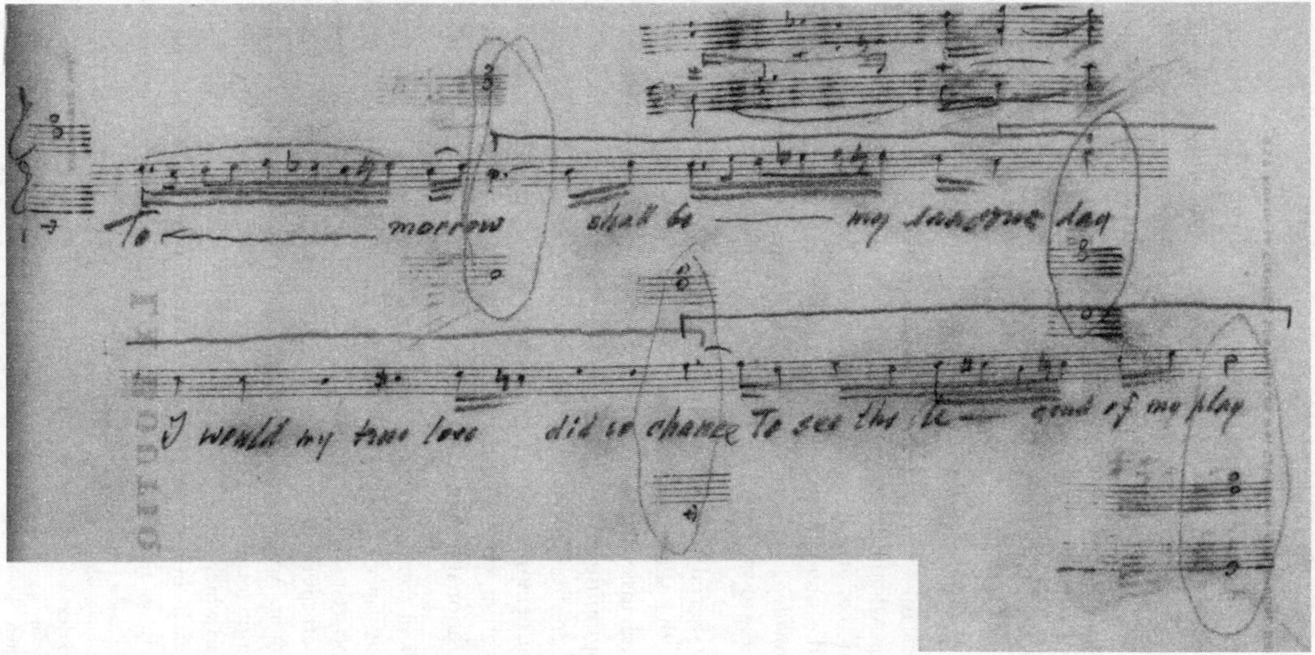

finished form (Example 2.5b). The initial series is unmarked, but its retrograde, inversion, and retrograde of the inversion are identified with analytical brackets. These brackets appear also in the published score of the *Cantata*, as do similar self-analytical annotations in *In Memoriam Dylan Thomas*. The presence in those scores of serial labels has been taken by some as a deliberate announcement of compositional intention and a public advertisement for his new compositional methods.[31]

It seems more probable, however, that their inclusion in the published score was inadvertent. Self-analytical markings persist at all stages of the compositional process and survive even in the most polished final drafts. It is likely, then, that Stravinsky simply neglected to delete them from the manuscript delivered to his publisher. Indeed, this was evidently the case with *Canticum Sacrum*, about which his editor in London, Erwin Stein, wrote him:

Your 12-tone rows will cause an upheaval in the musical world and will keep analysts busy. I do not know whether you should help them by the arrows you have indicated in the score. It is a question of principle about which I should be happy to know your opinion. Is it necessary that the listener knows the rows or is it sufficient that he feels the unity of form which the rows provide? . . . [Here Stravinsky wrote in the margin of the letter: "as always, I forgot to delete the arrows."][32]

Stravinsky's serial self-analyses had primarily a private function, to confirm for the composer the serial derivation of the notes he was writing. Throughout this period, Stravinsky became increasingly strict about the serial credentials of his music. Beginning with *Threni*, there are no passages, melodies, or even individual notes that are free from the serial constraints Stravinsky imposed upon himself. In this rigorous environment, his deliberate self-analyses serve as a form of reassurance and verification, confirming for the composer himself that he is effectively realizing his compositional design. As Craft explains,

Stravinsky still composes at the piano but not exclusively, at least not in the preliminary stages. Music paper, or styluses and unlined paper, are close to hand on all of his peregrinations, and he seems to be visited with a great deal of what may or may not be inspiration on airplanes; perhaps the perfect composing conditions for him would be found on an interplanetary flight. Any scrap of paper – bit of an envelope, back of a menu or programme, napkin, margin torn from a magazine – will do for notations, which is why the pages of the notebooks in which these sketches are pasted look like collages. Stravinsky dates each sketch and marks each choice of serial route in colored pencils, for the simple reason, he says, that it is otherwise so difficult to check errors, though obviously it is more than that; in fact the

---

[31] See, for example, Glenn Watkins, "The Canon and Stravinsky's Late Style," in *Confronting Stravinsky*, ed. Jann Pasler (Berkeley: University of California Press, 1986), 225, which refers to them as "overt methodological advertisements."

[32] Letter written November 3, 1955. Quoted, along with Stravinsky's response, in *Pictures and Documents*, 431. Similarly, with respect to *In Memoriam Dylan Thomas*, Stravinsky wrote, "In correcting the proofs I forgot to erase in the prelude these brackets left over from my final sketches, where they were put *throughout* the work, this complicating the reading of the instrumental and vocal score" (quoted without cited source by the Editor of *Tempo* at the end of Hans Keller, "'In Memoriam Dylan Thomas': Stravinsky's Schoenbergian Technique," *Tempo* 35 [1955], 13–20).

manifestation of a powerful compulsion for order. Stravinsky's compositional procedures seem not to have changed in late years. He almost always begins with a melodic idea, which in the first writing may be expressed only by its rhythmic values. He will often compose this single line, in isolation it seems, to a point where larger shapes become clear to him. The piano is not resorted to in this melody-forging stage, but only when harmonic and contrapuntal ideas begin to appear; it is then that Stravinsky will say he has invented (i.e., discovered) something which he now intends to compose (i.e., develop).[33]

Both the melody-first approach and the serial self-analysis are evident in the sketches for "Surge, aquilo," the second movement of *Canticum Sacrum* and Stravinsky's first entirely twelve-tone movement. From some initial, fragmentary melodic sketches, Stravinsky evolves the series, and its derivative forms, shown in Example 2.6a.[34] The row chart contains what for Stravinsky were the basic forms of the series, identified here in brackets as P, I, R, and IR. Stravinsky's own arrows indicate that P and I are related by inversion ("Riv.") and begin on the same note, as do R and IR.[35] To the right of the chart is a summary by Craft of a standard way of naming series forms (under the column marked "me") and of Stravinsky's idiosyncratic nomenclature (under the column marked "S"). What Craft refers to as O, I, R, and IR, Stravinsky calls O ("original"), R ("riversion"), C ("cancrizans"), and CR ("cancrizans riverse"). Under Craft's R, Stravinsky has inserted the abbreviation "canc." to clarify his own understanding of the label. Stravinsky's nomenclature has changed since "Full fadom five," discussed above, but never became reliably conventional throughout his compositional life, despite Craft's apparent effort to reform him.

    With his series in place, Stravinsky was in a position to write the tenor vocal line for the movement, which he did in its entirety before adding accompanying parts. For most of the melody, Stravinsky supplies analytical markings, as in Example 2.6b. This portion of the melody, mm. 50–55 in the score, consists of the first six notes of R (indicated by Stravinsky in blue pencil with an open dotted bracket pointing ahead to its later completion); the first six notes of IR (the "riverse" of R) transposed to E♭ (indicated in red pencil with a solid bracket); and concludes with a complete statement of R (indicated by the completion of the blue bracket and backward pointing arrow labeled "resume"). The three segments of the melody overlap with shared pivot notes: the last note of the first hexachord of R is E♭, which serves also as the first note of the transposition of IR that follows. The last note of the second segment is A, which also signals the return to the beginning of

---

[33] *Dialogues*, 14.

[34] The process of evolving the series from the initial melodic sketches is detailed in Susannah Tucker, "Stravinsky and His Sketches: The Composing of *Agon* and Other Serial Works of the 1950s" (D.Phil. dissertation, Oxford University, 1992), 117–18. The sketches in Example 2.6 and portions of their interpretation are based on Tucker, 121–23. Tucker identifies the row chart in Example 2.6a as sketchleaf CS68; the melodic sketch in Example 2.6b as sketchleaves CS75, CS76, and CS78r.

[35] Stravinsky's nomenclature is both idiosyncratic and inconsistent. Here, "riversion" obviously means inversion. Elsewhere (e.g. the sketches and published score for *In Memoriam Dylan Thomas*), the same term refers to retrograde.

Example 2.6 *Canticum Sacrum*, "Surge, aquilo'
(a) Stravinsky's row chart with annotations by Craft
(b) sketch for tenor melody, mm. 50–55, with Stravinsky's analytical markings

R. The use of common tones to link series forms is a common principle of serial combination in Stravinsky's music.[36]

The self-analysis here reveals the somewhat complex serial derivation of the resulting score. Indeed, as a general matter, the more complex the derivations in Stravinsky's music, the more intensive the self-analysis. When the serial going got tough, Stravinsky wanted to be sure that he was maintaining strict fidelity to his precompositional schemes. At this relatively early stage in his serial evolution, the series still function to some extent as register-specific lines of pitches, rather than, as becomes increasingly the norm, more abstract lines of register-free pitch classes. In the melodic line of Example 2.6b, for example, the contour of the melody follows exactly the contour of the series as written in the chart of Example 2.6a. The relationship of the melody to its serial source is therefore extremely close.

Stravinsky's melody has a self-contained, autonomous quality. It is shaped as an elegant double arch, one in which every leap is promptly filled in, creating a continuous chromatic cluster from its lowest note to its highest. The serial derivation,

---

[36] This is a trait Stravinsky shares with Webern, although it is hard to know if this is influence or coincidence.

as revealed in the self-analysis, and the internal qualities of the melody confirm its independence within what would later, with the addition of other serial melodies, become an elaborate contrapuntal setting.[37]

For the most part, Stravinsky conceived his serial music in terms of independent lines, each with its own internal serial and musical logic, which could then be combined in polyphonic layers. In the compositional process, the creation of the melodic lines was one phase, and their combination was another, later phase.[38] Within each discrete section of the music, each distinct textural block, the music was thus built up in layers.

ARRANGING THE BLOCKS

The final phase of composition involved arranging the sections or blocks in a suitable order. The composition of *Epitaphium* reveals each of the stages of the compositional process, including this last one. Example 2.7 reproduces Stravinsky's sole compositional sketch for the work.[39] The top two staves present a duet for flute and clarinet. The bottom two staves contain isolated phrases intended for harp. Arrows indicate that these harp gestures are to be inserted at regular junctures within the flute–clarinet duet. In the middle Stravinsky writes his four usual series forms and identifies them with labels: O, I, R, and IR (in this instance he has adopted the conventional nomenclature). The same labels appear also in the music above and below the row chart.

Stravinsky has described the process in some detail:

I began the *Epitaphium* with the flute–clarinet duet (which I had originally thought of as a duet for two flutes and which can be played by two flutes . . . In the manner I have described in our previous conversations I heard and composed a melodic-harmonic phrase. I certainly did not (and never do) begin with a purely serial idea and, in fact, when I began I did not know, or care, whether all twelve notes would be used. After I had written about half the first phrase I saw its serial pattern, however, and then perhaps I began to work towards that pattern . . . Only after I had written this little twelve-note duet did I conceive the idea of a series of funeral responses between bass and treble instruments and, as I wanted the whole piece to be very muffled, I decided that the bass instrument should be a harp. The first bar of the harp part was, however, written last . . . There are four short antiphonal strophes for the harp, and four for the wind duet, and each strophe is a complete order of the series – harp: O, I, R, RI; winds: O, RI, R, I.[40]

Stravinsky thus began with the first phrase of the duet for woodwind instruments, massaging it in the direction of a twelve-tone idea, in the manner of Example 2.2 above. When the series eventually emerged, he wrote it down along with its usual associates (I, R, and IR). He then completed the woodwind duet, carefully

---

[37] Craft, commenting on the composition of "Surge, aquilo," points to the independence of the contrapuntal parts and their serial integrity: "[Stravinsky's] usual procedure is to unfold complete statements of the series as often in the voice as in the instruments, either playing these simultaneously or superposing them in canon" (*Avec Stravinsky*, 160).   [38] The combination of contrapuntal lines is one of the subjects of Chapter 3.

[39] Document No. 109–0403 in the Stravinsky Archive at the Paul Sacher Foundation.

[40] *Memories and Commentaries*, 105–06.

Example 2.7 Compositional sketch for *Epitaphium*, with woodwind duet on top, series chart in the middle, and harp part at the bottom identifying its serial credentials with analytical labels. At that point, having already composed a continuous and essentially complete piece, Stravinsky decided to inter-polate contrasting phrases for harp, again with clear serial identifications. He thus radically disrupted the continuity of the duet in favor of a virtual collage of eight discrete blocks of sound, each embodying a single series statement. There are sig-nificant intervallic and motivic links among the blocks, but their centripetal force is barely enough to counteract the strong centrifugal energy of the antiphony.

The fragmentary, discontinuous nature of the composition of the work is reflected in the physical layout of the published score (see Example 2.8). In tradi-tional scores, each instrumental part is notated on continuous staves, with rests to hold and fill the space when the instrument is momentarily silent. In the scores of Stravinsky's late period, however, beginning with the *Epitaphium*, instruments are notated only when they actually play. As a result, the scores present a fragmentary visual appearance vividly reflective of the aural discontinuities of the music.

Stravinsky's music, both early and late, often gives the impression of an assem-blage of discrete units, or a collage. It sounds, in many cases, as though the blocks of music had been cut out and pasted together – and that is sometimes literally true. Stravinsky himself described the practice to his old friend Nicholas Nabokov with regard to the final scene of *Orpheus* (1947), one of the last works of the pre-serial period:

"Here, you see, I cut off the fugue with a pair of scissors." He clipped the air with his fingers. "I introduced this short harp phrase, like two bars of an accompaniment. Then the horns go on with their fugue as if nothing had happened. I repeat it at regular intervals, here and here again." Stravinsky added, with his habitual grin, "You can eliminate these harp solo interruptions, paste the parts of the fugue together, and it will be one whole piece."[41]

In principle, the textural blocks might contain any distinctive musical material, provided only that it was reasonably self-contained and complete in itself. But in the late music, the textural blocks become increasingly identified with serial units. Each of the blocks in *Epitaphium*, for example, corresponds to a single series state-ment. In the major works beginning with *Movements*, similar blocks, and indeed the entire melodic and harmonic fabric, are shaped by Stravinsky's rotational arrays. In his quest for strict precompositional limits within which to exercise compositional freedom, these arrays proved the most productive and represent his most original and important contribution to the theory and composition of twelve-tone music.

[41] Nicholas Nabokov, *Old Friends and New Music* (London: Hamish Hamilton, 1951), 152. Stravinsky made many other comments along similar lines. For example, with regard to *Symphonies of Wind Instruments*: "The chorale which concludes the Symphonies was composed June 20, 1920, in Carantec, a fishing village in Finisterre . . . The music was finished in abbreviated score by July 2, but a few days later I added two adumbrative bits of chorale to the body of the piece" (*Themes and Conclusions*, 39). See Stephen Walsh, "Stravinsky's Symphonies: Accident or Design?," in *Analytical Strategies and Musical Interpretation: Essays in Nineteenth- and Twentieth-Century Music*, ed. Craig Ayrey and Mark Everist (Cambridge: Cambridge University Press, 1996), pp. 35–71 for discus-sion of interpolation as a compositional strategy in this work. See also the sketch for *Agon* reproduced in *Strawinsky: Sein Nachlass, Sein Bild*, 160 which shows that the cello/contrabass figures at mm. 8–9 and 21–22 were late insertions into a continuous musical fabric.

Example 2.8   *Epitaphium*: published score of entire work

CHARTS AND ARRAYS

For all of his major pieces from 1960 until the end of his career (*Movements, A Sermon, a Narrative, and a Prayer, The Flood, Abraham and Isaac, Variations, Introitus, and Requiem Canticles*), Stravinsky constructed serial charts and arrays in a standard, consistent way. After constructing a series, he divided it into its two linear hexachords, each of which is rotated systematically to create a six-row chart of simple rotations. Then the simple rotations are transposed so that they all begin on the same first note, creating an additional six-row chart of transposed rotations. Finally, the other principal series forms (R, I, and IR) are treated the same way, their hexa-chords used to generate charts of simple and transposed rotations.[42]

Example 2.9 reproduces the serial charts derived from the P-form of the series for *Movements*, previously shown in Example 1.9b.[43] The charts that contain simple, untransposed rotations of the series hexachords are labeled with the Greek letters α (the first hexachord) and β (the second hexachord). The rotations are numbered with roman numerals I through V. The charts that contain the transposed rotations are labeled γ (in which the rows of the α chart are transposed to begin on E♭, the first note of the first hexachord) and δ (in which the rows of the β chart are trans-posed to begin on C, the first note of the second hexachord). In works subsequent to *Movements*, Stravinsky sometimes used the vertical columns of his transposed-rotation charts as chordal simultaneities, giving rise to homophonic, chorale-like passages. Typically, such passages consist of either six or twelve chords, each repre-senting a vertical slice through a transposed-rotation chart.[44] In *Movements*, however, and throughout most of his subsequent work as well, he draws primarily on the horizontal rows of these charts as a source of melodic material.

Stravinsky's late serial melodies weave through the rows of these charts. Sometimes, the melodies work their way through the charts in a systematic fashion, row by row. Often, however, they move through the charts in a more idiosyncratic way. Example 2.10a reproduces Stravinsky's sketch for what later became the flute melody in mm. 13–17 of *Movements*.[45] The melody is constructed from segments, none longer than four notes, extracted from the rows of the γ and δ charts, as shown in Example 2.10b.[46] The first three notes of the melody are notes 1, 2, and 3 from row I (i.e. the first rotation) of the γ chart. The next three notes of the melody are notes 4, 5, and 6 from row I of the δ chart, and so on. On his sketch for this

[42] There are local variations in this standard procedure. In *Movements*, for example, Stravinsky produces transposed rotations for some but not all of the series forms. In *Introitus*, he rotates the tetrachords rather than the hexa-chords. In *Variations*, he rotates the series forms as wholes, in addition to rotating their hexachords indepen-dently.   [43] Document No.110–0309 in the Stravinsky Archive at the Paul Sacher Foundation.

[44] The verticals of the rotational arrays will be discussed in detail in Chapter 4.

[45] In the published score, Stravinsky transposes this melody up a major third, possibly to accommodate the range of the flute by avoiding the low A♭3 of the sketch. The melody forms the basis of the larger section of music, mm. 7–21, that contains it. I discuss the melody and its larger musical context in Chapter 3. A significant literature has grown up around this melody, beginning with Stravinsky's comment that "No theorist could determine the spelling of the note order in, for example, the flute solo near the beginning. . . simply by knowing the original order [of the series]" (*Memories and Commentaries*, 100). See additional commentary in Eric Walter White, *Stravinsky: The Composer and His Works* (Berkeley: University of California Press, 1966), 464–66; Milton Babbitt, "Order, Symmetry, and Centricity in Late Stravinsky," in *Confronting Stravinsky*, ed. Jann Pasler (Berkeley: University of California Press, 1986), 255; Milton Babbitt, *Words About Music*, ed. Stephen Dembski and Joseph N. Straus (Madison: University of Wisconsin Press, 1987), 113; Milton Babbitt, "Stravinsky's Verticals and Schoenberg's Diagonals: A Twist of Fate," in *Stravinsky Retrospectives*, ed. Haimo and Johnson, 28; Douglas Rust, "Stravinsky's Twelve-Tone Loom: Composition and Precomposition in *Movements*," *Music Theory Spectrum* 16/1 (1994), 62–76; and Shaugn O'Donnell, "Transformational Voice Leading in Atonal Music" (Ph.D. dissertation, City University of New York, 1997). Stravinsky's sketches are transcribed in Christoph Neidhöfer, "Analysearbeit im Fach Komposition/Musiktheorie über die Movements for Piano and Orchestra von Igor Stravinsky" (Master's thesis, Musik-Akademie der Stadt Basel, 1991) and Rust, "Stravinsky's Twelve-Tone Loom."

[46] The analytical summary in Example 2.10b is Example 2 from Rust, "Stravinsky's Twelve-Tone Loom."

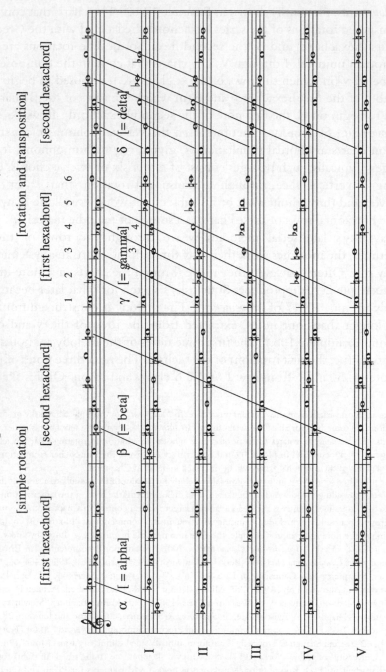

Example 2.9 Serial charts for *Movements* (P-form only)

Example 2.10 *Movements*
(a) sketch for flute solo in mm. 13–17 with Stravinsky's analytical markings
(b) γ and δ charts with segments of the flute melody identified

melody in Example 2.10a, Stravinsky himself has indicated the serial derivation of the entire melody. The intensity of the self-analysis is in proportion to the complexity of the serial derivation and underscores the importance of the charts in Stravinsky's compositional process – at this stage in his compositional life, he never wrote a note for which he did not have an explicit source in the charts.

Stravinsky created his melodies by weaving purposeful musical paths through his charts. Sometimes, as in Example 2.10, the path may appear fragmented and unpredictable, almost deliberately obscure. More commonly, the path involves forging common-tone links among the rows of the arrays. The note or notes that conclude one row become the note or notes that begin the next (see Example 2.11). Example 2.11a shows the remaining charts for *Movements*, based on the I ("Inv."), R ("Riv."), and IR ("Riv.-Inv.") forms of the series.[47] The circled rows form the basis for the sketch in Example 2.11b, which shows Stravinsky tracing a path through these charts. Across the top line of the sketch, he writes out the entire bottom row of his IR-chart ("RIV-INV V"). All twelve notes are present but, because the hexachords

---

[47] The charts of Example 2.11a and the sketch in Example 2.11b are found on Documents No. 110–0309, No. 110–0310 and No. 110–0316 in the Stravinsky Archive at the Paul Sacher Foundation.

Example 2.11 *Movements*
(a) Stravinsky's I–, R–, and IR–charts (circles added)

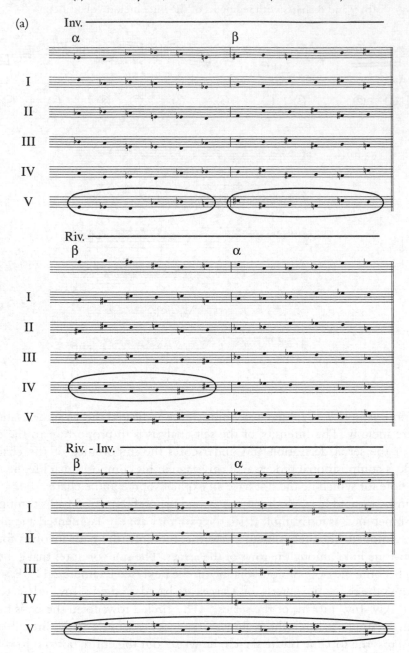

Example 2.11 (*cont.*)
(b) compositional sketch for mm. 68–73
(c) mm. 68–73 of the published score, with Stravinsky's analysis superimposed

(b)

(c)

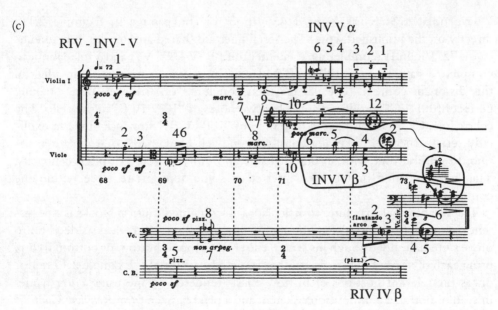

are rotated independently, this succession is not a form of the original series. Beginning on the second line of the sketch and continuing on the third, Stravinsky writes out the entire bottom row of the I-chart in reverse order with F♯–C♯ appearing twice ("INV V"). The vertical alignments and the vertical lines suggest that Stravinsky is looking for common-tone links among the rows. The F♯ in particular is singled out in that way. On the fourth and final line of the sketch, Stravinsky writes out the fourth rotation of the "β" hexachord of the R-chart ("Riv IV"), one that conspicuously ends with the perfect fifth F♯–C♯, just as the second line of the sketch did.

Example 2.11c contains the passage for which this sketch provides the serial structure. The passage is one of the self-contained "Interludes" that, at a relatively late stage in the compositional process, Stravinsky decided to insert between the previously composed "Movements." The Interludes thus constitute discrete musical units, to be literally cut out and pasted in. In Stravinsky's words, they are

introductions rather than codas; the conductor should pause *before* them. I like these caesuras, incidentally, and I want the seams and sutures in my music to show.[48]

I have notated Stravinsky's serial derivation for the passage in Example 2.11c directly on the published score. The serial lines are shared among the instruments. In m. 72, Violin II (completing a statement of "RIV-INV V") and Viola (about to complete a statement of "INV V β") play F♯ in octaves, a striking sonic effect in this dissonant context. The passage then concludes on the even more striking perfect fifth F♯–C♯, produced as the last two notes of "RIV IV β" in the cello. The cello's final C♯ serves also as the final note of "INV V β." Stravinsky uses an explicitly serial structure, internally consistent and self-contained, to articulate a distinctive musical unit with an unmistakable and unifying sense of pitch centricity. That self-contained unit is then inserted at some appropriate place within the composition.

The use of serial structures to articulate self-contained musical blocks is a persistent feature of Stravinsky's late music. Equally persistent is Stravinsky's decision to move systematically through his arrays, either from top to bottom or bottom to top, using each of its rows in turn as a source of melodic material.[49] Example 2.12 reproduces the relevant portions of his row chart (rendered by me using letter names instead of notes), a compositional sketch, and a brief passage from *Requiem Canticles* (Interlude, mm. 176–92).[50] The charts in Example 2.12a involve the usual transpositions and rotations. Each of the hexachords of the series, labeled α and β, is rotated independently and transposed so that all of the rows within each hexachordal array begin on the same first note.[51] The sketch in Example 2.12b is actually a composite of four separate fragments of paper taped onto a single sheet, suggesting

[48] *Themes and Episodes*, 25.   [49] Systematic progressions of this kind are discussed in detail in Chapter 3.

[50] The sketch is reproduced as Plate 15 of *Pictures and Documents*.

[51] The charts labeled α and β in Example 2.12 correspond to the γ and δ charts from *Movements*, discussed above with reference to Example 2.9.

Example 2.12 *Requiem Canticles*, Interlude, mm. 176–92
(a) row charts

(a)   P-chart, or O-chart (for Row 2)

	Alpha-hexachord						Beta-hexachord					
I	F	C	B	A	A♯	D	C♯	D♯	G♯	F♯	E	G
II	F	E	D	D♯	G	A♯	C♯	F♯	E	D	F	B
III	F	D♯	E	G♯	B	F♯	C♯	B	A	C	F♯	G♯
IV	F	F♯	A♯	C♯	G♯	G	C♯	B	D	G♯	A♯	D♯
V	F	A	C	G	F♯	E	C♯	E	A♯	C	F	D♯
VI	F	G♯	D♯	D	C	C♯	C♯	G	A	D	C	A♯

again the collage-like nature of Stravinsky's compositional process. The sketch reveals Stravinsky's intention to use the second of two series for the work (hence the label II in red ink) and to begin with a statement of the α hexachord of the P-form (or O-form) of the series. The α hexachord is followed by the six rotations of the β hexachord labeled, in order, β1, β2, β3, β4, β5, and β6. The β2–β3 succession is circled in red ink, and Stravinsky intends to substitute for it the music written directly below it. The β2–β3 unit is thus treated as a chunk or block, subject to insertion or deletion as a self-contained, integral unit.

At a higher level, the progression as a whole is treated in the same way. Having completed a systematic movement through the β-chart, Stravinsky intends to do the same thing again, but with the rhythms and registers of the notes modified. The second half of the sketch describes the same progression – a statement of the first hexachord followed by a progression, in order, of β1, β2, β3, β4, β5, and β6. This modified repetition is both circled in green ink and, apparently, cut out from another sheet and pasted into proximity with the first half of the sketch. In addition, portions of the second half are themselves cut out and pasted on. The serial units of the larger progression are thus treated as discrete, manipulable blocks, as is the progression in its entirety. Small blocks are embedded within larger ones, and, at every level of structure, the blocks are articulated by explicit serial schemes. The sketch is striking both for its collage, cut-and-paste format and the intensity of its serial self-analysis, which I have reproduced directly on the published score in Example 2.12c.

SERIAL "MISTAKES"

One measure of Stravinsky's commitment to his serial schemes is his attitude toward serial "mistakes," that is, inconsistencies within his serial charts or discrepancies

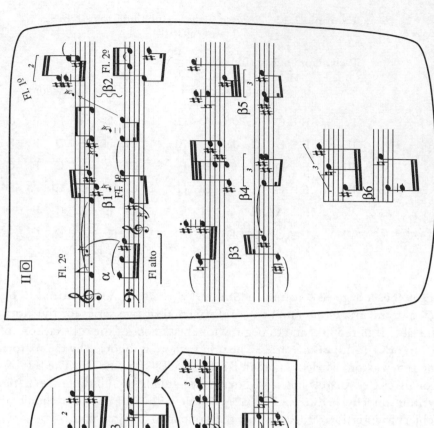

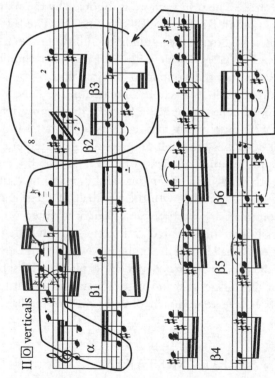

Example 2.12 (*cont.*)
(b) sketch with serial self-analysis

(b)

Example 2.12 (*cont.*)

(c) published score of mm. 176–92, with Stravinsky's self-analysis superimposed

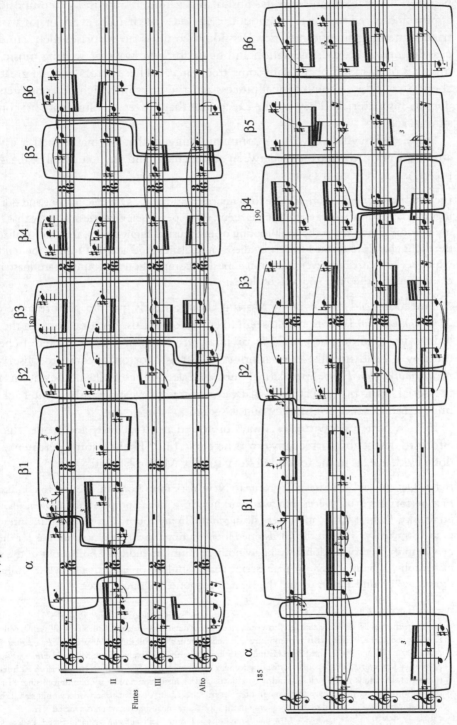

(c)

between a serial scheme and its musical realization.[52] Stravinsky's compositional approach evolved rapidly throughout this period – in virtually every major work he tried something significantly new. It should come as no surprise, then, amid this ceaseless musical experimentation and quest for new ways of writing music, that mistakes of this kind occur with some frequency.[53] These errors reveal a great deal about Stravinsky's compositional process and the ways in which he constructs and deploys his materials. They are the exceptions that prove and illuminate his compositional rules.

Some of Stravinsky's written comments suggest that he maintained a cavalier attitude toward discrepancies between serial charts and their musical realizations, preferring to rely on his ear:

I regard my feelings as more reliable than my calculations . . . Our calculations and our feelings overlap and they may even be congruent. I will persist, nevertheless, and say that I trust my musical glands above the foolproofing of my musical flight charts, though I realize that the flight charts are formed in part by these same glands; and add that I think the tendency which seeks to attribute every factor in a musical composition to a punch-card master plan could constrict the "free" options of the ear.[54]

An anecdote told by Lawrence Morton about an early, private performance of *In Memoriam Dylan Thomas*, would seem to corroborate this: "At one point in the preluding dirge-canons, he paused to say in a conspiratorial whisper, "Here I cheated the row – I did not like the harmony."[55] But as Morton goes on to observe, *In Memoriam Dylan Thomas*, in its final published version, contains no deviations from the serial plan, no "cheating" whatsoever. Stravinsky apparently went back and imposed strict serial consistency on the score.

In fact, Stravinsky virtually always preferred not to cheat, and made vigorous efforts to detect and correct any errors he could find. There is some pertinent anecdotal evidence, as in the following story told by Milton Babbitt:

In late December 1958 Stravinsky came to New York from London. He was to conduct the first performance of *Threni*, but was working on a new composition: *Movements*. Mrs. Stravinsky, Robert Craft, and I were sitting in the living room (as it turned out, anteroom) of the Stravinskys' suite at the Gladstone Hotel waiting for Stravinsky to join us for dinner; he was in the bedroom, doing we knew not what until he suddenly bolted out of the room in his robe, waving a page of manuscript paper, smiling broadly that pixylike smile, and shouting: "I found a mistake, and the right note sounds so much better."[56]

---

[52] See Joseph Straus, "Stravinsky's Serial 'Mistakes,'" *The Journal of Musicology* 17/2 (1999), 231–71.

[53] Notes in the published score that are "row-incorrect" are a persistent feature of music by all serial composers. See Edward Cone, "Editorial Responsibility and Schoenberg's Troublesome 'Misprints,'" *Perspectives of New Music* 11/1 (1972), 65–75; and Ethan Haimo, "Editing Schoenberg's Twelve-Tone Music," *Journal of the Arnold Schoenberg Institute* 8/2 (1984), 141–57 for discussions of the problem in Schoenberg's music. Both authors agree that serial deviations require close scrutiny by editors, and Haimo's conclusion is uncompromising: "I believe that a thorough examination of serial inconsistencies in Schoenberg's twelve-tone works would reveal that the vast majority of them would make more sense in the global and local spheres when corrected" (154).

[54] *Dialogues*, 55–56.   [55] Lawrence Morton, "Stravinsky at Home," in *Confronting Stravinsky*, ed. Pasler, 343.

[56] Milton Babbitt, "Order, Symmetry, and Centricity in Late Stravinsky," in *Confronting Stravinsky*, ed. Pasler, 248.

Stravinsky's self-analyses, discussed above, confirm the importance he attached to serial derivation. He wanted to be sure he had a reliable serial explanation for every note he wrote.

Another kind of documentation is found in correspondence between either Stravinsky or Robert Craft and the composer Claudio Spies.[57] At Stravinsky's request, Spies proofread the scores for *Abraham and Isaac, Variations, Introitus,* and *Requiem Canticles* – Stravinsky's last four major works – prior to their publication. Spies did an independent twelve-tone analysis, usually without the benefit of any of Stravinsky's charts or sketches, and communicated lists of serial deviations either directly to Stravinsky or indirectly through Craft.[58] In virtually every case, Stravinsky made the changes necessary to bring the music into exact conformity with the apparent serial plan.

The interaction of Spies, Craft, and Stravinsky on the subject of a single note in the Lacrimosa movement of *Requiem Canticles* illustrates their working methods and Stravinsky's attitude toward serial errors. On September 20, 1966, in preparation for analyzing the work, Spies copied Stravinsky's own serial charts, one of which is reprinted in Example 2.13. This chart is written in Stravinsky's standard format. A hexachord, in this case the second hexachord of the retrograde-inversional form of the first of the two series for *Requiem Canticles*, is written across the top. The rows of the chart systematically rotate that hexachord and transpose it to start on the same first note. *Requiem Canticles* uses sixteen such charts, eight for each of its two series (four basic series forms, with two hexachords each), and these sixteen charts originally contained seven errors, that is, seven deviations from their otherwise systematic organization. In each case, Stravinsky either simply miscalculated an interval or wrote an interval ascending when it should be descending, or vice versa. Of the seven errors, only two had an effect on the music – the defective portions of the other charts were never employed.[59] One of the two is circled in Example 2.13 – the last note in the fifth row should be B♮, not B♯.

Example 2.14 reprints a portion of the movement that makes use of the chart in Example 2.13. The contralto solo works systematically upward through the rows of the chart. The accompanying chords move equally systematically through the

---

[57] Spies has generously made all of his correspondence as well as his annotated photocopies of Stravinsky's manuscript scores available to me.

[58] These analyses formed the basis of a series of articles by Spies on *Introitus, Variations, Abraham and Isaac,* and *Requiem Canticles*: "Some Notes on Stravinsky's Requiem Settings," *Perspectives of New Music* 5/2 (1967), 98–123; reprinted in *Perspectives on Schoenberg and Stravinsky,* ed. Boretz and Cone, 223–50; "Some Notes on Stravinsky's *Variations*," *Perspectives of New Music* 4/1 (1965), 62–74; reprinted in *Perspectives on Schoenberg and Stravinsky,* ed. Boretz and Cone, 210–22; and "Some Notes on Stravinsky's *Abraham and Isaac*," *Perspectives of New Music* 3/2 (1965), 104–26; reprinted in *Perspectives on Schoenberg and Stravinsky,* ed. Boretz and Cone, 186–209. More than thirty years after their publication, these remain among the best sources of analytical information about these works.

[59] In all of *Requiem Canticles,* only three notes are potentially implicated, and all occur in the Lacrimosa movement. Two of these – the B♮ in the contralto solo in m. 235 and the Flute II part in mm. 238–42 – are discussed in what follows. The third is the F♯ in the second tenor trombone in m. 244 (indicated in the relevant chart incorrectly as G). All three are correct in the published score.

Example 2.13 Spies's copy of a rotational array from *Requiem Canticles* (based on the second hexachord of the IR form of the first series), with an error circled and the correct note provided by Spies

columns of the chart. (The uncircled notes in Example 2.14 are drawn from other charts, as part of a richly multi-layered counterpoint.) The last note of the contralto solo in m. 235 and the note in Flute II sustained in m. 238–42 are both the correct B♮ rather than the incorrect B♯ of Stravinsky's original chart. How were these corrections made?

At some time before the end of 1966, Spies identified the errors in the charts and communicated them to Stravinsky. On January 19, 1967, Spies wrote to Craft identifying two errors in the Lacrimosa movement, indicating "I find that there are two very bad errors in the score, and these *must* be corrected for the printed thing." The first error involved the lower harp note in m. 263 – it should be C♯, not C.[60] The second error involved the Flute II note in mm. 238–42, shown in Example 2.14, which should be B♮, not B♯. This is precisely the point at which the chart was defective. Spies points out that "this B♯ was corrected to B♮ in the contralto [in m. 235]," thus reminding Stravinsky that he had already corrected the chart and its

---

[60] The correct C♯ is present in the sketch reproduced as Plate 24 in *Pictures and Documents*. The sharp sign was omitted in the subsequent manuscript from which Spies worked, and was reinstated, at his suggestion, in the published score.

linear manifestation in the voice part, and should therefore make the same change in the chord in mm. 238–42.

On January 23, 1967, Craft responded: "Mr. S. says the harp should be C♯ (not C), but he can't understand the flute B♯ and asks you to send him your chart of it." Five days later, Spies responded directly to Stravinsky, enclosing a copy of the relevant chart and score page: "Since there had been a slight error in your chart *precisely* in connection with the vertical factor that I have called (5) [i.e., the fifth row on the chart], I presume this error was communicated to Flute II inadvertently. (You will recall that we spoke of this error in your chart in New York, and that *this very same note* had been written as B♯ for the contralto in her phrase only 3 measures before.) Now, since that B♯ was duly corrected to B♮, I assume that the vertical of which that B♮ is factor should yield B♮ for Flute II. And – I hope you will not think me impertinent for suggesting it – it sounds much better as B♮, without doubling the contrabass' C." In a subsequent undated response, Stravinsky accepted and initialed the change. B♮ is thus authoritatively confirmed and appears as such in the published score.

In accepting both the correction of his charts and the modification of music based on them, Stravinsky acknowledged that deviations both within the precompositional charts and between the charts and the score should be treated as mistakes. When Spies identified the apparent error in Flute II, Stravinsky wanted proof that the note was wrong with regard to the charts. He didn't just play the chord both ways and decide which one he liked best; rather, he wanted to know which was serially correct. Once confronted with irrefutable serial evidence, Stravinsky made the change. The documentation is not as extensive for all of the corrections suggested by Spies, but the result is almost always the same: Spies identifies serial errors and Stravinsky corrects them.

Stravinsky's serial mistakes confront us with conflicts among various kinds of compositional intentions. There are the intentions embodied in the charts, their systematic regularities, and the structural principles on which they are based. Then there are the occasionally contradictory intentions embodied in the compositional sketches, drafts, and manuscripts, as well as the published scores and the recordings based on them. It is clear that Stravinsky himself placed a high value on serial consistency. That is the irrefutable sense of the elaborate charts he constructed, of the careful self-analyses he provides on so many sketches and drafts, and of the near-perfect serial accountability of the published scores themselves. That is also the sense of Stravinsky's documented reliance on Spies. For Stravinsky, the compositional process in his late works involved a strict and uncompromising commitment to his serial constructions.[61]

---

[61] When critical editions of these late works finally do appear, they must not attempt to gloss over the tensions and contradictions between precompositional plans and compositional realizations. Rather, they will have to present a range of options that corresponds to the range of Stravinsky's demonstrable intentions. On balance, and in virtually every case, disputes will normally be resolved in favor of serial consistency.

Example 2.14 Compositional realization of the chart from Example 2.13 in *Requiem Canticles*, mm. 235–42 (roman numerals indicate rows of the array; arabic numerals indicate columns of the array)

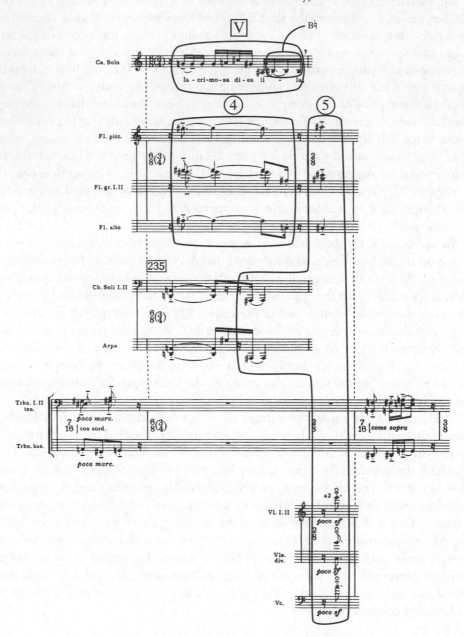

Example 2.14 (cont.)

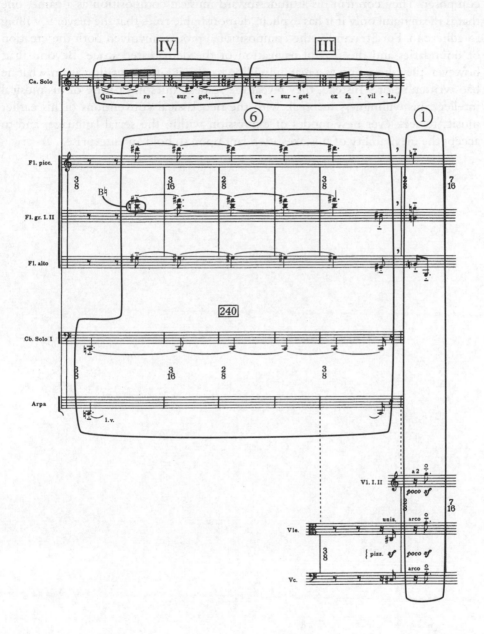

Stravinsky's serial mistakes, by revealing his vulnerabilities, bring us closer to the composer. They confirm his attitude toward musical composition as a game, one that is meaningful only if it has explicit, demonstrable rules that the player is willing to adhere to. For Stravinsky, the compositional process involved both the creation of boundaries and the playful navigation of the demarcated space. Beyond that, however, they show him as a man unwilling to play it safe by writing again what he had written before. Instead, they reveal the restless, questing nature of his musical intellect, his willingness to break with the neoclassical conventions of his earlier music, to seek ever new modes of expression within the serial language, and to accept the inevitability of mistakes attendant upon so bold an enterprise.

3

FORM

THE FORM PROBLEM: CONTINUITY AND DISCONTINUITY

Stravinsky's music, including his late music, is highly sectionalized, built up from discrete, static blocks. We have seen, in Chapter 2, the extent to which Stravinsky treated distinct musical blocks as preformed elements in a kind of musical collage, to be moved, inserted, or deleted as necessary. Sectionalization is one of the most characteristic features of his music, one of the defining elements of the distinctive Stravinskian sound.[1] His music deploys strong centrifugal forces, with each of the formal units pulling away from the others by asserting its own independence and integrity.

But the centripetal forces are equally strong, holding the sections together. The result in Stravinsky's music is not the gentle harmonious reconciliation of opposing tendencies, but rather a furious tension, at all levels, between the forces of integration and disintegration. Stravinsky's music gives no sense of spontaneous growth from a single seed, of a seamless fabric, a single improvisatory sweep. It is vigorously anti-organic and anti-developmental; its jagged edges are everywhere apparent. The forces of abruption, however, are everywhere balanced by equally strong ties that bind the music together.

This formal tension between part and whole is evident at all levels of musical

---

[1] This feature of Stravinsky's music has been widely acknowledged. See, for example, Pieter van den Toorn, *The Music of Igor Stravinsky* (New Haven: Yale University Press, 1968), where the phenomenon, termed "block juxtaposition," is identified as a "peculiarly Stravinskian conception of form" (p. 454). Jonathan Kramer, "Discontinuity and Proportion in the Music of Stravinsky," in *Confronting Stravinsky*, ed. Jann Pasler (Berkeley: University of California Press, 1986), describes Stravinsky's music as "overtly sectionalized": "Although the delineation of sharply juxtaposed sections has its origin in harmonic stasis, the resulting discontinuity is generally supported by other means – contrast of instrumentation, texture, motivic material, tempo, formal design, and even compositional procedure. Not all of Stravinsky's music is discontinuous, of course, just as not all of his harmonies are static, but discontinuity is crucial to his style" (p. 174). Taruskin calls this feature "Drobnost," defined as "splinteredness; the quality of being formally disunified, a sum-of-parts" (*Stravinsky and the Russian Traditions* [Berkeley: University of California Press, 1996], 1677). Taruskin considers "Drobnost" one of Stravinsky's most basic style characteristics. Glenn Watkins, *Pyramids at the Louvre* (Cambridge, Mass.: Harvard University Press, 1994) relates Stravinsky's procedure of combining and juxtaposing musical fragments to the "collage assemblages of the Cubists" (234). Jonathan Cross, *The Stravinsky Legacy* (Cambridge: Cambridge University Press, 1998) considers Stravinsky's "block forms" a principal source of his influence on later composers. For a consideration of continuity both within works and across style periods, see Anthony Pople, "Misleading Voices: Contrasts and Continuities in Stravinsky Studies," in *Analytical Strategies and Musical Interpretation: Essays on Nineteenth- and Twentieth-Century Music*, ed. Craig Ayrey and Mark Everist (Cambridge: Cambridge University Press, 1996), 271–87.

Table 3.1

X→X	literal repetition
X→Tn(X)	transposition, transpositional symmetry, transposed repetition
X→I(X)	inversion, inversional symmetry
X→R(X)	retrograde, retrograde symmetry
X→RI(X)	retrograde-inversion, RI-chains

structure, in the combination of intervals to create motives; the combination of motives to create melodies (which, in the later music, are usually coextensive with a series form); the combination of melodies horizontally to create melodic periods and vertically to create contrapuntal units (which, in the late music, are usually coextensive with textural blocks); the combination of textural blocks into larger sections or entire movements; and the combination of movements to create larger, multi-movement works.

At each level of structure, Stravinsky deploys the same integrative forces, the same strategies of combination. Musical units of whatever size are combined, via repetition, transposition, inversion, retrograde, or retrograde-inversion to create larger units. Table 3.1 summarizes the possibilities.

In Table 3.1, X represents any distinctive bit of musical material, ranging in scope from a simple interval to an entire movement. Larger units are created by combining or juxtaposing smaller units with repetitions or transformations of themselves.

FROM INTERVAL TO MOTIVE

For Stravinsky, the interval rather than the pitch or pitch-class is the basic atomic musical unit. The idea of generating structures upward from intervals and combinations of intervals is central to his musical constructions, and not only in the late period. Rather, it represents a source of continuity among the music of his different style periods.[2] There is a tension inherent in the process of generation. The constituent intervals retain their identity and integrity, and Stravinsky often finds musical means to articulate and isolate them. At the same time, they combine with other intervals, or with their own transpositions or inversion, to form the trichords and tetrachords that subsume but do not efface them.

The smallest interval, the semitone, plays a primal role in this process, joining with its own transposition or inversion at various levels to create the trichords and tetrachords that are most characteristic of Stravinsky's melodies.[3] Two different

---

[2] This is a central contention of Marianne Kielian-Gilbert, "Relationships of Symmetrical Pitch-Class Sets and Stravinsky's Metaphor of Polarity," *Perspectives of New Music* 21/1–2 (1982–83), 209–40.

[3] When intervals are discussed as ordered or directed (one note occurs before the other), only transposition (T) and inversion (I) will be considered. Retrograde (R) and retrograde-inversion (RI) are disregarded because, when only a dyad (pair of notes) is involved, RI is indistinguishable from T and R is similarly indistinguishable from I. When intervals are discussed as unordered, I becomes indistinguishable from T, and therefore only T is considered here.

Table 3.2

Semitone combined with its transposition at T_n	Resulting set-class	Musical example
T_1 or T_{11}	(012)	C–C♯ + C♯–D = C–C♯–D
T_2 or T_{10}	(0123)	C–C♯ + D–D♯ = C–C♯–D–D♯
T_3 or T_9	(0134)	C–C♯ + D♯–E = C–C♯–D♯–E
T_4 or T_8	(0145)	C–C♯ + E–F = C–C♯–E–F
T_5 or T_7	(0156)	C–C♯ + F–F♯ = C–C♯–F–F♯
T_6	(0167)	C–C♯ + F♯–G = C–C♯–F♯–G

semitones can be combined to create six different trichords or tetrachords (Table 3.2 summarizes the possibilities).

Of these combinations, the first three are by far the most common in Stravinsky's music. The first two are simple segments of the chromatic scale. The third, sc(0134), is a familiar segment of the octatonic scale, although it is portrayed here as the result of generation from a semitone rather than segmentation of a large referential collection.[4] The remaining three tetrachords have at most a limited life in Stravinsky's music. In the musical motives of his late music, Stravinsky simultaneously isolates semitones as atomic units and combines them to create larger shapes.

Example 3.1 describes two of Stravinsky's serial melodies in terms of semitones that assert their independence and simultaneously combine to form larger shapes. The melody from the *Double Canon* (Example 3.1a) begins with a descending semitone, F♯–F, which is immediately combined with its transposition at T_3, A–G♯, to create a form of sc(0134). A–G♯ is overlapped by a third descending semitone, G♯–G, related by T_2 to the initial F♯–F. The five notes together form a tight chromatic cluster, from F to A. The next five notes of the melody form another chromatic cluster, from C to E. Once again, the chromatic cluster is partitioned into discrete semitones, only these are now ascending: D–D♯ overlapped with D♯–E in an upper strand and C–C♯ in a lower strand. C–C♯ relates back to D♯–E at T_3 (creating sc(0134)) and to D–D♯ at T_2. Understood in this way, the second group of five notes appears as the exact retrograde of the first five, creating a sense of unified balance and melodic closure. To this self-contained ten-note melodic gesture, one final semitone is adjoined, B–A♯. This final semitone is relatively isolated from the rest of the melody by phrasing and dynamics, but is nonetheless linked to the concluding semitones of the two five-note gestures, G♯–G and C–C♯, by the same transpositions that unified the five-note gestures themselves: T_2 and T_3. Furthermore, the final B–A♯ fills in the gap between the two-five note groups,

---

[4] Set-class (0134) can also be described in other ways. Stravinsky himself described it, with reference to the *Symphony of Psalms*, as "two minor thirds joined by a major third," or, in the terms I am using here, a minor third combined with its transposition at T_1 (*Dialogues*, 45). For a related approach to generating larger collections, particularly the octatonic, through combinations of intervallic cells, see Richard Cohn, "Bartók's Octatonic Strategies: A Motivic Approach," *Journal of the American Musicological Society* 44 (1991), 262–300.

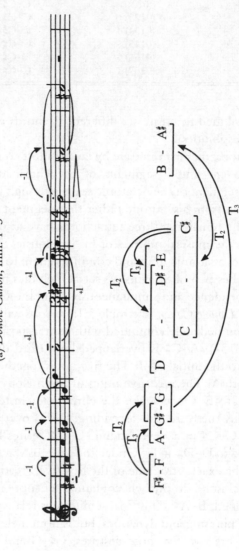

Example 3.1 Motives generated from the combination of a semitone with its transpositions
(a) *Double Canon*, mm. 1–5

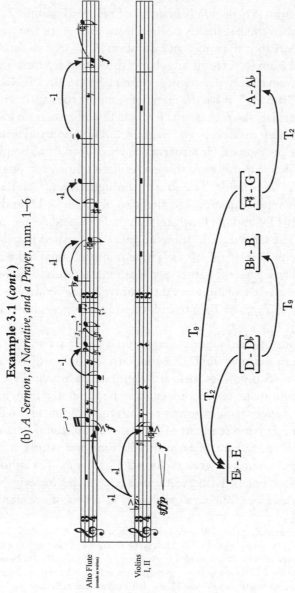

Example 3.1 (cont.)

(b) *A Sermon, a Narrative, and a Prayer*, mm. 1–6

creating a contiguous twelve-note span from F up to E. The isolation of the final semitone is thus contested by its strong intervallic bonds with the rest of the melody.

In the melody from *A Sermon, a Narrative, and a Prayer* (Example 3.1b), it is the first semitone rather than the last that is isolated from the rest of the melody by its distinctive instrumentation, dynamic, and duration. The second semitone, D–D♭, is also distinguished from its surroundings by its three-fold repetition. This oscillation of two notes is a remarkably persistent feature of Stravinsky's melodic lines, which he described as a "stutter."[5] It has the effect of stopping the musical motion, drawing attention to a singular, discrete event. Even at this microscopic level of structure, then, the constituent parts have a tendency toward isolation and insulation.

The intervals thus assert their structural integrity, and the boundaries between them are sharply delineated. Across those boundaries, however, purposeful transpositions create links and bonds. The fourth through eleventh notes of the melody consist of four discrete semitones. The first two of these, D–D♭ and B♭–B, combine at T_9 to create sc(0134) and the third and fourth, F♯–G and A–A♭, combine at T_2 to create sc(0123). The same transpositions connect the isolated initial semitone in the melody, E♭–E, with D–D♭ and F♯–G. These transpositional links do not eradicate the boundaries that separate the intervals. Rather, a tension is felt between the tendency of the intervals to isolation and the countervailing tendency of the transpositions (usually $T_{1/11}$, $T_{2/10}$, or $T_{3/9}$) to link them into larger wholes (usually sc(012), (0123), or (0134)).[6]

Motivic trichords and tetrachords are also built up from combinations of a whole tone with its transpositions. Table 3.3 summarizes the possibilities. Of these, the first three are most common as melodic fragments in Stravinsky's late music. Set-class (0123), the chromatic tetrachord, can also be generated from a semitone, as we have seen. (024) is a recurring segment of both the diatonic and whole-tone scales, while (0235) is a recurring segment of both the diatonic and octatonic scales. Set-class (0246), another segment of both the diatonic and whole-tone scales, occurs only once among Stravinsky's serial melodies (*Elegy for J. F. K.*) although, along with (0257) and (0268), it occurs with greater frequency as a harmony (see Chapter 4).

Example 3.2 describes four serial melodies in terms of combinations of whole

---

[5] Stravinsky calls the alternation of two notes a whole-tone or semitone apart "a melodic-rhythmic stutter characteristic of my speech" (*Themes and Episodes*, 58). The expressive impact of the "stutter" is discussed in Chapter 5.

[6] Partly as a consequence of their similar mode of generation, the two melodies in Example 3.1 share a large number of linear segments. This kind of self-borrowing, in which melodic gestures are repeated from piece to piece, is common throughout Stravinsky's late period. For example, the collection [G, G♯, A], one of the segments shared by *Double Canon* and *A Sermon, A Narrative, and A Prayer*, occurs also as a segment of the series for the Septet (second and third movements); *Canticum Sacrum*, "Surge, aquilo" (it occurs here as the first two notes (A♭–G) plus last one (A); *Agon*, Triple Pas-de-Quatre, Coda, and Pas-de-Deux; *Epitaphium*; *The Flood*; *Abraham and Isaac*; and *The Owl and the Pussycat*. The segment D–D♭–B♭–B, so prominent in the series for *A Sermon, a Narrative, and a Prayer*, is found also as the four-note series for the "Pas-de-Deux" in *Agon*. The first two notes of the series for *A Sermon, a Narrative, and a Prayer*, E♭–E, are also the first two notes of the series for *Movements*, while the series for *Threni* and "Full fadom five" from *Three Shakespeare Songs* also begin on E♭. Extensive self-borrowings of this kind enhance a sense of Stravinsky's late work as a single, coherent enterprise.

Table 3.3

Whole-tone combined with its transpositions at T_n	Resulting set-class	Musical example
T_1 or T_{11}	(0123)	C–D + C♯–D♯ = C–C♯–D–D♯
T_2 or T_{10}	(024)	C–D + D–E = C–D–E
T_3 or T_9	(0235)	C–D + E♭–F = C–D–E♭–F
T_4 or T_8	(0246)	C–D + E–F♯ = C–D–E–F♯
T_5 or T_7	(0257)	C–D + F–G = C–D–F–G
T_6	(0268)	C–D + F♯–G♯ = C–D–F♯–G♯

tones. The melody from the beginning of the first movement of the *Canticum Sacrum* (Example 3.2a) is based on one of Stravinsky's early, diatonic series. It consists of four notes, A–B–C–D, which can be understood as two whole tones related at T_9 to produce (0235). That tetrachord-type is extremely common as a segmental subset of Stravinsky's serial melodies, and it is often realized by these particular notes.[7]

The melody from *Anthem* (Example 3.2b) contains five segmental whole tones, indicated with solid brackets, and an additional registral whole-tone, indicated with a dotted bracket.[8] Stravinsky uses an oscillation of tones, his familiar "stutter," to isolate two of these, F♯–E and B–C♯, from their surroundings. But purposeful transposition creates links across the articulative boundaries. The stuttered whole-tone F♯–E initiates a chain of T_3, each link of which is a member of sc(0235): [E, F♯, G, A], [G, A, B♭, C], and [B♭, C, C♯, D♯]. The stuttered whole-tone B–C♯ initiates a chain of T_2, each link of which is a member of sc(024): [B, C♯, D♯] and [C♯, D♯, F]. The stuttered whole tones assert their independence, but the unifying transpositions enmesh them within the rest of the melody.

In the melody from *Abraham and Isaac* (Example 3.2c), the descending whole-tone B–A is repeated no fewer than twelve times, probably Stravinsky's most protracted stutter.[9] This whole-tone seems to stand alone, cut off from its

---

[7] Other series that embed [A, B, C, D] as a segmental subset: Septet, first movement; *Variations*; *Requiem Canticles*, Row 1. This tetrachord often forms part of a melodic and harmonic complex that centers on A and has a consistent, demonstrable expressive impact (see Chapter 5).

[8] The melody in Example 3.2b represents the P-form of the series for *Anthem*. It does not occur first in the piece, but is identified as such by Stravinsky in his sketches. The series for *Anthem* shares the BACH-tetrachord [A, B♭, B, C] and the dyad D♭–E♭ with the series for "Surge, aquilo," from *Canticum Sacrum*.

[9] The melody in Example 3.2c represents the P-form of the series for *Abraham and Isaac*, designated as such by Stravinsky in his sketches (see *Strawinsky: Sein Nachlass, Sein Bild*, ed. Hans Jörg Jans and Christian Geelhaar [Basel, Kunstmuseum, 1984], 176) and confirmed by Craft ("Pluralistic Stravinsky," in *Present Perspectives*, 309). Numerous published analyses of this work, including Arnold Whittall, "Thematicism in Stravinsky's *Abraham and Isaac*," *Tempo* 89 (1969), 12–16; Anthony Payne, "Two New Stravinsky Works (*Abraham and Isaac* and *Elegy for J. F. K.*)," *Tempo* 73 (1965), 12–15; Norbert Jers, *Igor Strawinskys späte Zwölftonwerke (1958–1966)* (Regensburg: Gustav Bosse Verlag, 1976), 186–209; Claudio Spies, "Some Notes on Stravinsky's *Abraham and Isaac*," *Perspectives of New Music* 3/2 (1965), 104–26; reprinted in *Perspectives on Schoenberg and Stravinsky*, ed. Benjamin Boretz and Edward Cone (Princeton: Princeton University Press, 1968), 186–209; and van den Toorn, *The Music of Igor Stravinsky* erroneously take the first twelve notes of the piece, G–G♯–A♯–B♯–C♯–A–B–D♯–D–E–F♯–F, as the P-form. As a result, their accounts of the serial structure are incomplete and unnecessarily convoluted.

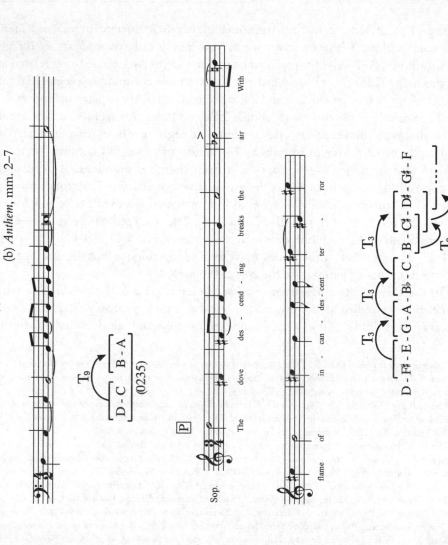

Example 3.2 Motives generated from the combination of a whole-tone with its tranpositions

(a) *Canticum Sacrum*, Dedicatio, mm. 1–4

(b) *Anthem*, mm. 2–7

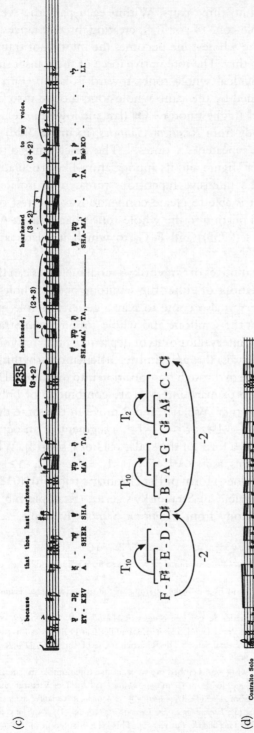

Example 3.2 (cont.)

(c) *Abraham and Isaac*, mm. 232–39

(d) *Requiem Canticles*, Lacrimosa, mm. 229–32

surroundings. But, in fact, it is one of six whole-tones in the melody (indicated with brackets), grouped into three pairs. Within each pair, the whole-tones are themselves related by whole-tone (T_2 or T_{10}), creating three instances of sc(024). In this way, the interval of the whole-tone becomes the interval of transposition that links the whole-tones together. The integrative force of the transpositions balances the tendency of the individual whole-tones toward isolation. Furthermore, the melody as a whole is framed by the same whole-tone motive it so conspicuously embeds: F (first note) – D♯ (highest note) – C♯ (last and lowest note).

In the Lacrimosa melody from *Requiem Canticles* (Example 3.2d), there is only one whole-tone: G♯–F♯, repeated six times.[10] The descending direction of the whole-tone in this "stutter" figure and its appoggiatura-like articulation give it the feeling of a lament.[11] The intensive repetitions threaten to isolate this interval within the melody. But it is able to create connections to the rest of the melody through its transpositional relation to the whole-tones that flank it: A–B, to which it relates at T_3, creating sc(0235), and F–G, to which it relates at T_1, creating sc(0123).

The most characteristic motives of Stravinsky's serial melodies can thus be understood in terms of combinations of either the semitone or the whole-tone with its transpositions. Other intervals also come to play a generative role, particularly in Stravinsky's last works, but the semitone and whole-tone remain Stravinsky's most common and characteristic intervallic points of departure. Stravinsky simultaneously isolates the individual intervals, through timbre, articulation, rhythm, and stutter-like repetition, and yokes them through transposition into meaningful larger shapes.

In many cases, these two primary intervals are combined not only with themselves, but also with each other. When 1 and 2 move in the same direction, as in <+1, +2>, <-1, -2>, <+2, +1>, or <-2, -1>, a segment of an octatonic or diatonic scale is produced, as is a form of the scalar trichord, sc(013). When the 1 and 2 move in different directions, as in <+1, -2>, <-1, +2>, <+2, -1>, or <-2, +1>, a "twist" motive results, as does a form of the chromatic trichord, (012).[12] The twist motive is particularly prevalent in Stravinsky's series (Example 3.3 provides two such melodies).[13] The melody from *Canticum Sacrum* (Example 3.3a) concludes

---

[10] This melody represents the sixth row of the rotational array derived from the second hexachord of the IR-form of Row 1.

[11] The lamenting alternation of G♯ and F♯ recalls the opening of the second scene of *Petrushka* (my thanks to David Smyth for this observation).

[12] The term "twist" comes from Charles Seeger (see *Studies in Musicology II, 1929–1979*, ed. Anne Pescatello [Berkeley: University of California Press, 1994], 137–49). Chandler Carter discusses this motive in *The Rake's Progress* in his article "Stravinsky's 'Special Sense': The Rhetorical Use of Tonality in *The Rake's Progress*," *Music Theory Spectrum* 19/1 (1997), 55–80.

[13] Twelve-tone series from the following works embed the twist motive (the number in parentheses indicates the number of occurrences): "Surge, aquilo" from *Canticum Sacrum* (1); "Ad Tres Virtutes" and "Brevis Motus" from *Canticum Sacrum* (2); Coda from *Agon* (4); *Movements* (3); *A Sermon, a Narrative, and a Prayer* (2); *The Flood* (3); *Anthem* (2); *Abraham and Isaac* (3); *Fanfare for a New Theater* (5); *Introitus* (1); *Requiem Canticles*, Series 1 (2); *Requiem Canticles*, Series 2 (2); *The Owl and the Pussycat* (1). This list is adapted from Jers, *Igor Strawinskys späte Zwölftonwerke*, 33– 35.

Example 3.3 Combinations of semitone and whole-tone into a "twist" motive
(a) *Canticum Sacrum*, Three Virtues, mm. 117–24
(b) *Fanfare for a New Theater*, mm. 1–4

with two statements of the "twist" motive, each of which is inversionally symmetrical: the first converges on G from Ab above and F♯ below; the second converges on Bb from Cb above and A below.[14] Furthermore, the two motives are themselves related by inversion: the first notes of the two motives, Ab and A in the bass trumpet, are flanked by F♯/Cb and G/Bb in the first trumpet. Stravinsky thus uses a combination of semitones and whole-tones to create a sense of inversional balance that operates both within and between the motives.

The serial melody from *Fanfare for a New Theater* (Example 3.3b) is entirely derived from the twist trichord. Each of its four discrete segmental trichords is a "twist" and a fifth one occurs across one of the trichordal boundaries.[15] As in the melody from *Canticum Sacrum* (Example 3.3a), the twist motive creates a sense of inversional balance as its notes either wedge outward from the first tone or converge on the last one.

Stravinsky thus creates his motivic shapes, his characteristic trichords and tetrachords, by "composing with intervals." The musical intervals have both resistance toward and affinity with each other, simultaneously asserting their integrity and

[14] The notes in the bass trumpet sound an octave lower than written, so these are symmetries of pitch-class, not pitch. The melody in Example 3.3a represents the P-form of the series for this "Three Virtues" movement of *Canticum Sacrum*.

[15] I will say more below about the relations among these trichords and the remarkable segmental invariance their equivalence enables.

seeking affiliation with others. Stravinsky creates affinities and affiliations by combining intervals, particularly semitones and whole-tones, with themselves (via
transposition) and with each other. In the process, he confronts at this very immediate level of structure the basic formal paradox of his music, namely the centrifugal
tendency of the musical units toward isolation and the centripetal tendency of the
transpositions and inversions to link them together into larger wholes.

FROM MOTIVE TO SERIAL MELODY

Just as intervals combine to form motives, so do motives combine (via transposition, inversion, retrograde, and retrograde-inversion) to form melodies. Stravinsky's
comment on the composition of the *Elegy for J. F. K.* gives a sense of this process: "I
had already joined the various melodic fragments before finding the possibilities of
serial composition inherent in them, which is why the vocal part could begin with
the inverted order and the clarinet with the reverse order – i.e. because the series
had been discovered elsewhere in the piece. There is virtually no element of prede-
termination in such a procedure."[16] As in the movement from interval to motive,
the movement from motive to series is fraught with a productive formal tension.
The motives assert their identity and integrity, both through musical means and by
virtue of their recurrence, but at the same time are juxtaposed to create larger
wholes. The constituent motives retain their distinctiveness – they are not sub-
sumed or effaced – but nonetheless are perceived as parts of a larger whole.

In Stravinsky's late music, melody is generally identified with series. Series are
presented melodically and each melodic phrase is usually coextensive with a series-
form. Within the serial melody, motives are often combined with their retrogrades,
inversions, or retrograde-inversion, manifesting an impulse toward mirroring and
balance. Stravinsky's motives are often asymmetrical and, as such, seek to create a
sense of balance by pairing themselves with their mirror images, either in register
(inversion), in time (retrograde), or both (retrograde-inversion).[17]

A particularly common strategy of motivic combination involves retrograde-
inversion. Often, motives are overlapped with their own retrograde-inversions to
create RI-chains.[18] In Example 3.4, two serial melodies deploy RI-chains involving
the twist motive. In the passacaglia subject from the second movement of the Septet
(Example 3.4a), the fourth through sixth notes state a form of the twist motive:
G–F♯–G♯. Later in the melody, the same three notes return, this time engendering
an RI-chain with three links: G–F♯–G♯, F♯–G♯–G, and G♯–G–A. The last of these

---

[16] *Themes and Episodes*, 59.

[17] The similar mirroring effect of inversion and retrograde has been noted by David Smyth: "Inversional pairing
may be viewed as a vertical analog to palindromic pairing in the horizontal dimension. Both play prominent
roles throughout Stravinsky's early serial works" [and the later ones, too, I might add] ("Stravinsky at the
Threshold: A Sketch Leaf for *Canticum Sacrum*," *Mitteilungen der Paul Sacher Stiftung* 10 [1997], 23).

[18] An RI-chain results when the last two notes of a motive become the first two notes of its retrograde inversion.
RICH (an abbreviation for RI-chain) is one of several serial transformations that are described and illustrated by
David Lewin in *Generalized Musical Intervals and Transformations* (New Haven: Yale University Press, 1987). I will
occasionally expand the application of RICH to refer to RI-related motives that share only one note.

Example 3.4 RI-chains involving the twist motive
(a) Septet, second movement, mm. 1–8
(b) *Agon*, Coda, mm. 198–203

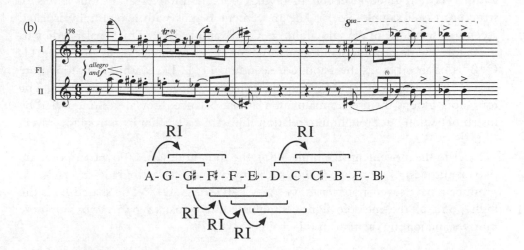

occurs as a segment in many of Stravinsky's series, as previously noted. It is isolated here through instrumentation – the only three-note group assigned to any single instrument and the only three notes played by the bassoon – but strongly connected to the rest of the line. This RI-chain simultaneously spins a melodic segment out of a single motive and helps to direct the melodic motion toward A, the eventual goal.

The melody from *Agon* (Example 3.4b) consists in virtually its entirety of an alternation of tones and semitones (only the eleventh note does not participate), producing forms either of the scalar trichord, sc(013), or the twist motive.[19] The

---

[19] This melody represents Stravinsky's first twelve-tone series. See Susannah Tucker, "Stravinsky and His Sketches: The Composing of *Agon* and Other Serial Works of the 1950s" (D.Phil. dissertation, Oxford University, 1992) for the chronology of Stravinsky's development as a twelve-tone composer. As Tucker observes (118), this series, A–G–G♯–F♯–F–E♭–D–C–C♯–B–E–B♭, bears a striking similarity to the next twelve-tone series he composed, for "Surge, aquilo" from *Canticum Sacrum*, a relationship that is most evident in its IR-ordering: A–G–F♯–G♯–F–E♭–D–C–E– C♯–B–B♭.

initial A–G–G♯ (that familiar trichord yet again) is overlapped with G–G♯–F♯ to create an RI-chain with two links. Another chain of the same kind, transposed up a perfect fifth, occurs later in the series. In between these two chains and connecting them, we find a different chain, one whose links consist of the scalar trichord (013). The succession of overlapping scalar segments in this melody – G♯–F♯–F, F♯–F–E♭, F–E♭–D, E♭–D–C – results in virtually a complete octatonic collection in scalar order (and the two missing notes, A and B, are near at hand).[20] The octatonic emerges here as a by-product of the motivic interplay; in other parts of *Agon*, and in other works, similar interplay produces other large collections. In both melodies of Example 3.4, larger melodies are spun out from the combination, via retrograde-inversion and RI-chains, of smaller motives, themselves the product of combination of a semitone and a whole-tone.

RI-relations and RI-chains are by no means confined to the twist and scalar trichords. The Pas-de-Deux from *Agon* reveals the process of generation and combination via retrograde-inversion involving different motives at various levels of structure (see Example 3.5).[21] The movement begins with a registrally isolated ascending semitone in the solo violin: F–G♭ (Example 3.5a). This is balanced by its inversion, the descending semitone A–A♭. Similarly, in the cello, an ascending 11, C–B, is balanced by its inversion, a descending 11, E–E♭. Within each four-note group, the constituent semitones are held apart, balanced against each other. The four-note groups themselves maintain a similar balance: they are distinguished by instrumentation but brought into relationship with each other by retrograde-inversion.[22]

Later in the movement (Example 3.5b), the four-note series (now transposed up two semitones) is conjoined and overlapped with its retrograde-inversion to produce a new, seven-note series: G–A♭–C♭–B♭–A–C–D♭.[23] The shared B♭ is the high point of the melodic figure, simultaneously separating the two four-note motives and joining them in an RI-chain.

---

[20] One result of all of this intensive RI-chaining is that the first ten notes of the series are RI-symmetrical in their entirety: the first five notes of the series are related, in reverse order and at T_8I, to the next five notes of the series. The result is extensive segmental invariance between the P (or R) and IR forms of the series, a point to which I shall return.

[21] The following discussion is indebted to Tucker, "Stravinsky and His Sketches," 182–231. Based on Stravinsky's compositional sketches, Tucker considers F–G♭–A–A♭ the prime ordering of the four-note series that underlies mm. 411–62.

[22] Here, the two RI-related series forms together produce an entire octatonic scale. As elsewhere in this discussion, however, I prefer to see the octatonic collection as a by-product, one among many, of the strategies of motivic combination. Stravinsky combines motives in various ways, often with a retrograde-inversion that maintains one or more common tones. In some cases but not in others, the octatonic scale results. What remains constant in this music, then, is the mode of formation, not the resultant collection. For the opposing perspective, see van den Toorn, *The Music of Igor Stravinsky*, 408–14.

[23] Tucker, "Stravinsky and His Sketches," 190–91 identifies a consistent use of RI-chains in which the last note of a P-form of a series becomes the first note of an RI-form. The seven-note series in Example 3.5b results from a conjunction of that kind. The result is a chromatic segment that spans a tritone. The same structure frequently emerges in "Musick to heare" from *Three Shakespeare Songs* and *In Memoriam Dylan Thomas* from conjunctions of forms of their respective four- and five-note series.

Still later (Example 3.5c), the four-note series (now back at its original transposition level) is the first link in an RI-chain that extends to the first nine notes of a twelve-tone series. The last four notes of the series create an additional form of the same resulting set-class (0134), but in a different, unrelated ordering. A subsidiary RI-chain with two links draws together D–D♭–E with D♭–E–E♭.

Retrograde-inversion also draws together entire statements of the twelve-note series. The passage in m. 520–26 (Example 3.5c) consists of two statements of the twelve-note series separated by the silence on the downbeat of m. 523. The silence articulates the two series into discrete sonic blocks; the retrograde-inversion creates a connection that spans over the articulative boundary. The process of combining units via retrograde-inversion thus extends from intervals, to a four-note series, to a seven- or twelve-note series, to combinations of twelve-tone series. At each level, one senses a complementary tendency of the constituent units to assert their distinctive identity and the power of the retrograde-inversion to conjoin them into meaningful wholes.

The conjunction of motives via inversion is an even more potent and far-reaching source of musical connection. Indeed, the inversional balance that results is a persistent preoccupation of Stravinsky's late music, one that manifests itself in a variety of ways. In the melodic domain, Stravinsky frequently juxtaposes motives related by inversion to create a sense of poised equilibrium, with the motives simultaneously held together and apart. This is the paradox of inversional balance: it simultaneously distinguishes and conjoins two elements by balancing them. They are brought into relationship with each other, but a relationship that emphasizes their individuality. They are poised against each other in a state of equilibrium and deadlock.

Example 3.6 shows two relatively early serial melodies both of which are arranged symmetrically in pitch space. The melody from "Full fadom five" (Example 3.6a), which represents the P-form of the series for that work, consists of a diatonic collection, the E♭ minor scale. Stravinsky has arranged it as a wedge, moving toward its symmetrical center on A♭. The A♭ is flanked by forms of (0235) above and below it related by inversion around A♭. These familiar motive shapes, which hark back to the Russian folk-like melodies of Stravinsky's earlier music, are distinguished by register and contour, balanced against each other even as they move toward each other.

The five-note melody from *In Memoriam Dylan Thomas* (Example 3.6b), representing its series, is also a wedge, but a chromatic one. The melody converges on its final D, balancing forms of (012) above and below it. It fills in a gap in chromatic space just as the A♭ in "Full fadom five" filled in a gap in diatonic space. In fact, the axis of pitch-class symmetry is the same in both cases – that is why D♭ is poised opposite E♭ in both excerpts.

When Stravinsky began writing music based on larger twelve-tone series, inversional balance and symmetry remained important constructive forces. In *The Flood*, for example, Stravinsky depicts the voice of God by combining two twelve-tone

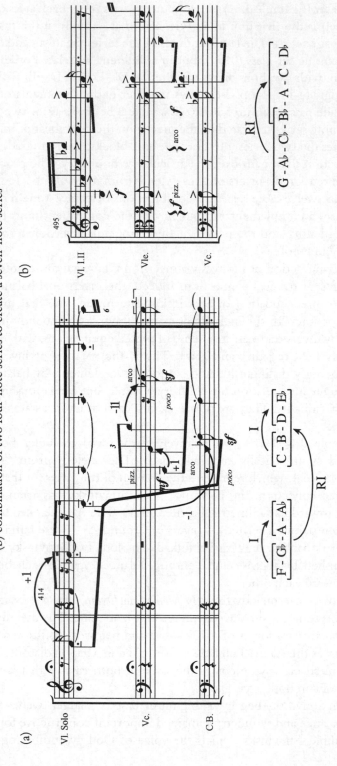

Example 3.5 Retrograde-inversion and RI-chains in *Agon*, Pas-de-Deux

(a) combination of two intervals to create a four-note motive, and of two four-note motives to create an eight-note (octatonic) collection

(b) combination of two four-note series to create a seven-note series

Example 3.5 (cont.)

(c) creation of a twelve-note series from a four-note series, and combination of two twelve-note series via RI

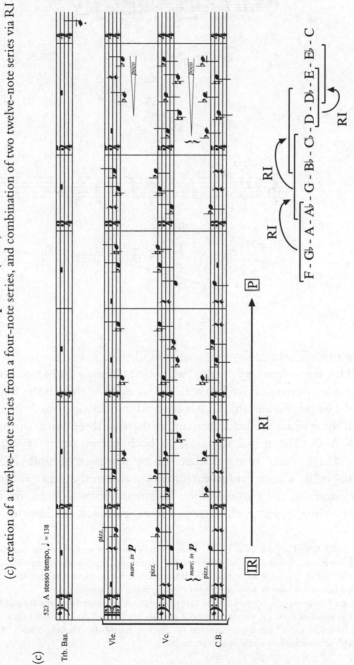

Example 3.6   Pitch symmetry
(a) "Full fadom five," from *Three Shakespeare Songs*, mm. 2–3
(b) *In Memoriam Dylan Thomas*, Prelude, mm. 1–2

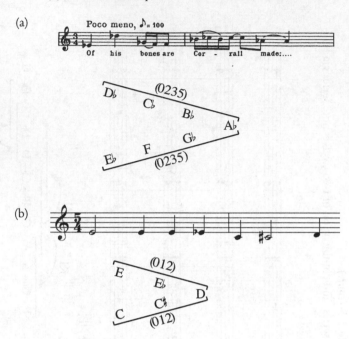

melodies that are related by inversion around their shared first note, G♯ (Example 3.7).[24] The upper melody begins with that familiar twist trichord, G♯–G–A, arranged as a symmetrical wedge, with the second and third notes fanning out from the G♯.[25] The second and third notes are held in balance around the initial G♯. As a result, all three notes are held invariant as the first three notes of the lower voice, now G♯–A–G. The initial trichords in both voices are internally symmetrical around G♯ and related to each other also by inversion around G♯. There is thus inversional balance both within each melody and in the relationship between the initial trichords of the two melodies. Inversion serves to poise musical elements, notes or motives, against each other in a static, balanced equilibrium.

---

[24] In *Elegy for J. F. K.* and *Introitus*, as in *The Flood*, the P- and I-forms, related by inversion around their shared first note, G♯, are frequently heard in close proximity. The series for all three works are structured so as to emphasize an internal sense of symmetry around G♯. This is the same pitch-class axis as the one referenced in the melodies from "Full fadom five" and *In Memoriam Dylan Thomas*, shown in Example 3.6.

[25] All published accounts of *The Flood* assume that these two melodies represent the P and I forms of the series. Stravinsky's sketches, however, identify them as R and IR. See Lynne Rogers, "Stravinsky's Serial Counterpoint and the Voice of God," paper presented to the Society for Music Theory, Atlanta, 1999. I will follow Stravinsky's designation here and throughout this book.

At the end of the top melody, stutter-like repetition helps to isolate the final three notes: C–B–C♯. Within the top melody, this motive relates, again through inversion around G♯, to the three notes that ended the previous phrase: E–F–D♯. Both of these motives are heard also in the lower voice (although D♯ is left out of the lower voice in this excerpt). Inversion around G♯ thus creates relationships within each voice even as it relates the two voices taken as wholes. Inversion simultaneously individuates motives and voices while bringing them into poised equilibrium with each other. In *The Flood*, inversional balance serves as a musical emblem of the perfect, balanced harmoniousness of God. In other works, where its expressive meaning may be less clear, it still serves as a distillation of the basic formal tension in all of Stravinsky's music between musical elements that are simultaneously independent but brought into relationship with each other.

Transposition, although it lacks the poised, balanced quality of inversion, can also be used to individuate and juxtapose motives to create serial melodies. "Surge, aquilo," from *Canticum Sacrum*, Stravinsky's first entirely twelve-tone movement, concludes with the three-voice canon in augmentation shown in Example 3.8. The tenor solo presents two series forms ($T_1(I)$ followed by P) and acts as the leading voice of the canon. Each of the three canonic voices relates to the other two by T_4 (Example 3.8a). This interval of transposition also shapes the relations among the segmental subsets of the series (Example 3.8b). The first four notes of the melody, A–B♭–C–E♭, are transposed in order at T_4 to become the sixth-through-ninth notes of the melody, D♭–D–E–G, the first three notes of which are themselves transposed at T_4 to become the last three notes of the melody, F–G♭–A♭. The melody thus projects a strong sense of cycling through the chromatic by ascending 4s. This sense is reinforced by Stravinsky's setting of the text: the two iterations of "Comedite" begin on A and D♭ followed by "amici" beginning on F. The transpositional relations thus simultaneously articulate the melody into segments and bring the segments into meaningful relationship with each other.

The intensity of the transpositional relations within the melody brings about a high degree of segmental invariance among the voices (Example 3.8c). All of the trichords bracketed in Example 3.8b occur as segments of all three canonic voices – the only exception is the conclusion of the third canonic voice (harp and English horn) which is truncated to permit a final cadence on the perfect fifth, A–E. The combination of motives within the series is thus reflected in the combination of serial melodies in a passage of three-part counterpoint.

The series for *Epitaphium*, like the series for "Surge, aquilo," makes extensive use of T_4 to articulate and link its constituent motives, in this case forms of sc(016) (see Example 3.9). Example 3.9a identifies three such forms in the series and links them together in a complete 4-cycle.[26] The remaining notes describe a related complete

---

[26] There is one additional form of sc(016) embedded in the series, B–F♯–F, which overlaps C–B–F♯ to create an RI-chain.

Example 3.7 *The Flood*, mm. 85–100: two melodies (representing the R and IR forms of the series) related by inversion around G♯

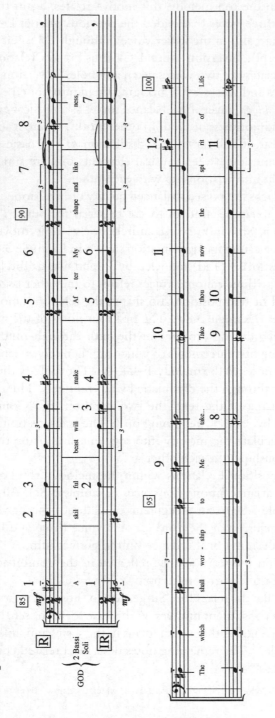

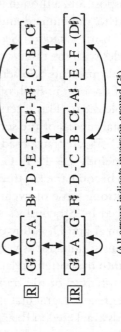

(All arrows indicate inversion around G♯)

Example 3.8 Motivic combination via transposition in *Canticum Sacrum*, second movement ("Surge, aquilo")

(a) cycle of T_4 among three voices in a canon in augmentation

(b) cycle of T_4 within the series

(c) segmental invariance

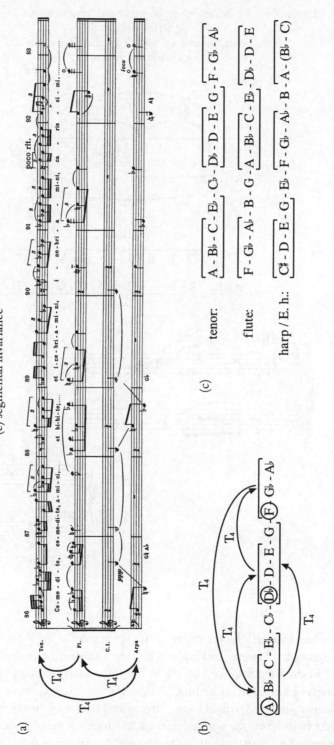

Example 3.9   Motivic combination via transposition in *Epitaphium*
(a) series embeds T$_4$
(b) segmental invariance between I and IR (related at RT$_4$)
(c) final two measures

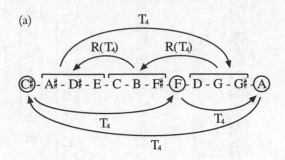

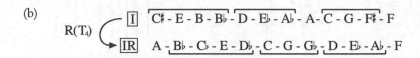

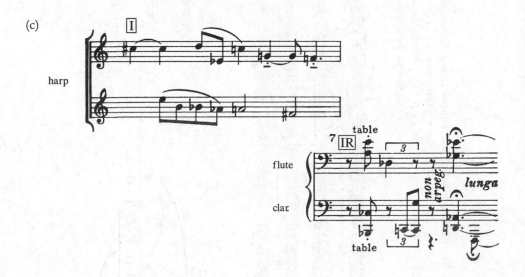

4-cycle. The I and IR forms of the series are related at R(T$_4$) and, as a result, share many segmental subsets (Example 3.9b). As the piece concludes with these two forms (I in the harp followed by IR in the flute–clarinet duet), these invariants are particularly prominent (Example 3.9c). As in "Surge, aquilo," T$_4$ is used in *Epitaphium* to link individual tones, three- and four-note motives, and entire series forms. At each level, the transpositional relationship simultaneously articulates the discrete structural units and draws them together into a connected network.

FROM SERIAL MELODY TO MELODIC PERIOD
(LINEAR COMBINATION)

In serial music, including Stravinsky's, much or all of the musical substance can be traced to forms of a series that are related by transposition, inversion, retrograde, or retrograde–inversion. In that sense, the combination of series via those operations to create larger musical units is an inevitable, definitional aspect of serial composition: the series is the basic unit and it is combined with its transpositions, inversions, retrogrades, or retrograde–inversions to create larger units. That is simply the nature of serial composition.

But in Stravinsky's serial music, there is more to the story. Specifically, the combinations of series tend to reflect the combinations of motives within the series in consistent, systematic ways. There is thus recursion among the structural levels: the same processes that forge intervals into motives and motives into serial melodies are also at work in creating larger melodic periods from constituent series.[27] We have already seen this briefly in the previous discussion of "Surge, aquilo" and *Epitaphium* (see Examples 3.8 and 3.9). In each of those works, the specific levels of transposition used to combine motives within the series were also used to combine series into melodic periods or contrapuntal complexes. Purposeful, directed transpositions of this kind play a role in creating larger melodic and contrapuntal shapes throughout Stravinsky's late music.

In the works prior to *Movements*, there is a good deal of transposition of the four basic forms, and these transpositions often reflect the internal construction of the series being transposed. Beginning with *Movements*, however, and the advent of the rotational arrays, the series-forms themselves are no longer transposed in their entirety. The smaller works use only the untransposed four basic forms of the series: P, R, I, and IR. The larger works use only rotational arrays derived from the four basic forms.[28]

Although transposition is banished outside the arrays, however, within them it is systematic and musically meaningful. Recall how the arrays are constructed: each hexachord of a twelve-note series is systematically rotated and the rotations are then transposed to begin on the same initial note. Example 3.10a shows the first hexachord of the I-form of the series for *A Sermon, a Narrative, and a Prayer*: E♭–D–G♭–E–F–A♭. The hexachord describes a particular succession of intervals, 11–4–10–1–3, to which the interval 7 is adjoined if the hexachord is imagined as wrapping around from its last note to its first. In Example 3.10b, the hexachord is

---

[27] I am using the term "period" in its general sense as "a complete musical utterance," corresponding to "the sentence (or period) in language. . .Periods may be joined to form larger periods (perhaps constituting a section of a movement) and whole movements or forms" (*The New Harvard Dictionary of Music*, ed Don Randel [Cambridge, Mass.: Harvard University Press, 1986], 625). I do not intend the more specific reference of the term to a combination of antecedent and consequent phrases.

[28] There are a few small exceptions. In *Elegy for J. F. K.*, Stravinsky uses the retrograde of I (=RI) as well as his standard IR. There is some local transposition of series in both *Movements* and *The Flood*, which also makes consistent use of the retrogrades of both I (=RI) and IR (=RIR).

Example 3.10   Directed transposition within a rotational array
(a) first hexachord of the I–form of the series for *A Sermon, a Narrative, and a Prayer*
(b) hexachord rotated and then transposed
(c) entire rotational array

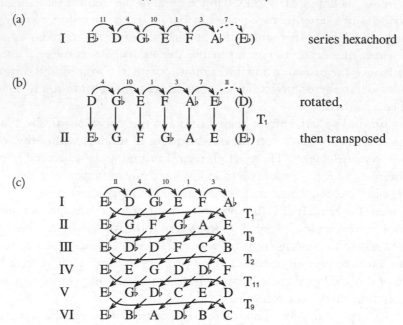

rotated to begin on its second note, D, thereby shifting the succession of intervals one place to the left. The rotated hexachord is transposed to begin on E♭. The interval of transposition, T_1, is the complement of the first interval of the original hexachord, i11. That is because, just as the first interval of the hexachord takes us eleven semitones from the first note, E♭ to the second, D, the complementary transposition is needed to take us from D, the first note of the rotated hexachord, back to E♭, the first note of the transposed rotation.

Example 3.10c shows the entire array of which Examples 3.10a and b contain the first two rows. In moving from Row I to Row II, as we have seen, we simultaneously rotate, thus shifting the intervals one place to the left, and transpose so that the rows begin on the same first note. The interval of transposition is the complement of the corresponding interval within the hexachord. In moving from Row II to Row III, similarly, we rotate and transpose by T_8, which is the complement of the second interval in the hexachord, 4. As we move through the array from Row I to Row VI, the transposition levels reenact, in order, the complements of the intervals within the generating hexachord.

Stravinsky frequently writes extended melodic lines by moving systematically from top to bottom through one of his rotational arrays. Example 3.10d reproduces a passage from *A Sermon, a Narrative, and a Prayer* that is based entirely on the array

Example 3.10 (*cont.*)

(d)*A Sermon, a Narrative, and a Prayer,* mm. 226–38, alto and tenor solo only
(e) summary of hexachordal progression

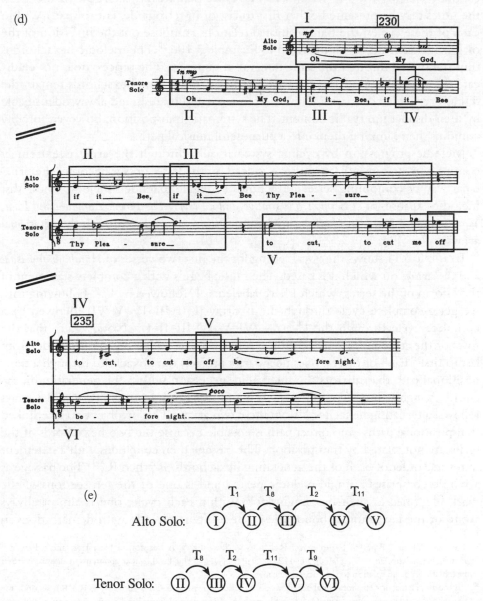

from Example 3.10c. The two voices are moving in canon through the array, with the alto solo traversing rows I–II–III–IV–V and the tenor solo, which leads it in canon, traversing rows II–III–IV–V–VI. (Note that within each row of the array, the notes may be presented either first to last or in retrograde, last to first.) Within each of these cycles, the transpositional relations compose out the inversion of the original hexachord, as summarized in Example 3.10e.[29] The melodic hexachord is thus transposed through the same intervals it contains. The process does not eradicate the musical boundaries between the hexachords. The hexachords remain the discrete, articulated structural units, often separated by rests and always identifiable by their distinct intervallic content. The systematic transposition, however, forcibly conjoins them, linking them into a purposeful musical path.

Melodic progression by cycling systematically through the array is extremely common in Stravinsky's late music – indeed, in the last works it becomes the principal way of conjoining series hexachords to create extended melodic lines. Vast melodic expanses of *A Sermon, a Narrative, and a Prayer*, *The Flood*, *Abraham and Isaac*, *Variations*, and *Requiem Canticles* arise from systematic cycles through the rotational arrays.

Example 3.11 shows the vocal setting for the first two verses of *Abraham and Isaac* and the arrays on which it is based. The music begins with a complete statement of the I-form of the series, which I have labeled as I_I^A followed by I_I^B.[30] Following this, we get a complete cycle through the I^A-array (I–II–III–IV–V–VI) followed by a complete cycle through the I^B-array (VI–V–IV–III–II–I). (Note, again, that the rows of the array may be stated either from first note to last or, in retrograde, from last to first.) Each of these cycles necessarily projects the hexachord through a transpositional path that mirrors the intervallic succession within the generating hexachord. A slightly more complicated cycle of hexachords from the R^A and R^B arrays follows, alternating hexachords from these two arrays. This involves two interlinked transpositional paths – no direct path is possible because the two hexachords of the series are not related by transposition. The passage then concludes with a statement in reverse order of each of the generating hexachords: R_I^B then R_I^A.[31] The passage as a whole comprises a single melodic period and is one of the ten sections of the work identified as such by Stravinsky.[32] Within each cycle, one is almost always aware of the hexachordal boundaries. These often coincide with demarcations in

[29] Thomas Clifton, "Types of Symmetrical Relations in Stravinsky's 'A Sermon, a Narrative, and a Prayer,'" *Perspectives of New Music* 9/1 (1970), 96–112, describes cycles of this kind, but is apparently unaware of their systematic aspect in relation to the rotational arrays.

[30] My nomenclature for the rotational arrays works as follows: First, the series form (P, I, R, IR); second, the hexachord written as a superscript (A for first hexachord, B for second hexachord); third, the row of the array written as a subscript using Roman numerals (I, II, III, IV, V, VI).

[31] It would be simpler to describe this twelve-note succession as P, but the derivation from the two hexachords of R relates it better to the cycles that precede it. Furthermore, this is Stravinsky's own derivation – the relevant compositional sketch, including a complete serial self-analysis, is reproduced in *Strawinsky: Sein Nachlass, Sein Bild*, 176.

[32] *Themes and Episodes*, 55. The formal plan for the work is described in detail in Spies, "Notes on Stravinsky's *Abraham and Isaac*."

the text and are marked by longer rhythmic values. Because of the structure of the array, the shared first note of each row becomes an audible signal that a hexachordal unit has just ended, or is just beginning. The constituent hexachords, then, are felt as discrete, integral units. At the same time, the larger melodic period of which they are part is unified by the purposeful transpositions that create links across the hexachordal boundaries.

In similar fashion, the melodic line of the Lacrimosa movement from *Requiem Canticles* is based entirely on complete, systematic cycles through the IR^B- and IR^A-arrays (see Example 3.12). For the most part, each row of the array is used to set a line or clause of the text, and the musical phrases are separated by instrumental interludes. The rows of the array are thus established as discrete musical units, each with its own distinct identity. But the tendency of the rows toward isolation is counterbalanced by strong forces of integration. These forces include the common tones that link the hexachords, particularly at the point where they begin or end, but even more so by the purposeful transpositions that connect them. Each is simultaneously a self-contained musical utterance and part of a larger musical motion that spans the entire movement.

In addition to these melodic combinations via transposition, Stravinsky also creates extended melodic periods by combining a serial melody with its inversion. The melodic period as a whole thus maintains a sense of inversional symmetry and balance. The Bransle Simple from *Agon* is based on two six-note series, which I have designated X and Y on Example 3.13.[33] Series X begins with the whole-tone D–E, and one can imagine those notes as related by inversion at I^D_E. That initial dyad is repeated and thus distinguished from the rest of the melody. The melody continues by adjoining another whole-tone, F–G, related to the initial D–E at I^D_G. The resulting tetrachord, a member of the familiar sc(0235), spans the perfect fourth D–G. That fourth (which is filled in by step) is combined with another fourth, F♯–B (left empty), which completes the six-note series. The series-form that follows is the one that inverts the two fourths onto each other: now the F♯–B is filled in and D–G is left empty. At four levels of structure – notes combine to create a dyad; dyads combine to create a tetrachord; tetrachords combine to create a series; series combine to create a melodic period – inversion simultaneously isolates the constituent structures and holds them in balance.

Series Y is generated and combined in a similar way. It begins with a whole-tone D–C and is spanned by another whole-tone, D–E. The initial D–C is conjoined with G–F to create an RI-chain that spans the first four notes of the series. The six-note series as a whole is then combined melodically with the inversion that preserves the whole-tone frame: the original form spans D–E and the inversion spans E–D. Like Series X, then, Series Y contains symmetrically balanced components (notes, dyads, trichords) and is itself balanced against its own inversion. Within the

---

[33] Stravinsky's sketches indicate that he composed Series X first, then derived Series Y as a transposition of the literal complement of Series X. Series X and Series Y are thus abstract complements of each other. See Tucker, "Stravinsky and His Sketches," 141–55.

Example 3.11 Cycles through rotational arrays
(a) *Abraham and Isaac*, mm. 12–45, voice part only

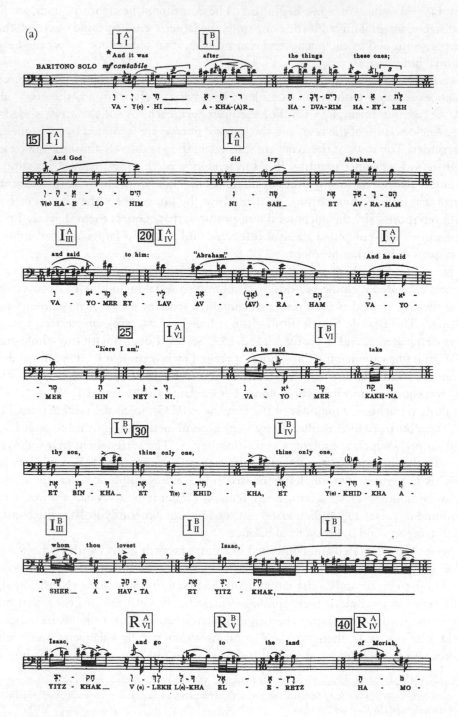

Example 3.11 (*cont.*)
(a) (*cont.*)
(b) rotational arrays

(a)

(b)

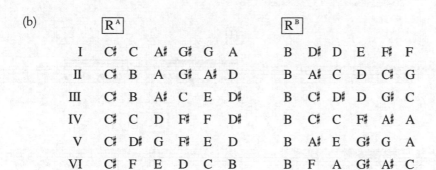

	R^A						R^B				
I	C♯	C	A♯	G♯	G	A	B	D♯	D	E	F♯	F
II	C♯	B	A	G♯	A♯	D	B	A♯	C	D	C♯	G
III	C♯	B	A♯	C	E	D♯	B	C♯	D♯	D	G♯	C
IV	C♯	C	D	F♯	F	D♯	B	C♯	C	F♯	A♯	A
V	C♯	D♯	G	F♯	E	D	B	A♯	E	G♯	G	A
VI	C♯	F	E	D	C	B	B	F	A	G♯	A♯	C

	I^A						I^B				
I	F	E	F♯	G♯	G	B	C♯	D♯	D	C	A♯	A
II	F	G	A	G♯	C	F♯	C♯	C	A♯	G♯	G	B
III	F	G	F♯	A♯	E	D♯	C♯	B	A	G♯	C	D
IV	F	E	G♯	D	C♯	D♯	C♯	B	A♯	D	E	D♯
V	F	A	D♯	D	E	F♯	C♯	C	E	F♯	F	D♯
VI	F	B	A♯	C	D	C♯	C♯	F	G	F♯	E	D

Example 3.12   Cycles through rotational arrays
(a) *Requiem Canticles*, Lacrimosa, mm. 229–65, voice part only

Example 3.12 (*cont.*)

(b) rotational arrays

(b)   IR^A   IR^B

I	A♯	C	B	F♯	G♯	A		G	D	E	F	C♯	D♯
II	A♯	A	E	F♯	G	G♯		G	A	A♯	F♯	G♯	B♯
III	A♯	E♯	G	G♯	A	B		G	G♯	E	F♯	A♯	E♯
IV	A♯	B♯	C♯	D	E	D♯		G	D♯	F	A	E	F♯
V	A♯	B	C	D	C♯	G♯		G	A	C♯	G♯	A♯	B
VI	A♯	B	C♯	C	G	A		G	B	F♯	G♯	A	F

extended melodic spans that result, one feels a constant sense of tension between the structural units and the transformations that conjoin them.

Inversion around D plays an important role in organizing the two melodies shown in Example 3.14. Stravinsky's first sketch as he began work on the vocal line for *In Memoriam Dylan Thomas* is shown in Example 3.14a.[34] It consists of the retrograde of the five-note series for the piece, D–D♭–C–E♭–F♭, and, aligned directly below it and written in red pencil, its inversion also beginning on D. That inversionally balanced combination is then composed-out in the melodic line for the first two lines of the text (all of the analytical markings on the sketch are Stravinsky's own).[35] By combining R and IR in this way, Stravinsky simultaneously emphasizes a sense of balance around the initial tone, D, and fills in the chromatic span of a perfect fourth, from C to F. After the R–IR combination, Stravinsky plans to have I (the retrograde of IR) and then repeat his initial R. So a path takes us from an initial idea (R), through its inversion (IR), the retrograde of that inversion (I), then the retrograde-inversion of that retrograde-inversion (R), which brings us back to the initial idea (these relationships are summarized in Example 3.14c). The initial R- and IR-forms are realized musically as discrete phrases, each devoted to a single line of poetic text. The concluding I- and R-forms are linked to form a single phrase. The result is an extended melodic line made up of audibly distinct units balanced against each other through either inversional or retrograde symmetry.

The second Ricercar from the *Cantata* begins with the melodic line shown in Example 3.14d. It consists of an eleven-note series, E–C–D–E–F–E♭–D–E–C–D, followed by its retrograde, its inversion around D (i.e. the inversion that exchanges the first two notes of the series, C and E), and the retrograde of that inversion.[36] The series contains only six different pitch classes, B–C–D–E♭–E–F, and is nearly

---

[34] Document No. 109–0696 in the Stravinsky Archive at the Paul Sacher Foundation.

[35] The sketch for the melody shown as Example 3.14b differs from the final published score slightly in the first two lines and entirely for the next two.

[36] Note that in this early work, Stravinsky uses RI instead of IR, which later became his standard procedure.

Example 3.13 Melodic extension via inversion: *Agon*, Bransle Simple, mm. 298–304

symmetrical around D. Only the E♭ lacks its inversional partner within the series. As a result, when Stravinsky inverts the series around D, he gets five common tones and one new note, C♯, the missing partner for E♭ (these relationships are summarized in Example 3.14e).[37] The combination also has the effect of filling in a chromatic space, this time a diminished fifth from B to F. The chosen inversion thus extends the melody to create a sense of inversional balance and to fill chromatic space.

In all of the melodic periods discussed, the seams between the constituent series tend to show. Sometimes the boundaries are obscured, but more often they are reinforced by melodic contour and phrasing. At this level of combining melodies into melodic periods, we observe the same formal tension we saw in the combination of intervals into motives and motives into melodies: the constituent units assert their identity and distinctiveness, in relative isolation from each other while, at the same time, they are juxtaposed in ways that bind them.

FROM SERIAL MELODY TO CONTRAPUNTAL UNIT (CONTRAPUNTAL COMBINATION)

Stravinsky's late music is generally contrapuntal in conception. Melodic lines are conceived independently, then layered polyphonically. Usually, the principal line is written first in its entirety, and then counterpoints are added to it, as discussed in Chapter 2. Stravinsky's comment about the *Elegy for J. F. K.* pertains equally to most of the music of this period: "I wrote the vocal part first and only later discovered the relationships from which I was able to derive the complementary instrumental counterpoint. Schoenberg composed his *Phantasie* in the same way, incidentally, the violin part first and then the piano."[38] The polyphonic parts thus maintain a high degree of independence. They are conceived separately, and each has its own individual quality, its own internal logic. They can never be bound into a single, seamless whole; the divisions among them will always be apparent. At the same time, as with the extension of melodies to create larger melodic periods, Stravinsky uses transposition, inversion, and, to a lesser extent, their retrogrades to create meaningful contrapuntal combinations in which the lines are brought into significant relationship with each other.

---

[37] As Babbitt explains ("Remarks on the Recent Stravinsky," *Perspectives of New Music* 2/2 [1964], 171–72): "In the Ricercar, although the six–note unit is so chosen that there is no inversional form which contains a duplication of the content of the original unit, there is one that contains five notes in common, with the result that there is maximum pitch intersection between these forms. The statements of the four forms of the unit, constituting the first section of the tenor solo, contain only seven different, chromatically contiguous notes. Since the order of forms is: prime, retrograde, then inversion, retrograde inversion, the first two forms employ only six pitches, and the following two – which as a compound unit are the retrograde inversion of the first two regarded as such a unit – similarly employ only six pitches, differing by one only from those associated with the first two forms."

[38] *Themes and Episodes*, 58. It is revealing that Stravinsky justifies his procedure by adducing the authority of Schoenberg.

Example 3.14 Melodic extension via inversion around D
(a) *In Memoriam Dylan Thomas*, initial sketch
(b) first sketch for vocal melody
(c) analytical summary
(d) *Cantata*, Ricercar I, mm. 2–8

(a)

(b)

(c)

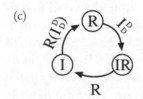

(d)

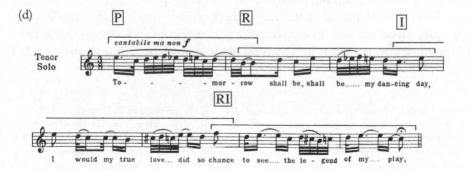

Example 3.14 (*cont.*)
(e) analytical summary

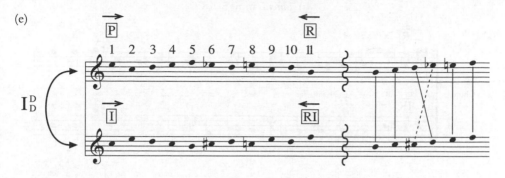

Contrapuntal duets in which the two parts are related by inversion are particularly common (see Example 3.15 for two such passages). In both cases, the sense of inversional balance around a shared D♯ axis is palpable. The counterpoint is largely note against note and one consistently hears notes sounded simultaneously with their inversional partners. Both texts are religious in nature and the inversional symmetry seems to suggest a divine balance and harmoniousness.[39] The lines maintain their independence, poised against each other in static equilibrium.

Although Stravinsky's melodic lines are conceived independently and maintain a high degree of autonomy, a sense that they nonetheless belong together is often enhanced by segmental invariance, that is, by groups of pitches that the lines have in common. Segmental invariance under inversion or retrograde-inversion is a particularly consistent feature of contrapuntal combination in Stravinsky's late music (see Example 3.16 for three such passages). In the passage from "Full fadom five" (Example 3.16a), the voice states the seven-note series for the piece: E♭–D♭–G♭–F–B♭–C♭–A♭. As previously discussed, this series consists of the seven notes of the E♭ minor scale ordered as a wedge collapsing inward toward its center, A♭ (refer again to Example 3.6a). The viola plays the same series in off-beat canon at the octave, starting a beat and a half later. The clarinet states the inversion of the retrograde, which concludes in the flute: A♭–F–G♭–C♭–B♭–E♭–D♭. This IR-form of the series shares three segmental dyads with the P-form – these are bracketed in the example. What is more, because of the internal inversional symmetry of the series around A♭, the IR-form, which begins on A♭, has exactly the same total content as the P-form. These two measures of music, then, present three tunes and two different forms of the series, but only seven different notes, namely the notes of the E♭ minor scale. The inversional combination of lines thus produces melodic variety but collectional stasis. The melodies are rhythmically independent, but joined by the shared collection of notes they mutually project.

[39] Refer back to Example 3.7 for a similar passage from *The Flood*. There, the inversional duet represents the actual voice of God.

Example 3.15   Inversional duets
(a) *Introitus*, mm. 42–49
(b) *Threni*, mm. 5–18

(a)

R   D♯ - G - F♯ - A - A♯ - B - F - E - C - D - C♯ - G♯

IR   D♯ - B - C - A - G♯ - G - C♯ - D - F♯ - E - E♯ - A♯

(b)

P   D♯ - G♯ - G - A♯ - C♯ - A - D - B - E - C - F - F♯

I   D♯ - A♯ - B - G♯ - F - A - E - G - D - F♯ - C♯ - C

Example 3.16 Contrapuntal combination via retrograde-inversion to create segmental invariance

(a) "Full fadom five" from *Three Shakespeare Songs*, mm. 2–4

In the passage from *Agon* (Example 3.16b), Flute I states IR while Flutes II and III state P virtually note against note (the other instruments present I at the same time). The extensive invariance between P and IR produces a virtual canon when the two are heard as a duet. This is because P is almost entirely RI-symmetrical in its internal construction, with its first five notes related by retrograde-inversion to its next five notes. The melodies are serially independent (each represents a distinct series form) but virtually merged musically.

In the conclusion of *Fanfare for a New Theater* (Example 3.16c), similarly, there is extensive invariance between the I and R forms of the series. Indeed, the four trichords of I, all twist motives, are also the four trichords of R. The staggered disposition of invariant trichords between the two lines here also produces a canonic effect. The lines are ordered as retrograde-inversions of each other, but their motivic identity could hardly be more complete.

In combining independent melodies into a contrapuntal complex, then, Stravinsky's standard procedure is to emphasize their motivic and pitch-class similarity. Occasionally, but more rarely, he takes the opposite tack, and combines lines so as to emphasize their complementary quality, their lack of shared segments. In the more extreme cases, Stravinsky combines lines, as Schoenberg does, to create aggregates through hexachordal combinatoriality. This is not Stravinsky's usual procedure — contrapuntal combinations are far more likely to create reinforcement, repetition, doubling between the parts rather than exclusion — but its occurrence in

Example 3.16 (cont.)
(b) *Agon*, Coda, mm. 234–41

$\boxed{\text{IR}}$ B♭ - E - A - G - G♯ - F♯ - F - E♭ - D - C - C♯ - B

$\boxed{\text{P}}$ A - G - G♯ - F♯ - F - E♭ - D - C - C♯ - B - E - B♭

Example 3.16 (*cont.*)

(c) *Fanfare for a New Theater*, last measure

Canticum Sacrum is so striking as to be worthy of notice (see Example 3.17).[40] In the first of the duets (Example 3.17a), Stravinsky begins by combining P and R. This combination creates hexachordal R–combinatoriality: by the time each series has traced its first six notes, an aggregate has been created between the parts, and the same is true in the combination of their last six notes. In the continuation of this duet, the combination of an I-form and an R-form also creates aggregates in this manner, now via RI-combinatoriality. The duet as a whole, then, is divided into four aggregates created between the parts.

The same is true in the second duet (Example 3.17b). Now Stravinsky has combined two I-related series forms (IR and R) to create aggregates between the parts via I-combinatoriality. Each of the melodies makes individual sense, with its own internal shape and structure, and is rhythmically independent of the other. Their relationship here is one of complementarity – each melody presents just those notes excluded by the other at that moment. Complementarity, like inversion, has the paradoxical effect of simultaneously holding the melodies together and apart. They are distinguished from each other by their exclusive pitch content, but poised against each other to create, together, the complete aggregate of all twelve pitch-classes.

It is notable that both duets of Example 3.17 end on a perfect fifth. This interval retains some of its traditional consonant resonance and its cadential force: it remains a "perfect" interval. Stravinsky's contrapuntal combinations, whether via inversion or transposition, are often directed toward producing cadential perfect fifths. That interval serves to bind the independent lines at a cadence.

---

[40] This aspect of *Canticum Sacrum* is discussed in Babbitt, "Remarks on the Recent Stravinsky," 178–79.

Example 3.17 Hexachordal combinatoriality to create aggregates: *Canticum Sacrum*, Three Hortatory Virtues
(a) mm. 154–62
(b) mm. 237–43

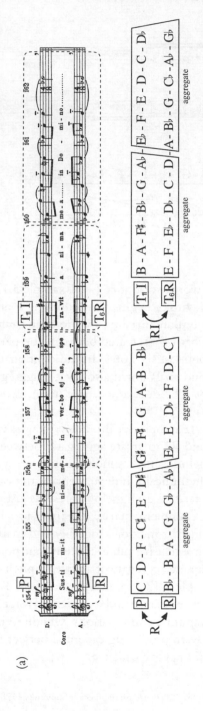

(a)

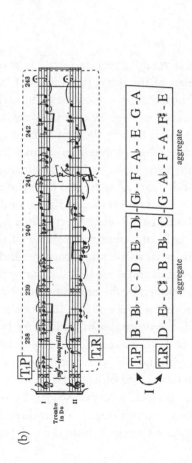

(b)

Example 3.18   Contrapuntal layering at T_7 to reflect the internal construction of the layered melodies: Septet, first movement, five measures at Rehearsal No. 8

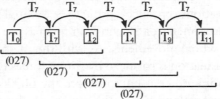

F - G - A♭ - B♭ - A - D - E

The binding effect of the perfect fifth, used as an interval of transposition, is evident in the passage from the Septet shown in Example 3.18. In the first movement of the Septet, the climactic passage shown in Example 3.18 leads to the recapitulation of the opening theme. A melodic series, previously heard as the subject of a fugato, is rearranged into a brief tune: F–G–A♭–B♭–A–D–E. Its last three notes are arranged as a symmetrical stack of perfect fourths, with D a perfect fourth above A and E a perfect fourth below it. The concluding trichord is a member of sc(027).

That tune is presented in a dense stretto of overlapping imitations, with each entrance seven semitones higher than the previous. Each group of three entries thus creates a form of sc(027) among the transpositional levels. The last three entries begin, successively, on D, A, and E, the same three notes, and thus the same set-class as the final three notes of the series. A, D, and E are also the first three notes of the movement (the head-motive of the principal melodic series) and form part of its final chord as well. Stravinsky thus binds the disparate melodies of his counterpoint in a characteristic way: they are transposed by the intervals they contain so as to produce significant pitch redundancies and emphases.

As with his combination of melodic segments into melodic periods, Stravinsky's combination of melodic lines into counterpoint is fraught with productive formal tension. The melodic lines are conceived independently and, in a variety of musical ways, assert their integrity. They resist integration with their contrapuntal partners. At the same time, they are brought into relationship with each other. These relationships may reveal similarities between the melodies, in the form of shared intervallic or pitch content. More generally, the relationships involve a sense of balanced equilibrium, a musical complementarity in which the lines simultaneously attract and repel, are held together and apart.

FROM MELODIC PERIOD AND CONTRAPUNTAL COMPLEX TO SECTION OR MOVEMENT

Stravinsky's melodies are extended in time and combined contrapuntally through purposeful, musically significant transpositions and inversions. These melodic and polyphonic combinations produce distinctive textural blocks, which in turn become the basic components of Stravinskian form as they are juxtaposed to create formal sections and whole movements. As with the melodies, the tendency of the blocks toward self-insulation is balanced by strong forces that bind them.

The principal binding force is transposition: the blocks are juxtaposed to create transpositional pathways along which the music can flow with a sense of purpose and direction.[41] In some cases, the transposed textural block may be as short as a single interval or note. In "Musick to heare," the first of the *Three Shakespeare Songs*, for example, the transposition of a single interval, the cadential perfect fifth, helps to shape the large-scale organization of the work. This song is organized almost entirely with reference to a four-note series: B–G–A–B♭. At the beginning and ending of the song, melodies derived from that series interact with a contrasting melody that consists of the first five notes of the C major scale, played in either ascending or descending order. The two kinds of melodies conjoin, at the end of the instrumental introduction and again at the end of the entire song, to make a strong cadence on the perfect fifth C–G, a vivid musical representation of the poetic text, which describes music as "a speechless song being many seeming one" (see Example 3.19).

At the final cadence, two serial streams converge on the cadential perfect fifth, C–G: I_{11} in the voice (C♭–E♭–D♭–C) and I_6 in the flute (G♭–B♭–A♭–G). Beneath

---

[41] I discuss these issues in "The Problem of Coherence in Stravinsky's Serenade in A," *Theory and Practice* 12 (1987), 3–10, and "A Strategy of Large-Scale Organization in the Late Music of Stravinsky," *Integral* 11 (1999), 1–36.

Example 3.19 A transpositional pathway in "Musick to heare" from *Three Shakespeare*
Songs, final thirteen measures

them, beginning at Rehearsal No. 9, the clarinet and viola trot up and down the
first five notes of the C major scale (C–D–E–F–G), coming finally to rest on the
two boundary tones, C and G. The preceding musical phrase, ending before
Rehearsal No. 9, ends on another cadential perfect fifth, G–D. It is produced by the
convergence of two serial strands: I_1 in the voice (D♭–F–E♭–D) and P_8 in the instruments (A♭–E–F♯–G). The large-scale progression leads from a perfect fifth on G to
another on C, thus composing-out the concluding interval, C–G. The larger path
from G to C is compressed into the final cadential interval. Just as the perfect fifths

draw together disparate melodic strands, the larger progression from G to C draws together separate formal sections of the song.[42]

Something similar happens on a much larger scale in the large central movement of *Canticum Sacrum*. This movement is in three sections which set biblical verses on the three hortatory virtues: *caritas* (charity), *spes* (hope), and *fides* (faith). Each section begins, and the third section ends, with a distinctive organ solo in octaves; the movement concludes with a coda in which the same music is scored for violas and contrabasses (see Example 3.20). The first four statements of this twelve-note melody are at different transposition levels; the coda restores the level of the third statement.[43] The melodies are identical rhythmically except for the fourth, which is a strict rhythmic diminution.[44] The melodies each form discrete, self-contained formal blocks, insulated from their immediate surroundings and widely separated from each other.

Despite their isolation, however, the melodies are bound together by the transpositions that connect them, which compose-out the intervallic patterns of the melody itself. For example, the first three notes of the first melody, A–G♯–B♭, describe the intervallic succession <-1, +2>, the familiar "twist" motive, which is heard immediately thereafter in inversion as C–C♯–B, or <+1, -2>. The original intervallic succession, <-1, +2>, also defines the transpositional relationships among the second, third, and fourth melodies, taken as wholes: the first notes of those three melodies are C–B–C♯. Similarly, the next three-note fragment in the first melody, E–D♯–F♯, describes an intervallic succession, <-1, +3>, that is heard in retrograde inversion in the transpositional relationships of the first three melodies, taken as wholes: the first notes of those three melodies are A–C–B. Intervals contained within the series thus shape the larger path along which the series itself as a whole is projected. The discrete textural blocks defined by the series are self-contained, isolated both from each other and their immediate surroundings, but linked together by purposeful, motivic transposition.

In mm. 7–22 of the first of the *Movements*, Stravinsky creates a large section of music by combining three textural blocks, all related to each other by transposition (see Example 3.21). The blocks contrast with each other and the boundaries between them are strongly reinforced. The first block is isolated by its instrumentation, for piano alone, and closed off by the cadential perfect fifth in the trumpets. The second block is dominated by a flute solo accompanied by sparse linear counterpoints. The flute breaks off abruptly as the third block begins with the reentry of the piano, accompanied by pizzicato chords.

---

[42] The "Sensus Spei" movement of *Threni* provides an even more striking example. It is punctuated by heavily doubled and sustained statements of single notes or pairs of notes which, taken together, describe a series statement that takes virtually the entire movement to unfold. In this case, transposed repetition is stripped down to its bare essentials. A single note, memorably orchestrated, acts as the distinctive bit of musical material to be transposed along a motivic path.

[43] The first tune in Example 3.20 is related at $T_{11}IR$ to the P-form of the series for the movement as a whole.

[44] The rhythm is a recurring thematic element throughout the movement, in the manner of a rhythmic *talea* in an isorhythmic motet. See Tucker, "Stravinsky and His Sketches," 124–26.

The relative autonomy of each block reflects Stravinsky's composition of the passage, which began with the flute melody in mm. 13–17.[45] This is the melody of which Stravinsky wrote "No theorist could determine the spelling of the note order in, for example, the flute solo near the beginning . . . simply by knowing the original order, however unique the combinatorial properties of this particular series," and, until the sketches became available, no theorist did.[46] The serial derivation is elaborate – it involves assembling fragments, none more than four notes in length, from the rotated and transposed hexachords of the original series.[47] Whatever the serial derivation, however, once the melody was written, Stravinsky treated it as a discrete block, subject to transposed repetition.

In the published score, the flute melody in mm. 13–17 begins on G, but Stravinsky initially wrote the melody a major third lower, beginning on E♭. He then transposed the melody up a major third into its present position, possibly to accommodate the range of the flute. Then he wrote the piano music at mm. 7–12 at the same pitch level, also starting on G, before transposing it down a step into its present position on F. Finally he wrote the music at mm. 18–32 at the original pitch level, E♭, indicating on his sketch, "follow the flute solo before (same series)." Thus we see Stravinsky working consciously and deliberately with blocks of material, arranging them in a particular transpositional pattern.[48]

The three blocks begin successively on F, G, and E♭; from the first block one ascends two semitones to the second and falls two semitones to the third. The relevant transpositional intervals have two sources, first in the series and second in the flute melody so elaborately derived from it. Within the series, these notes, and the set-type they represent, sc(024), do not occur together as a segment of the series. They do, however, occur as a kind of wraparound: the series begins with E♭ and ends with G and F (see Example 3.22a). Furthermore, these are the first and/or last notes of all the principal series forms. Within each series form, the interval from first to last note is two semitones, the featured large-scale interval of transposition. Whole-steps appear four times among the segmental dyads of the series, and no other interval is represented more. Within the flute melody, there are frequent ascending and descending whole-tones delineated either by adjacency or by register. The first six notes of the melody, for example, can be entirely parsed in that way

[45] My description of the chronology and content of the compositional sketches for *Movements* is based on Christoph Neidhofer, "Analysearbeit im Fach Komposition/Musiktheorie über die Movements for Piano and Orchestra von Igor Strawinsky" (Master's thesis, Musik-Akademie der Stadt Basel, 1991) and on my own study of the sketches.

[46] *Memories and Commentaries*, 106. See Chapter 2, footnote 45, p. 65 above for references to the extensive literature on this flute solo.

[47] The serial derivation is explained in Douglas Rust, "Stravinsky's Twelve-Tone Loom: Composition and Precomposition in *Movements*," *Music Theory Spectrum* 16/1 (1994), 62–76 and Neidhofer, "Analysearbeit."

[48] The transpositional relationship among these three blocks of music has been described in Martin Boykan, "Neoclassicism and Late Stravinsky," *Perspectives of New Music* 1/2 (1963), 155–69; William Walden, "Stravinsky's Movements for Piano and Orchestra: The Relationship of Formal Structure, Serial Technique, and Orchestration," *Journal of the Canadian Association of University Schools of Music* 9/1 (1979), 73–95; Rust, "Stravinsky's Twelve-Tone Loom," 62–76; and Neidhofer "Analysearbeit."

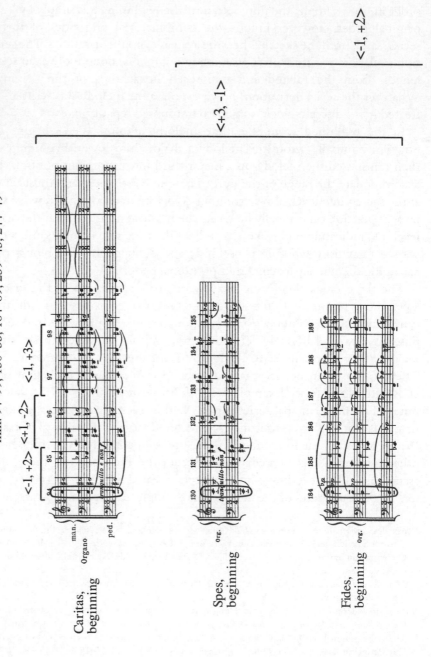

Example 3.20 Transposition of a distinctive melody: *Canticum Sacrum*, "Ad Tres Virtutes Hortationes," mm. 94–99, 130–35, 184–89, 239–43, 244–49

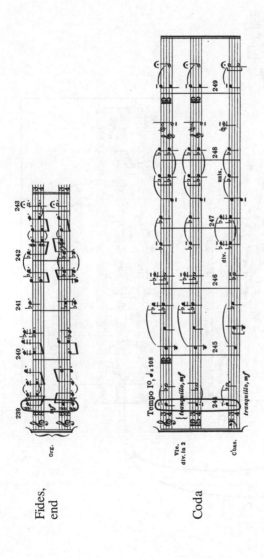

Fides, end

Coda

Example 3.21 Three transpositionally related blocks: *Movements*, mm. 7–22

Example 3.22   Ascending and descending whole-tones as surface elements in *Movements*
(a) in the four basic forms of the series
(b) in the first six notes of the flute melody
(c) in the contour of the flute melody as a whole

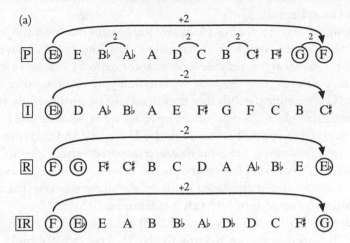

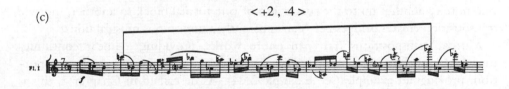

(see Example 3.22b). Furthermore, the contour of the entire flute melody projects the motive <+2, -4> in its succession of melodic high points (see Example 3.22c).[49] The pattern of transposed repetition from block to block thus replicates the pattern of intervals within the block, both in its immediate, note-to-note successions and in its larger design.

The linking of discrete, formal blocks by purposeful transposition is a persistent feature of large-scale design in Stravinsky's late music. We have seen how Stravinsky's rotational arrays provide a context for melodic extension via transposition: melodies are created by moving systematically up or down through the rows of an array. The melodic periods that result can also be purposefully transposed in their entirety. Example 3.23a reproduces a passage from *Abraham and Isaac* that consists of two complete cycles, first through the IR^B-array and then through the I^A-array. The two generating hexachords are transposed retrogrades of each other; their intervals are thus complementary and in reverse order (see Example 3.23b). The transpositions among the hexachords of the array describe the same or the complementary successions of intervals (see Example 3.23c).

The entire arrays (shown in Example 3.23d) are related at T$_2$. Compare the first row of the IR^B-array with the last row of the I^A-array (see Example 3.23e). The first notes of the two rows are related at T$_2$, as are the remaining five notes, but in reverse order. The same is true of the second row of the IR^B-array and the second-to-last row of the I^A-array, the third row of the IR^B-array and the third-to-last row of the I^A-array, and so on. The arrays as a whole are thus related at T$_2$, in this very precise sense. Interval 2 is represented twice within the hexachord – no interval is represented more – and thus twice also within the transpositional relations among the hexachords. In Example 3.23d, we see the same motivic interval composed-out at a still higher structural level. At each structural level, then, from the succession of one note to another up to the succession of one formal block to another, motivic transposition creates bridges between apparently autonomous musical units.

Motivic transpositions can span entire works, providing a linear continuity through many disparate textural blocks. *Epitaphium*, a work of very modest proportion, provides an example (see Example 3.24). As described in Chapter 2, this is among the most fragmented of Stravinsky's compositions. It was conceived originally as a duet for flute and clarinet, divided into four distinct phrases, each derived from a single series form. At a later stage, four additional phrases were written for harp and inserted into the gaps between the flute–clarinet phrases. Stravinsky literally cut and pasted this work together.

The boundaries between the blocks, however, are bridged by motivic transpositions. The series for the work, as discussed previously with reference to Example 3.9, can be understood entirely in terms of transposition of notes or segments at T$_4$ (Example 3.24a). The four basic forms of the series, the only forms to occur in the work, all begin and end on A, C♯, or F (Example 3.24b). The discrete phrases of

---

[49] Robert Morris, "New Directions in the Theory and Analysis of Musical Contour," *Music Theory Spectrum* 15/2 (1993), 205–28, provides a systematic approach to large-scale contour. I apply his "contour reduction algorithm" to this melody in "A Strategy of Large-Scale Organization in the Late Music of Stravinsky."

Epitaphium, each of which is derived from a single series-form, thus all begin and end on one of these three notes. One has a constant sense in the piece of moving along that particular cycle of major thirds. The cycle is particularly audible in the lowest three notes of the piece: A–C♯–F. In this way, Stravinsky makes reference at the highest structural level to the musical concerns of the intermediate and surface levels. The textural blocks are highly independent in this piece, which is one of the most fragmented he ever wrote. Nonetheless the blocks are bound together by the larger musical pathway described by the lowest notes.

Transpositional paths can extend over entire movements, and bind together many discrete textural blocks. Example 3.25 shows the beginnings of the first three textural blocks from the Septet, first movement. The first block is an A-majorish fanfare (but with both C♮ and G♮ present). The melody presents the first of two series that provide much of the musical material for the movement: A–E–D–C–B–A. After the fanfare concludes, the music changes character radically, and shifts to the E-centered music at Rehearsal No. 1. That new, contrasting block then itself yields to the D-majorish music at Rehearsal No. 3. Those three pitch centers replicate, in order, the first three notes of the series: A–E–D. The disparate blocks are thus linked together along this transpositional path. Despite their manifest dissimilarity, and despite the obvious discontinuities and disruptions their juxtaposition creates, they are nonetheless bound to each other in their mutual projection of this large-scale motive.[50]

FROM SECTION TO MOVEMENT TO MULTI-MOVEMENT WORK

The same strategies of combining musical elements with their transpositions, inversions, or retrogrades apply also at the highest levels of structure, binding sections into movements and movements into multi-movement works. But, in part because of the large musical spans involved, their binding force is diminished. At the lower levels of structure, the music expresses a continual conflict of centrifugal and centripetal forces held in a tense, uneasy balance. But as one approaches the highest structural levels, the tension is often dissipated in favor of a sense of transcendence. Works occasionally end where they began, with repetitions (direct, transposed, or retrograded) of where they began. But, more often, they end with a transformation of earlier material that is so thorough as to virtually preclude any sense of repetition. Instead, one has a sense of opening out into a new realm. The centripetal forces finally relax, and the music is permitted to move beyond its initial structures and premises.

Among the binding operations, inversion (and retrograde-inversion) play very little role at the highest levels. Only two movements in all of late Stravinsky bear the impact of a large-scale inversion. In *Agon*, the brief Saraband–Step is clearly divided

---

[50] The transpositional path described here continues through the entire movement and creates two large-scale statements of the series, the first interrupted and the second complete. See Chapter 5 for a complete discussion.

Example 3.23 Linking of formal blocks

(a) two complete cycles through rotational arrays in *Abraham and Isaac*, mm. 65–79

Example 3.23 (*cont.*)
(b) comparison of the two generating hexachords
(c) intervals of transposition within the arrays
(d) interval of transposition between the arrays
(e) comparison of the first row of the IR^B-array with the last row of the I^A-array

(b)

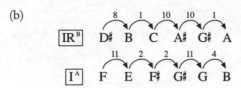

(c)

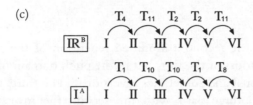

(d)

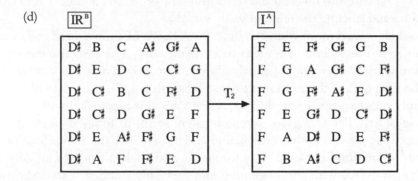

(e)

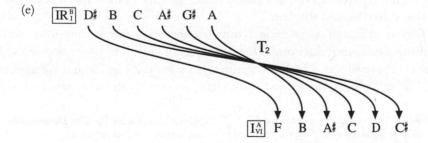

Example 3.24   Projection of T_4 and A–C♯–F at various levels of structure
(a) series for *Epitaphium*

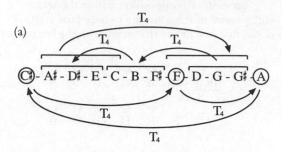

into two halves, with the second a modified repetition of the first. The second largely inverts the contours of the first, but in the pitch domain, the relationship is sometimes transpositional and sometimes inversional. The third movement of the Septet is divided into three parts with the second the inversion of the first. Stravinsky confirms this division and relationship by providing double bars between the sections and labeling the relevant series forms.

Retrograde is used more widely to bind the sections of a movement and even to relate different movements of a multi-movement work. The central scene of *The Flood*, the musical depiction of Noah's flood, is strictly retrograde-symmetrical. From the midpoint of the movement (downbeat of m. 427), the music of the first half simply runs backward, and the movement ends as it began (but with the notes in reverse order). The retrograde symmetry here seems to imply continuations in both directions, toward both a time before and a time after the flood. Stravinsky's depiction of the flood is a kind of synecdoche: a part taken from the middle of a much longer event, with the beginning and end only implied.[51] In Stravinsky's words, "This 'La Mer' has no 'de l'aube à midi' but only a time experience of something that is terrible and that lasts."[52]

In *Canticum Sacrum*, retrograde symmetry serves to frame the entire work.[53] Apart from a brief introduction ("Dedicatio"), this work is in five movements. The central third movement ("Ad tres virtutes"), by far the biggest and weightiest, is flanked by two others, the second and fourth, of roughly the same size and weight

---

[51] My thanks to Elliott Gyger for this observation.   [52] "Working Notes for *The Flood*," in *Dialogues*, 78.

[53] The five-part symmetry of the work is presumed by commentators to reflect the architecture of St. Mark's Cathedral in Venice where the work had its premiere: "The five domes of the cathedral may have inspired the five movements, with the lengthy middle movement in three parts symbolic of the cathedral's central dome" (van den Toorn, *The Music of Igor Stravinsky*, 415). *Threni* has similar five-part design, but without any overt, large-scale retrograde. According to David Smyth ("Stravinsky as Serialist: The Sketches for *Threni*," unpublished manuscript), "*Threni*'s special relationship to *Canticum Sacrum* involves the tripartite subdivision of the central movement. Stravinsky's unorthodox ordering of the three virtues in *Canticum Sacrum* (not Faith, Hope, and Charity but Charity, Hope, Faith) is reflected in *Threni*'s Querimonia, Sensus Spei, and Solacium (that is, Complaint, Perceiving Hope, and Compensation), in which Hope is again the centerpiece of a triptych with a reassuring ending. It is important to recognize that this subdivision is entirely the composer's invention, and has no counterpart in the biblical Lamentations."

Example 3.24 (*cont.*)
(b) four basic forms of the series
(c) within phrases and across entire piece

(b)

P	C#	A#	D#	E	C	B	F#	F	D	G	G#	A
I	C#	E	B	Bb	D	Eb	Ab	A	C	G	F#	F
R	A	G#	G	D	F	F#	B	C	E	D#	A#	C#
IR	A	Bb	B	E	C#	C	G	F#	D	Eb	Ab	F

(c)

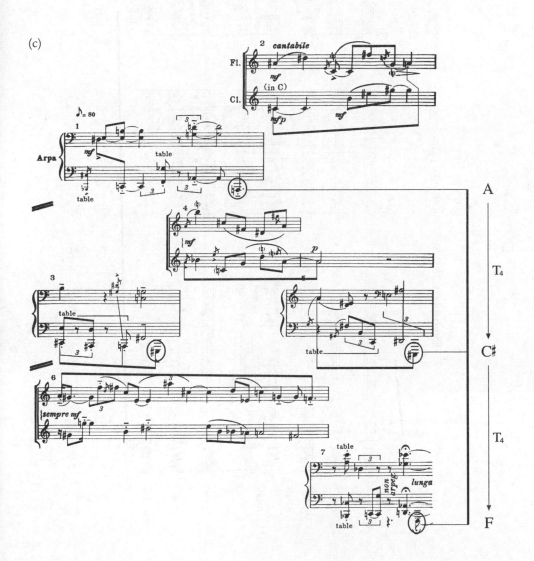

Example 3.25 A transpositional path: Septet, first movement

("Surge, aquilo" and "Brevis Motus"). The work as a whole is framed by the relatively brief first and fifth movements ("Euntes in mundum" and "Illi autem profecti"), with the fifth an almost exact retrograde of the first. This use of retrograde as a way of relating two separate movements is unique in Stravinsky's music. As a general matter, although retrograde and retrograde symmetry are common phenomena at the lower levels of structure, they play little role at the highest levels.

As a framing device for large works, Stravinsky much more frequently turns to exact or slightly modified repetition of opening material. *The Flood* and *Agon*, for example, both conclude with extended recapitulations of music heard at or very near the beginning of the work.[54] *In Memoriam Dylan Thomas* is framed by a Prelude and Postlude scored for string quartet and trombone quartet. The music is substantially the same, with two important exceptions: the music assigned to the strings in the Prelude is played by the trombones in the Postlude, and vice versa; and the music played by the trombones in the Prelude is transposed down two semitones by the strings in the Postlude.[55]

Literal recapitulations (or transposed recapitulations), however, are not common at the highest level of structure in late Stravinsky. When opening material is recalled at the end, it is substantially modified. Often, the opening music is presented in an attenuated, fragmented fashion, as though the earlier music were heard from a great distance. The music conveys a sense of dissolution, of motion from a vivid, concrete present to a more indistinct, ethereal realm.

Movements, for example, begins and ends with a complete statement of the P-form of the series (see Example 3.26). Complete series statements are rare events in *Movements*, and the one that ends the piece strongly recalls the one that begins it. But despite the similarity in the pitch–class succession, the expressive impact of the two moments is entirely different. While the first statement is vigorous, sudden, and abrupt, the last is quiet, gentle, and ruminative. The moments are linked, but the second is more a transformation than a recapitulation of the first.

In *Variations*, similarly, the ending may be understood as a modified repeat of the opening.[56] The specific serial derivations are different, although both passages are scored largely as chorales and are derived as verticals of the rotational arrays. As in *Movements*, the end of *Variations* conveys a sense of opening out, of motion from something confined to something expansive and rapturous. Again, it is hard to talk of recapitulation in this context. The opening is not so much repeated as darkly remembered as though in a dream.

The ending of the third movement of the Septet has a similar effect. This work is unique among Stravinsky's late music in its degree of inter-movement

---

[54] Stravinsky made the decision to end *The Flood* with a modified recapitulation relatively late in the compositional process (I am indebted to Lynne Rogers for this information). The same is true of the recapitulation in *Agon*, which I discuss at length in Chapter 5.

[55] I talk about this transposition, from E-centered to D-centered music, at length in Chapter 5.

[56] The published literature on *Variations* has generally understood it in this way. See, for example, Claudio Spies, "Some Notes on Stravinsky's *Variations*," *Perspectives of New Music* 4/1 (1965), 62–74; Paul Phillips, "The Enigma of Variations: A Study of Stravinsky's Final Work for Orchestra," *Music Analysis* 3/1 (1984), 69–89; and Christopher Hasty, "Phrase Formation in Post-Tonal Music," *Journal of Music Theory* 28/2 (1984), 167–90.

Example 3.26 Series statements in *Movements*
(a) the beginning
(b) the end

(a)

(b)

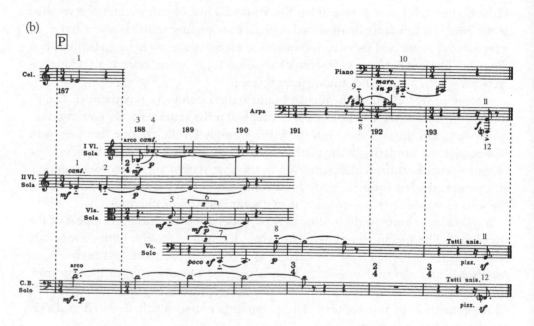

integration.[57] The initial series for the first movement is modified and expanded to become the passacaglia subject for the second, which in turn serves as the series for the third. At the end of the third movement, the initial tune of the first movement is recalled as if from a distance (see Example 3.27).[58] The tune occurs in the first movement as part of a brilliant, rapid fanfare (Example 3.27a). In the last movement, at Rehearsal No. 58, the tune comes again in the clarinet, but in slower, more ruminative fashion, in canon with the bassoon (a fourth lower) and the horn (in inversion). It appears briefly amid the chattering in the piano, which continues before, during, and after. When the tune quickly ends, after only two-and-a-half measures, we may wonder if we ever heard it at all. The distant reminiscence vanishes first in the continuous, oblivious activity in the piano, and then in the rapturous final chords. The distance between the initial fanfare tune and its repetition at the end of the last movement is so wide, the context is so altered, and the transformation is so extensive, that one can hardly speak of the second as a repeat of the first. The rhetorical move is one of transcendence, not recapitulation.

And it is here, at the highest level of structure, that Stravinsky's combinational strategies that permitted him to bind intervals into motives, motives into melodies, melodies into melodic periods and contrapuntal complexes, and textural blocks into sections and entire movements, begin to relax. Inter-movement connections of any kind, beyond the sorts of common motivic and intervallic concerns that result from mutual use of a series, are rare. Only in comparing beginnings and endings of works can one find a use of large-scale repetition, transposition, or retrograde as in the levels closer to the surface. And even there, the sense of repetition or recapitulation is often attenuated to the vanishing point.

In truth, the most characteristic kind of ending for Stravinsky, in his late music as in his earlier music, is the extended, rapturous coda in which the concrete concerns of the preceding work seem to melt away in a sense of timeless ecstasy.[59] *Introitus, A Sermon, a Narrative, and a Prayer, Requiem Canticles*, and other works conclude with solemn, devotional chorales. These chorales engage the substance of the music that precedes them, but only in an abstract, insubstantial way. Rather than offering any kind of recapitulation, they serve to open the piece out, to point beyond the boundaries of the piece, to refuse closure at the ultimate moment. At the more immediate levels, up to and including the relations among the discrete textural blocks, the music engages in a dialectic of continuity and discontinuity, of closure and openness, of binding and severing. Much of the expressive impact of Stravinsky's music, early and late, resides precisely in the intensity of the conflict it embodies between the isolation of its parts and the countervailing pressure of the whole. Only at the very highest level of structure, in the relationship of large sections or entire movements to entire multi-movement works, does the dialectic lose its force. At this level, the music ultimately bespeaks a transcendence of constraint and a release of all bonds.

---

[57] Robert Craft observes the close relationship among all three movements in "Analyses par Robert Craft," *Avec Stravinsky*, 144.

[58] The procedure is reminiscent of earlier works, including *Les Noces, Symphony in C*, and *The Fairy's Kiss*.

[59] I discuss the Stravinskian coda as a rhetorical topic in Chapter 5.

Example 3.27   Statement of principal tune in Septet
(a) beginning of the first movement
(b) end of the last movement

(a)

(b)

4

HARMONY

THE HARMONY PROBLEM: COUNTERPOINT AND CHORD

Stravinsky's serial music is generally contrapuntal in texture. The series tend to function as themes, melodies, or polyphonically independent lines. Often, the harmonies are by-products of the contrapuntal activity, and are thus difficult to account for in any systematic way. And the problem is not merely analytical in nature. Stravinsky himself, to judge by his compositional sketches and the finished works themselves, worked carefully and consciously to devise solutions to his perceived harmony problem.[1] Indeed, the evolution of his music during this period can be understood, at least in part, in terms of evolving solutions to the problem of writing serial harmony.

Stravinsky himself understood the importance of serial harmony, and understood also the extent to which his concern with harmony distinguished him from some of his colleagues:

Always I have been interested in intervals. Not only horizontally in terms of melody, but also the vertical results that arise from the combinations of intervals. That, by the way, is what is wrong with most twelve-tone composers. . .They are indifferent to the vertical aspect of music. The intervals of their horizontal counterpoint I approve of and admire. But they are terribly deaf to the logic of vertical combination.[2]

In Stravinsky's late music, "the logic of vertical combination" occasionally involves the replication, in the harmonic dimension, of transposed or inverted segments of the serial melodies. In the concluding measures of *Anthem*, shown in Example 4.1, for instance, many of the harmonies represent set types also found in

---

[1] For discussions of Stravinsky's serial harmony, see Milton Babbitt, "Remarks on the Recent Stravinsky," *Perspectives of New Music* 2/2 (1964), 35–55; reprinted in *Perspectives on Schoenberg and Stravinsky*, ed. Benjamin Boretz and Edward Cone (Princeton: Princeton University Press, 1968), 165–85; Charles Wolterink, "Harmonic Structure and Organization in the Early Serial Works of Igor Stravinsky, 1952–57" (Ph.D. dissertation, Stanford University, 1979); Pieter van den Toorn, *The Music of Igor Stravinsky* (New Haven: Yale University Press, 1983); George Perle, *Serial Composition and Atonality* (6th edn., Berkeley: University of California Press, 1991); Susannah Tucker, "Stravinsky and His Sketches: The Composing of *Agon* and Other Serial Works of the 1950s" (D.Phil. dissertation, Oxford University, 1992); and Christoph Neidhofer, "An Approach to Interrelating Counterpoint and Serialism in the Music of Igor Stravinsky, Focusing on the Principal Diatonic Works of his Transitional Period" (Ph.D. dissertation, Harvard University, 1999).

[2] Interview with Jay S. Harrison, *New York Herald Tribune*, 21 December 1952 (cited in Tucker, "Stravinsky and His Sketches," 187). It is not clear which composers Stravinsky has in mind.

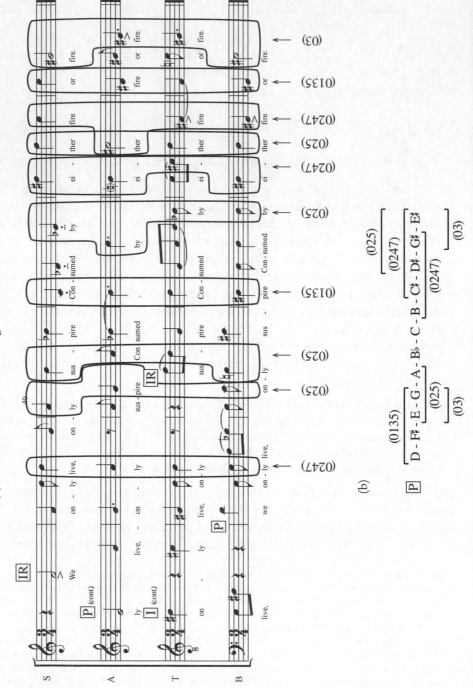

Example 4.1 Integration of melody and harmony
(a) *Anthem*, mm. 38–43, with linear series forms and vertical harmonies identified
(b) P-form of the series with segmental subsets identified

the series from which the melodies are derived.[3] In this way, Stravinsky achieves a kind of integration of musical space: the same musical ideas are projected simultaneously as melody and harmony.[4] The series embeds certain three- and four-note segments which, in this case, are often diatonic in quality. The melodic lines, which express forms of the series, necessarily contain the same segments. Harmonies related to these by transposition or inversion are then created as chords, formed by the lines sounding together. Moreover, this identity of harmony and melody becomes increasingly apparent as the passage approaches its cadence. The final chord is simply a vertical statement of the last two notes of the prime ordering: G♯–E♯.

It has to be quickly admitted, however, that exploitation of this kind of "associative harmony" in a serial "secondary dimension," with the same musical ideas projected simultaneously in melody and harmony, is far from being Stravinsky's standard procedure. Much more commonly, it is only the harmonies right at a cadence that make audible musical sense, either on their own terms or in relation to the melodic lines. In the Prelude to *In Memoriam Dylan Thomas*, for example, the chords are generally unrelated to the melodic lines, but the passage comes into harmonic focus at the cadence (see Example 4.2).[5] Beginning in m. 3, where the third voice enters, none of the harmonies is equivalent to a melodic segment. And even among themselves the harmonies show no particular consistency. Nonetheless, the counterpoint is strongly directed toward the cadence, with the last two chords describing a progression from an F♭-minor to an F♭-major triad.[6] Like the cadential perfect fifths discussed in Chapter 3, the consonant triads here retain their cadential force, their sense of repose and completion. Through most of the passage, the harmonies do not make consistent sense, either on their own terms or in relation to the melodic lines, but a sense of cadential convergence draws the independent lines together at the end of the phrase.

Occasionally, the cadential progressions take on a degree of independent structural life without reference either to traditional perfect fifths or consonant triads. In the three passages shown in Example 4.3, a strong sense of harmonic progression leads to the final chord. The Bransle Double from *Agon* (Example 4.3a) is based on

[3] In the bass, the second note of P (F♯) is omitted. This may be a serial "error," but if it is, it is not easily corrected.

[4] The same feature of harmonic organization in Schoenberg's music has attracted considerable analytical attention. The simultaneities in his music are often related by transposition or inversion to segmental subsets of the series. This phenomenon is called "associative harmony" by Babbitt and Haimo. See Milton Babbitt, "Some Aspects of Twelve-Tone Composition," *The Score and I.M.A. Magazine* 12 (1955), 53–61; Ethan Haimo, *Schoenberg's Serial Odyssey: The Evolution of His Twelve-Tone Method, 1914–1928* (London: Oxford University Press, 1990). The same phenomenon is described as a "secondary dimension" by Martha Hyde. See "Musical Form and the Development of Schoenberg's Twelve-Tone Method," *Journal of Music Theory* 29 (1985), 85–143; "The Roots of Form in Schoenberg's Sketches," *Journal of Music Theory* 24 (1980), 1–36; and *Schoenberg's Twelve-Tone Harmony: The Suite Op. 29 and the Compositional Sketches* (Ann Arbor: UMI Research Press, 1982).

[5] For a detailed discussion of harmony in this passage, but using Howard Hanson's somewhat idiosyncratic nomenclature, see W. Ronald Clemmons, "The Coordination of Motivic and Harmonic Elements in the 'Dirge-Canons' of Stravinsky's *In Memoriam Dylan Thomas*," *In Theory Only* 3/1 (1997), 8–21.

[6] I will have more to say about this cadential arrival on F♭ (or E) in Chapter 5.

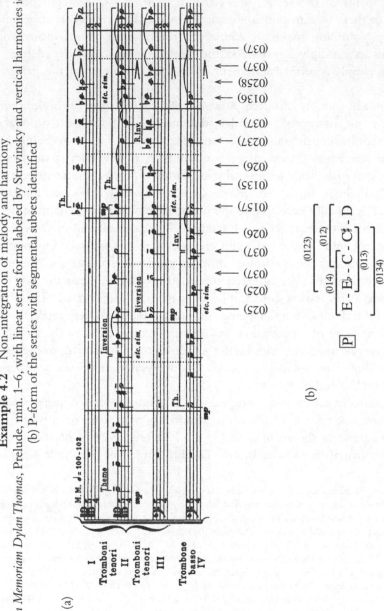

Example 4.2 Non-integration of melody and harmony

(a) *In Memoriam Dylan Thomas*, Prelude, mm. 1–6, with linear series forms labeled by Stravinsky and vertical harmonies identified

(b) P-form of the series with segmental subsets identified

a twelve-note series whose hexachords are treated independently. In the final cadence of that movement (Example 4.3a), three series-forms are unfolding simultaneously at different rates: the P-ordering of the second hexachord in the soprano (A–Bb–C–Db–Eb–Ab); the I-ordering of the first hexachord in the alto (D–C–B–A–Bb–F); and the IR-ordering of the second hexachord in the bass (Ab–Db–Eb–E–F♯–G). By sustaining the concluding Ab and F in the soprano and alto while moving from F♯ to G in the bass, Stravinsky creates the chord progression summarized beneath the music: the inversion that exchanges Ab and F also sends F♯ onto G.[7] The inversional symmetry of the two-chord progression thus creates a sense of balance and completion appropriate to a cadence.

In the final cadence of *Abraham and Isaac* (Example 4.3b), two melodic hexachords are combined to create a strong harmonic progression involving members of sc(026). The voice sings a hexachord from the R^A-array while the accompaniment provides a hexachord from the IR^A-array. The first three notes of the accompanimental hexachord, C–E–F♯, isolated in the viola solo, describe a form of sc(026). Three additional members of the same set class are formed as vertical harmonies between the two linear hexachords. The first chord inverts onto the second around $I^C_{C♯}$, which is also the operation that relates the two linear hexachords to each other. The second chord inverts onto the third around $I^{C♯}_{D♯}$. These axial notes are repeated in the accompaniment and their mutual mapping is what sends the penultimate melody note G onto the final A. The harmonic progression here is meaningful, powerful, and easily audible.

In the opening phrase of the *Requiem Canticles* (Example 4.3c), transposition directs the harmonic motion toward the cadential chord. The melodic hexachord, A♯–C–D–A–G–C♯, is the sixth row of the P^B-array; the accompaniment, F–C–B–A–(A♯)–D, is the first row of the P^A-array, but with A♯ omitted. These hexachords share the same total interval content, but are not related to each other by transposition or inversion.[8] Nonetheless their combination produces a strong, unifying harmonic progression. The first three notes of the passage, [B, C, F], map onto the last three, [C♯, D, G], at T_2. This harmonic gesture, a partial harmonic stutter, reflects the whole-steps within each melody, most notably the thrice-repeated A♯–C in the melody. This distinctive melodic gesture is thus coordinated with the larger, phrase-spanning harmonic gesture.

The three harmonic progressions of Example 4.3 are striking in their binding effect: they serve to link the disparate melodic lines into a single, coherent musical gesture. The harmonic progression is as meaningful as the counterpoint. This is not the usual case in Stravinsky's late music, however. Amid the prevailing contrapuntal textures, intervals and harmonies between the voices sometimes come into focus,

---

[7] Elsewhere I refer to progressions of this kind as a "static voice exchange," in which the inversion that maps two sustained notes onto each other also sends the remaining notes of the first chord onto their inversional partners in the second. See my "Voice Leading in Atonal Music," in *Music Theory in Concept and Practice*, ed. James Baker, David Beach, and Jonathan Bernard (Rochester: University of Rochester Press, 1997), 237–74.

[8] This is the familiar Z-relation of atonal set theory.

Example 4.3 Harmonic progression via inversion or transposition
(a) *Agon*, Bransle Double, mm. 381–86
(b) *Abraham and Isaac*, mm. 252–54

(a)

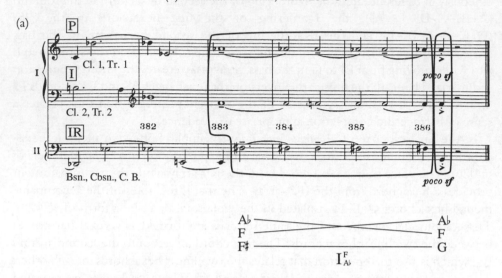

(b)

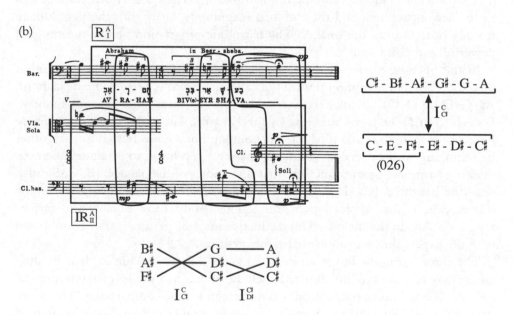

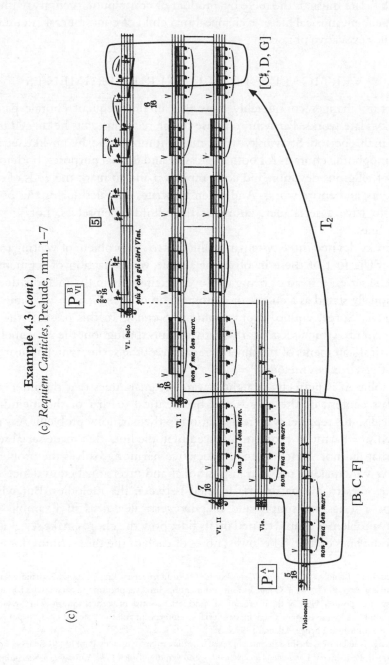

(c)

Example 4.3 (cont.)
(c) *Requiem Canticles*, Prelude, mm. 1–7

particularly at cadences. But as a general matter, the "logic of vertical combination" in his late music is often difficult to perceive. The vertical harmony in much of Stravinsky's late music is the mere by-product of contrapuntal activity, with little or no independent musical life – "a chance-born child of contrapuntal circumstances" in Brindle's evocative phrase.[9]

VERTICALIZATION OF SERIES SEGMENTS

The picture changes considerably, however, in the frequent chorale passages in Stravinsky's late works. Partly in response to the religious texts he turned to so frequently in this period, Stravinsky wrote many homophonic, hymn-like settings. He used homophonic chorales for both expressive and formal purposes, both to convey a sense of religious devotion and contemplation and to mark the ends of sections, movements, and entire works. And when he writes chorales during this period, he wanted to have a serial derivation for the chords themselves, not just for the melodic lines.

Stravinsky devised three systematic solutions to the problem of writing true serial chorales. The first of these involves the simple verticalization of segments of his series. The series, instead of being deployed exclusively in the melodic dimension, is occasionally stated as a chord, or a progression of chords, as in Example 4.4 (the opening of "Surge, aquilo," from *Canticum Sacrum*). In this passage, the somber opening chords, which recur at articulative points throughout the movement, comprise vertical statements of the three tetrachords of the series, which is heard immediately afterwards as a melody.[10]

This solution is perfectly straightforward. It guarantees that the intervallic and pitch-class content of the chords will be identical to that of the melodies. But, theoretically, this represents no real solution to the harmony problem. As originally presented, the harmony problem involved melodic lines that made serial sense and chords that did not. Schoenberg's "associative harmony" solves the problem in an elegant way by making use of transpositional and inversional equivalence to relate serial melodies to the harmonies formed between the melodies. But when segments of a series are simply and literally verticalized, as in Example 4.4, the harmony problem is simply turned on its side: now the chords make serial sense and the melodic lines do not. The lowest notes of each of the three chords, for example,

[9] Reginald Smith Brindle, *Serial Composition* (Oxford: Oxford University Press, 1966), 85. Brindle is referring to a particular passage in *Canticum Sacrum*, but his comment has broad application in Stravinsky's late music. For a generally more positive view of the degree of compositional control of vertical sonorities in Stravinsky's serial counterpoint, see Lynne Rogers, "Stravinsky's Serial Counterpoint and the Voice of God," paper presented to the Society for Music Theory, Atlanta, 1999.

[10] This passage is adduced as the first instance of serial harmony in Stravinsky by Babbitt ("Remarks on the Recent Stravinsky"), Perle (*Serial Composition and Atonality*), and van den Toorn (*The Music of Igor Stravinsky*), although there are precedents in *Agon* and, if a single dyad is counted as a verticalized series segment, the Septet (see Table 4.1).

Example 4.4 Verticalization of series tetrachords: "Surge, aquilo," from *Canticum Sacrum*, mm. 46–49

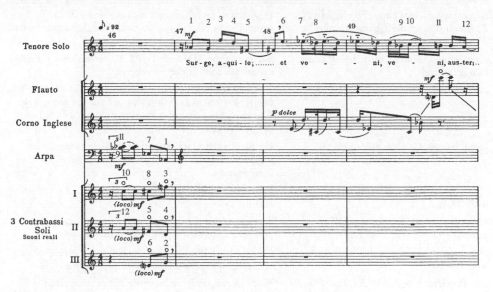

descend Bb–Eb–Ab. That makes a clear succession of descending perfect fifths, but it has nothing whatsoever to do with the series, which embeds no perfect fifths or stacks of fifths. Either because he sensed this theoretical problem, or for some other reason, Stravinsky rarely creates harmony by verticalizing segments of his series (see Table 4.1).

Once he begins using rotational arrays, however, Stravinsky does occasionally present the rows of the array as chords. Example 4.5 shows a passage from *The Flood* and the array on which it is based. The music depicts Lucifer in his pride, leaping boldly about.[11] Each of his leaps is marked by a new chord including an initial C♯, and each of the chords represents a row of the P^A-chart shown in Example 4.5b.[12] The progression moves systematically through the chart from its last row to its first.

The last of the chords (Row I in the chart) is arpeggiated and describes the succession of intervals <10, 1, 6, 9, 2>. The same succession of intervals in reverse order also describes the transpositional progression among the hexachords, as

---

[11] "With the recitative 'Lucifer was vain,' the Lucifer dancer begins to move. He jumps to a higher rock with each chord, but misses the last one, and at measure 130, the *arioso*, is at floor level dancing a lithe, athletic 'twist'" (Stravinsky and Balanchine, "Working Notes for *The Flood*," reprinted in *Dialogues and a Diary*, 74). "Satan walks on a carpet of complex and sophisticated music, unlike God, and his vanities are expressed, to a certain extent, by syncopation. The music that accompanies the avowal of his ambitions is also, you will notice, the music that accompanies his fall" (*Expositions and Developments*, 124).

[12] Recall that I am following Stravinsky's own designation of C♯–B–C–F♯–D♯–F–E–D–Bb–A–G–G♯ as the P-form of the series. All previous published accounts describe this as the R-form.

Table 4.1 *Verticalization of series segments*

Septet, second movement, Rehearsal No. 22 (beginning of the eighth variation)	First two notes of the sixteen-note series, E–B, verticalized in the piano. Vertical dyad initiates chorale-like variation.
Agon, Bransle Simple, mm. 308–09 (last two measures)	Six-note series (D–E–F–G–F♯–B) verticalized as final, cadential chord of the movement.
Agon, Bransle Gay, mm. 311–31	The two trichords of the six-note series (B–D–C–F–E♭–B♭) presented as chords throughout the movement. The remaining six notes comprise the final chord of the movement.
Agon, Bransle Double, mm. 336–86	Frequent vertical statements of two- and three-note segments from the two series, both individually and in combination.
Agon, Pas-de-Deux, mm. 411–13, 427–29, and 492	Four-note series (B♭–B–D–D♭) verticalized as cadential chord.
Canticum Sacrum, "Surge, aquilo," mm. 46–93	Tetrachords of the twelve-note series verticalized at points of articulation throughout the movement.
A Sermon, a Narrative, and a Prayer, mm. 98–101	One trichord from each of the four basic series forms verticalized to create four-chord progression.
The Flood, mm. 1–7, 401–53, and 490–96	Work begins with twelve-note chord to signify the formless void before creation, and later to depict the flood.
The Flood, mm. 24–25 and 44–45	Last six notes of I verticalized as cadential chord.
The Flood, mm. 248–50	"Building of the Ark" scene begins with verticalization of R into two chords (notes 1–7 and 8–12) to signify the initial hammer strokes.
The Flood, mm. 383–86	R presented as three vertical tetrachords.

shown in Example 4.5c. And when Lucifer begins to sing, he presents another version of the same succession, now with each interval replaced by its complement mod 12. The progression from chord to chord thus reflects the intervals found within each chord.

Cyclic motion through an array is much more commonly a generator of extended melodic lines, as discussed in Chapter 3. When the rows of a rotational array are used as chords, as in Example 4.5, the actual voicing of the chords – their arrangement in register – is not easy to account for. The voice leading is generally conjunct, with common pitch-classes retained as common pitches. Occasionally, the registral voices move by the appropriate transpositional interval – the bass voice, for example, begins by moving up a step from G to A (T_2) and then down a minor third from A to F♯ (T_9). But, in general, the linear motions of the voices are not part of any apparent serial design. As when series segments are verticalized, the harmony problem has simply been redefined into a voice-leading problem: now the chords make serial sense and the lines do not. The harmony problem has not been solved, merely relocated. Perhaps as a consequence, verticalization of the rows of

Example 4.5   Verticalizing the rows of a rotational array
(a) *The Flood*, mm. 127–31
(b) P^A-chart
(c) progression of hexachords

(a)

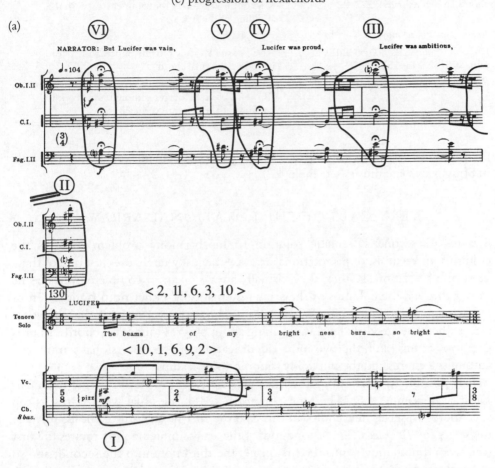

(b)

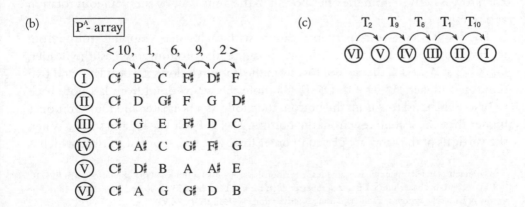

Table 4.2 *Verticalization of rows of the rotational arrays*

The Flood, mm. 127–30, 146–49 (same chords an octave lower), 277–82	Rows of the P^A-array for Lucifer's pride and his fall; rows of the IR^A-array for hammer strokes in the Building of the Ark
Abraham and Isaac, mm. 16–17, 51	I^B_{II}, I^A_{II}, IR^B_I
Requiem Canticles, Rex Tremendae, mm. 206–09, 214–15, 226–28	Rows of the I^A-array provide punctuating chords, including the final chord
Requiem Canticles, Libera Me, throughout	Entire movement consists of verticalized rows from the IR^B, I^A, I^B, and R^B arrays (although usually only portions of the rows are verticalized)

the rotational arrays, like the verticalization of series segments, occurs infrequently in Stravinsky's late music (see Table 4.2).[13]

VERTICALS OF THE ROTATIONAL ARRAYS

Stravinsky's second systematic solution to his harmony problem involves the columns, or verticals, of his rotational arrays. Stravinsky rarely uses just one of these verticals in isolation. Rather, they virtually always occur in complete cycles, as he moves through the columns of the array systematically, either from right to left or left to right (see Table 4.3). When talking about the verticals of the rotational arrays, then, we are virtually always talking about progressions of six chords. In progressions of this kind, the two most salient features are the inversional symmetries among the chords and the implicitly canonic voice leading.

It is possible to see both of these features operating in the R^A-array from *The Flood* (see Example 4.6). The array is constructed in the usual way. Across its top row, there is a series hexachord, in this case the first hexachord of the R-form of the series for *The Flood*. The second row of the array simultaneously rotates the first (the second note moves into the first place; the third note into the second; and so on) and transposes the new row to begin on the same note as the first, namely G♯. Each row is derived from the one above it in the same way, by simultaneous rotation and transposition.

The result is a six-voice perpetual canon, with each voice wrapping around from its last note back to its first. If we imagine the bottom row as the leader, G♯–C–B–C♯–D–F♯, the second row from the bottom follows it a beat later and two semitones higher, A♯–D–C♯–D♯–E–G♯ (note the wraparound from last note back to first). The third row from the bottom then follows a beat later and four semitones higher than the second row from the bottom, D–F♯–F–G–G♯–C, and so on. When the verticals of the array are played in order from first to last or last to first, which is

---

[13] As previously noted, my nomenclature for the rotational arrays works as follows: First, the series-form (P, I, R, IR); second, the hexachord written as a superscript (A for first hexachord, B for second hexachord); third, the row of the array written as a subscript using Roman numerals (I, II, III, IV, V, VI).

Table 4.3 *Verticals of the rotational arrays*

A Sermon, A Narrative, and A Prayer, mm. 75–85	A single pass through the twelve verticals of the R^A- and R^B-arrays. (NB: This, not *Movements*, is the first use.)
The Flood, mm. 180–247	R^A, R^B, I^B, I^A, P^B. (NB: longest passage involving verticals in all of Stravinsky)
The Flood, mm. 289–93	P^B
The Flood, mm. 329–34	P^A and P^B interspersed
The Flood, mm. 375–79	IR^B and R^A
The Flood, mm. 479–86	R^A and R^B
Abraham and Isaac, mm. 69–72	R^B
Abraham and Isaac, mm. 89–90	IR^A
Abraham and Isaac, mm. 173–77	R^B
Abraham and Isaac, m. 186	I^A
Abraham and Isaac, mm. 195–96	I^B
Abraham and Isaac, mm. 203–205	I^B
Abraham and Isaac, mm. 220–22	IR^A
Abraham and Isaac, mm. 229–39	P^B (penultimate passage of work)
Variations, mm. 1–5	R
Variations, mm. 73–85 (entire Variation VI)	P^A
Variations, mm. 130–41 (entire Variation XI)	P^B, P^A, P^A, P^B
Introitus, mm. 50–53	I
Requiem Canticles, Exaudi, mm. 76–80	R^A (Series 1 – there are two series in use in this work)
Requiem Canticles, Dies Irae, mm. 83–84, 86, 97–102	Single vertical from IR^B of Series 2 used as punctuating chord
Requiem Canticles, Rex Tremendae, mm. 202–07	R^A and R^B (Series 1)
Requiem Canticles, Lacrimosa, mm. 229–65 (entire movement)	Verticals from IR^B (Series 1) comprise one of three musical strands
Requiem Canticles, Postlude, five "chords of death"	Verticals from arrays of both Series 1 and 2 combined

Stravinsky's normal procedure, the voice leading will thus always be canonic. This is inherent in the structure of these arrays, not dependent on the design of any particular hexachord.

To make the canon easily audible, the rows of the array would have to be realized as musical lines, probably registral lines, and the lines would share the same pitch contour. Example 4.7 attempts a realization of that kind. Each melodic line corresponds to a row of the array. The lowest voice leads, and the voices above it follow at some rhythmic and intervallic distance, with each voice wrapping back around to the beginning.

Example 4.6   Rotational array (R^A) from *The Flood*

G♯	G	A	A♯	D	E
G♯	A♯	B	D♯	F	A
G♯	A	C♯	D♯	G	F♯
G♯	C	D	F♯	F	G
G♯	A♯	D	C♯	D♯	E
G♯	C	B	C♯	D	F♯

Example 4.7   Canonic voice leading in a hypothetical realization of the
R^A-array from *The Flood*

Inversional symmetry is also inherent in the structure of these arrays, irrespective
of the hexachord from which they are generated. A single note occurs six times in
the first vertical, and that note becomes an axis of symmetry for the rest of the array.
Vertical 2 is related to Vertical 6 by inversion around that note, as are Verticals 3 and
5. Vertical 4 is internally symmetrical around the same note. In the case of the R^A-
array from *The Flood*, all of these symmetries take place around G♯, the first note of
the generating hexachord.[14] To make these symmetries most immediately audible,

---

[14] To understand the inversional symmetry of this array, focus on the first interval of the first row, the descending
semitone G♯–G. When the first row is rotated and transposed to become the second row, the G moves up a
semitone to G♯ as it moves into the first position, and the G♯ from the first row moves up a semitone to A in the
last position of the second row. So G in the second position of the first row, a semitone below G♯, is balanced by
A in the last position of the second row, a semitone above G♯. Now consider the first interval in the second row,
the ascending whole-tone, G♯–A♯. When the second row is rotated and transposed to become the third row, the
A♯ moves down a whole-tone as it moves into the first position in the third row. At the same time, the G♯, the
first note of the second row, moves down a whole-tone to F♯, the last note of the third row. So A♯ in the second
position of the second row, two semitones above G♯, is balanced by F♯ in the last position of the third row, two
semitones below G♯. Each note in the second position in some row of the array is thus balanced around G♯ by
the note in the last position of the next row below. The second vertical as a whole is thus related by inversion
around G♯ to the last vertical as a whole. The third and fifth verticals are also related by inversion around G♯,
only now each note in the third position in some row of the array is balanced by the note in the fifth position *two*
rows below. Within the fourth vertical, each note is balanced by its around-G♯ partner found, also within the
fourth vertical, *three* rows below. The fourth vertical is thus self-symmetrical around G♯.

Example 4.8   Inversional symmetry in a hypothetical realization of the
R^A-array from *The Flood*

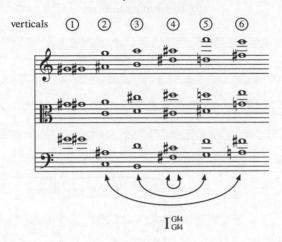

they would probably have to be realized in pitch space. Example 4.8 attempts such a realization. The realization begins with a six-times reinforced statement of a single pitch: G♯4. Around that pitch, the second chord balances the sixth, the third chord balances the fifth, and the fourth chord balances itself. In this realization, only the first three notes in each melody correspond to the rows of the array; the remaining notes have been reordered to emphasize the inversional symmetry of the chords.

Stravinsky's own compositional realizations of the array, however, are not nearly as literal-minded as my two hypothetical realizations. In composing with the verticals of his rotational arrays, Stravinsky makes use of canonic voice leading and inversionally symmetrical harmonic progressions only in a subtle, suggestive, inconclusive manner. In Example 4.9, a passage from *The Flood* based on the R^A-array from Example 4.6 maintains six distinct voices throughout. When a pitch-class occurs twice in some column of the array, it is doubled at the octave in the realization. None of the voices conforms to any of the rows of the array in its entirety, although row segments do appear intact. As a result, canonic voice leading is apparent only intermittently. Similarly, the inversional symmetry among the array verticals is only partially apparent in the actual chords of the music. Chords 3 and 5 are inversions of each other in actual pitch space and Chord 4 is its own inversion also in pitch space, but the inversion in both cases is around D, the axial partner of G♯, not around G♯ itself.

Later in *The Flood*, Stravinsky provides a somewhat different compositional realization of the same array (see Example 4.10). The pitch-class doublings have generally been eliminated so the chords now contain only four or five, rather than six, notes. As in the earlier realization (Example 4.9), none of the registral voices conforms in its entirety to any of the rows of the array, so canonic voice leading is only

Example 4.9　A realization of the R^A-array from *The Flood*
(a) mm. 180–90
(b) harmonic summary

Example 4.10   Another realization of the R^A-array from *The Flood*
(a) mm. 479–82
(b) harmonic summary

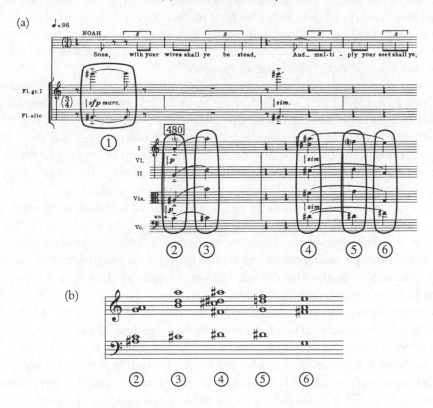

intermittently present. As for inversional symmetry, it exists only in pitch–class space – there is no registral reinforcement of it.

Still, both passages manage to create coherent, self-contained harmonic progressions. This is true in the first instance because of a striking similarity in sound of all of the chords. All of the verticals in the array, and thus all of the chords in both passages, are diatonic subsets. The second and sixth chords are members of sc(0235); the third and fifth are members of sc(0135); and the self-symmetrical fourth chord is a member of sc(0258). There is thus a certain aural consistency within the progression. The verticalities also maintain an intermittently audible degree of both inversional and retrograde symmetry, with the first chord in each progression equivalent to the last and the second to the second-to-last.

The voice leading of the chords is somewhat more problematic. It is implicitly canonic, but the canons are not a salient feature of the musical setting. The spacing of the chords tends to be somewhat open (no semitones between adjacent voices) and the voice leading is fairly smooth (notes tend to move to the nearest available position within the next chord), but beyond that, it is difficult to make persuasive generalizations about the voice leading in these passages. In principle, Stravinsky has achieved an elegant solution to his harmony problem by using the columns of his arrays as a source of chords and the rows of his arrays as a source of voice-leading continuity from chord to chord. In practice, however, his actual musical settings do not vigorously underscore the most salient structural properties of the arrays in either the melodic or the harmonic dimension.

Similar observations may be made about the penultimate passage of *Abraham and Isaac* (see Example 4.11). The chords come from the P^B-array. They are not diatonic chords but, naturally, they maintain the inversional symmetry of all of these rotational arrays. None of the instrumental or registral voices traces the rows of the array, although some do in part (indicated with brackets). The voicing of the chords obscures both the canonic structure of the array and its inversional symmetry, which remain implicit, somewhat concealed beneath the musical surface.

These progressions of verticals thus represent a kind of sublimation of what were, in the earlier Stravinsky, overt style characteristics. In progressions based on the verticals of the rotational arrays, canon (with its ostinato-like repetition) and inversional symmetry go underground, embedded deeply with the structure of the array. They manifest themselves on the musical surface only in fleeting ways, but their influence at a deeper level is profound.

Normally Stravinsky's rotational arrays are generated from series hexachords. *Variations*, however, uses arrays (and their verticals) generated from entire twelve-note series and *Introitus* uses arrays (and their verticals) generated from series tetrachords. *Introitus* is particularly interesting for the tension between its array origins and its perceptible surface. The work is based on arrays like the one shown in Example 4.12a. The chart and all of its notations, excluding the circles around some of the notes, are taken directly from Stravinsky's own compositional sketch.[15] He has written the I-form of the series across the top and labeled its tetrachords α, β, and γ. Each tetrachord is then rotated and transposed in the usual manner – Stravinsky adds diagonal lines to trace the rotations. The first column of the chart contains four iterations of G♯, the first note of the α tetrachord. Similarly, the fifth and ninth columns contain four iterations of C, the first note of the β tetrachord, and G, the first note of the γ tetrachord respectively. The remaining columns contain four-note chords that are the result of the transposed rotations. The nine chords in Example 4.12b are Verticals 2–4, 6–8, and 10–12, that is, all of the verticals that consist of more than a single note.[16]

But there are five wrong notes in the chart, circled by me in Example 4.12a, and these affect five of the chords in Example 4.12b.[17] These result from simple

---

[15] The sketch is reproduced as Plate 21 in *Pictures and Documents* and in *Strawinsky: Sein Nachlass, Sein Bild*, 178.

[16] Note that the harp is written in bass clef.

[17] The mistakes in the portion of the chart derived from the α tetrachord also affect mm. 46–47. There, Stravinsky presents three chords derived from the reverse diagonals of the I-chart. The second and third chords, from the β and γ tetrachords, are correct, but the first chord should be [E, G♯, A♯, A], not [E, G♯, A♯, B]. It would be easy to replace the incorrect B with the correct A, and this correction should probably be made.

Example 4.11 Harmony and voice leading in a rotational array
(a) *Abraham and Isaac*, mm. 229–35

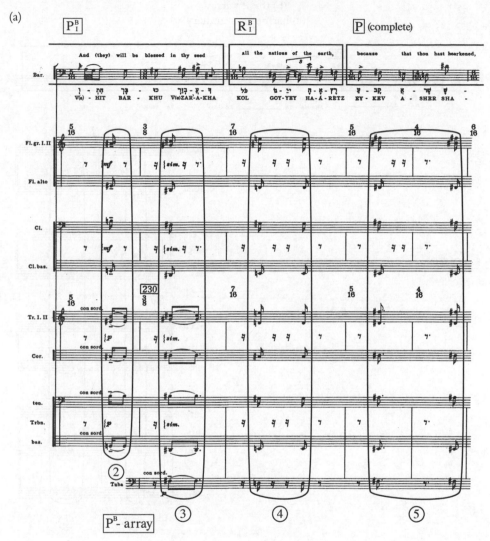

miscalculation. In the second row of the chart, for example, the second note should be G, a semitone below G♯, rather than A, a semitone above G♯. The subsequent notes, B and D♯, should also be a whole-tone lower. Similarly, in the last row of the chart, the seventh and eighth notes should be F–B, a semitone higher than Stravinsky's E–A♯. All of the notes I have circled in the chart result from simple mistakes in maintaining its intervallic consistency. In addition to the mistakes within the chart, Stravinsky also makes mistakes when he transfers notes from the chart to the score. The bottom row of the chart is written in treble clef, but when

Example 4.11 (*cont.*)
(a) (*cont.*)
(b) the P^B-array
(c) harmonic summary

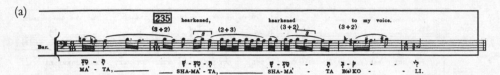

(b)

①	②	③	④	⑤	⑥
A	G	G♯	A♯	C	C♯
A	A♯	C	D	D♯	B
A	B	C♯	D	A♯	G♯
A	B	C	G♯	F♯	G
A	A♯	F♯	E	F	G
A	F	D♯	E	F♯	G♯

(c)

⑥ [G, G♯, B, C♯] = (0146)
⑤ [A♯, C, D♯, F, F♯] = (01368)
④ [D, E, G♯, A♯] = (0268)
③ [C, C♯, D♯, F♯, G♯] = (01368)
② [F, G, A♯, B] = (0146)

Example 4.11 (*cont.*)
(d) instrumental lines
(e) registral lines

(d) mm. 229–239: instrumental lines

	②	③	④	⑤	⑥
Fl. 1	B	C#	E	F#	G#
Fl. 2	A#	G#	A#	B#	G#
Fl. alto	E#	B#	D	D#	G
Cl.	B	F#	G#	A#	B
Cl. bass	G	D#	E	E#	G
Tr. 1	B	C#	E	F#	G#
Tr. 2	E#	G#	D	D#/F#	G
Horn	A#	B#	A#	B#	G#
Trb. ten.	B	B#	G#	A#/D#	B
Trb. bass	G	D#	E	E#	G
Tuba		F#	D	F#/A#	C#

(e) registral lines

②	③	④	⑤	⑥
B	C#	E	F#	G#
A#	B#	A#	B#	G#
E#	G#	D	D#	G
B	B#	G#	A#	B
( )	F#	D	F#	C#
G	D#	E	E#	G

he uses the chart to compose, Stravinsky sometimes inadvertently assumes a bass clef.[18]

The errors both within the chart and in constructing chords based on it affect seven of the nine chords in the passage, some more than once. In Example 4.12b, notes resulting from errors within the chart are circled and notes resulting from errors in reading a clef are placed in triangles. In the third chord of the passage, for example, based on Vertical 4, the E♭ in the harp derives from the incorrect note in the second row of the chart and the A♯ in the contrabass derives from a misconstruction of the treble-clef F♯ on the lowest row of the chart. The sixth chord of the passage, derived from Vertical 8, is harder to explain. The A♮ in the viola may be a simple misprint for A♯ on the bottom row of the chart (itself, of course, incorrect within the chart). Or, the C♯ in the contrabass may be a clef-incorrect realization of the same chart-incorrect note. In any case, the passage is permeated by serial mistakes of the kind Stravinsky normally preferred to correct, as discussed in Chapter 2.

Nonetheless, despite all of these problems, the nine-chord progression has a certain musical logic, and makes interesting connections that would be lost if the errors were corrected (see Example 4.13). Chords 10 and 12 are serially correct

---

[18] Clef errors of this kind are reasonably persistent throughout Stravinsky's late music, as discussed in Chapter 2 and, at greater length, in my article, "Stravinsky's Serial 'Mistakes,'" *The Journal of Musicology* 17/2 (1999).

Example 4.12 *Introitus*

(a) Stravinsky's I–array based on rotation of tetrachords (incorrect notes circled) final
measures, with nine chords

(b) final measures, based on verticals 2–4, 6–8, and 10–12 (chart errors indicated with
circles; clef errors indicated with triangles)

(a)

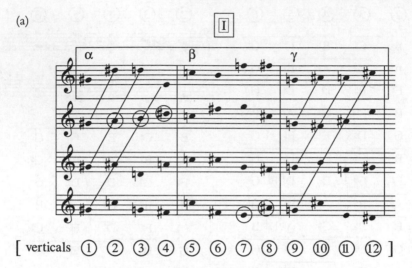

(b)

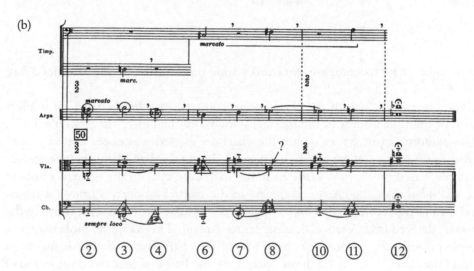

Example 4.13   The concluding chord progression of *Introitus*
(a) the chords
(b) connections via transposition and inversion
(c) a single coherent gesture

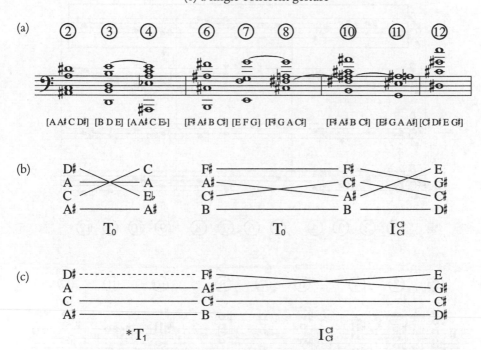

and, as a result of the structure of the array, are related by inversion. The clef mistake in Chord 6 makes it identical in content to Chord 10, and thus links it also to Chord 12. Chords 2 and 4 should be related by inversion, but the mistakes in both chords render them instead identical in content. Furthermore Chord 2 can be related to Chord 6 by what I call "near-T_1," which means that all but one of the notes move by T_1.[19] As a result, the progression as a whole can be understood as a single, coherent harmonic gesture.

Example 4.14a provides a correct version of the chart and Example 4.14b a corrected chord progression in which I have tried to maintain Stravinsky's spacing to the greatest extent possible. This chord progression now has some of the attractive features predicted by the structure of the array on which it is based. Chords 2 and 4 are related by inversion around G♯, the first note of the α tetrachord, and Chord 3 is self-inversional on the same axis. Chords 6 and 8 are related by inversion around C,

---

[19] See Straus, "Voice Leading in Atonal Music" for a discussion of "near-transposition." In Example 4.13, transpositions that are "near" are indicated with an asterisk and a dotted line connects notes that do not participate in the prevailing motion. Lewin talks about the same kind of voice leading, which he calls "quasi-transposition," in his "Some Ideas About Voice Leading Between Pcsets," *Journal of Music Theory* 42/1 (1998), 15–72.

Example 4.14   Conclusion of *Introitus* corrected
(a) correct serial chart
(b) serially correct chord progression

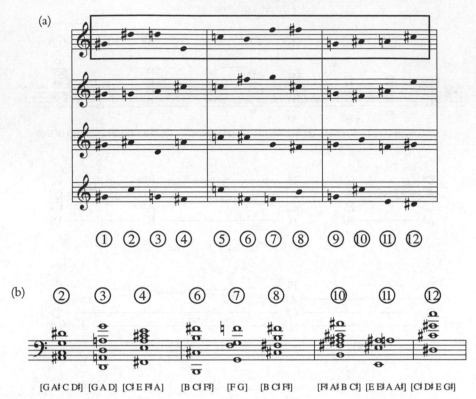

the first note of the β tetrachord (as it happens, they are actually identical in content) while chord 7 is self-inversional on the same axis. Chords 10 and 12 are related by inversion around G, the first note of the γ tetrachord – just as they are in the published version of the score – and Chord 11 is self-inversional on the same axis. These patterns of repetition and inversional symmetry are built into the structure of the array and almost entirely obliterated in Stravinsky's faulty realization of it. Nonetheless, Stravinsky's published version has its own logic, and its own stony, evocative quality, and I would not be in a rush to make corrections in this case. In both its incorrect, published version and my correct, hypothetical version, the final progression of *Introitus* has an impressive effect – a slow, austere, chorale. All of Stravinsky's experimentation with verticals of his rotational arrays, whether generated from tetrachords, hexachords, or entire series, has the aim of producing that effect, and of guaranteeing a legitimate serial harmony that is more than a mere contrapuntal by-product.

ARRAYS OF TWO, FOUR, AND EIGHT PARTS

Stravinsky's third systematic solution to his harmony problem involves a layering of two, four, or eight series forms from which chords are created as vertical slices through the array (see Table 4.4).[20] Arrays of this kind typically come into play at important formal positions in Stravinsky's music, particularly conclusions of sections and movements where they give rise to chorale-like successions of chords in a homophonic texture. The four-part arrays in particular assume a standardized formal and expressive role in Stravinsky's late music.[21]

The concluding passage of *A Sermon, a Narrative, and a Prayer* is typical of Stravinsky's procedure (see Example 4.15, which reproduces the passage [excluding harp, piano, contrabass, and percussion] together with the four-part array on which it is based).[22] The array consists of Stravinsky's four basic forms of the series: a prime (P), its inversion starting on the same note (I), its retrograde (R), and an inversion of the retrograde starting on the first note of the retrograde (IR). The chords in the passage are vertical slices of the array. They all contain four notes, one from each of the series forms. When there are pitch-class duplications in the array, Stravinsky realizes them as octave doublings.

The Stravinskian four-part array, like the one in Example 4.15, can be thought of as two pairs of inversionally related series: P and I related by inversion around their shared first note (the first note of the prime ordering) and R and IR by inversion around their shared, and necessarily different, first note (the last note of the prime ordering)(see Example 4.16). This is probably how Stravinsky thought of them and the two-part arrays in his music almost always combine two series-forms related by inversion, either P+I or R+IR. Because the first note of P and I is E♭, or pitch-class 3, the dyads in the first pair of series all sum to 6; because the first note of R and IR is F, or pitch-class 5, the dyads in the second pair all sum to 10. Both of these sums are even because each series-pair begins on the same pitch class, and all the vertical dyads in that pair balance around that pitch class. Each dyad thus consists of one note n semitones above the axis and another n semitones below it. The vertical interval is 2n, which is always an even number.

Each vertical dyad contains an even number of semitones and is thus a member of

---

[20] Apart from the prototypical passages in the Septet, I include only situations in which the creation of meaningful, audible, serial chords seems to be a primary purpose in the layering of series forms. In most cases, the compositional sketches confirm the primacy of the chords in these passages, and most have a reasonably simple note-against-note or chorale texture.

[21] For a thorough, technical account of these arrays, see my "Stravinsky's 'Constructions of Twelve Verticals': An Aspect of Harmony in the Serial Music," *Music Theory Spectrum* 21/1 (1999), 43–73.

[22] In Chord 5, the A♭ in the viola substitutes for the G♭ of the array. In moving from the array to the music, Stravinsky may have momentarily confused the treble and alto clefs. His serial charts indicate that he intended G♭, but his compositional manuscripts all confirm the serially incorrect A♭. Such discrepancies between serial plan and compositional realization, often resulting from an apparent misreading of clef, are reasonably common in Stravinsky's serial music and pose interesting editorial and interpretive challenges, as discussed in Chapter 2. In my discussion of Example 4.15, I will assume that the note should be the serially correct G♭, and I believe it should be so corrected in any performance of the work.

Table 4.4 *Arrays of two, four, and eight parts*

Septet, second movement, eighth variation, Rehearsal Nos. 22–23	Combination of four series forms (with RI instead of the later standard IR) and with the rows of the array still realized as instrumental lines
Septet, second movement, ninth and final variation, Rehearsal No. 23–end	Combination of P + RI, still more a contrapuntal prototype than a true two-part array
Agon, Coda, mm. 185–253	Two-part array: verticals created from R and IR
Threni, mm. 1–6	Two-part array: verticals created from R and IR (as in *Agon*)
Threni, mm. 166–93 and 322–83	Two-part arrays: Punctuating chords setting Hebrew letters involve various two-part combinations
Threni, mm. 309 and 321	Eight-part arrays involving segmental tetrachords from eight different series forms
Threni, 405–19 (conclusion of work)	Four-part array: First full-fledged instance, involving P + I + R + IR with twelve verticals
Movements, second movement, all	Begins with two two-part arrays (R + IR, as in *Agon*, then I + IR). Concludes with standard four-part array.
Movements, Interlude between fourth and fifth movement	Eight-part array based on simultaneous statements of hexachords from the four basic forms of the series
Movements, fifth movement, mm. 141–50, 167–71, 184–86 (leading to final statement of series that concludes the entire work)	Standard four-part array, but folded to produce combinations of Verticals 1 + 7, 2 + 8, 3 + 9, 4 + 10, 5 + 11, and 6 + 12
A Sermon, a Narrative, and a Prayer, mm. 138–41	Two-part array combining R + IR (as in *Agon*)
A Sermon, a Narrative, and a Prayer, mm. 183–85	Two-part array combining P + I
A Sermon, a Narrative, and a Prayer, mm. 207–15 (conclusion of Narrative)	Standard four-part array
A Sermon, a Narrative, and a Prayer, mm. 267–75 (conclusion of Prayer, and thus of entire work)	Standard four-part array
The Flood, mm. 62–82 (accompaniment for spoken narration of the creation story)	Standard four-part array
Abraham and Isaac, mm. 91–101	Two-part arrays based not on the series but on the linear hexachords of the rotational arrays
Requiem Canticles, Exaudi, mm. 71–76	Standard four-part array (Row 1)
Requiem Canticles, Interlude, mm. 136–46, 159–60, 194–96	Standard four-part array (Row 1)
Requiem Canticles, Postlude, mm. 290–92, 294–97, 300–02	Four-part arrays that combine two series-forms based on Series 1 and two series-forms based on Series 2

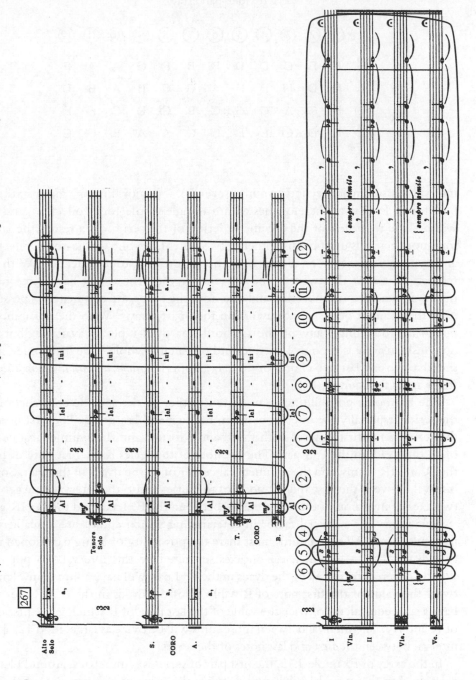

Example 4.15 Conclusion of *A Sermon, a Narrative, and a Prayer*

(a) mm. 267–75 with chords labeled (harp, piano, contrabass, and percussion excluded)

Example 4.15 (*cont.*)

(b) four-part array

(b)

	①	②	③	④	⑤	⑥	⑦	⑧	⑨	⑩	⑪	⑫
P	Eb	E	C	D	Db	Bb	B	F#	G	A	Ab	F
I	Eb	D	F#	Fb	F	Ab	G	C	B	A	Bb	Db
R	F	G#	A	G	Gb	Cb	Bb	C#	D	C	Fb	Eb
IR	F	D	C#	Eb	Fb	Cb	C	A	Ab	Bb	Gb	G

interval-class 2 (major second or minor seventh), 4 (major third or minor sixth), or 6 (tritone). Each dyad therefore lies within a single whole-tone collection, and this will be true regardless of the specific ordering of the series. As a result, the larger four-note verticals must consist either of two notes from one whole-tone collection and two from the other, or all four from the same whole-tone collection. With this restriction, ten of the twenty-nine tetrachord-types, those that have three notes from one whole-tone collection and one from the other, are eliminated as possibilities: they cannot occur in a Stravinskian four-part array.[23] With the possibility of pitch-class doublings, any of the trichord- or dyad-types is available, but the Stravinskian array is strongly biased toward producing whole-tone harmonies, as in the first two and last two chords of the array from *A Sermon, a Narrative, and a Prayer* (refer again to Example 4.15).

The harmonic possibilities are restricted further by the specific construction of the series, especially the interval between the first and last notes. The first note of the series is the first note of both the P and I forms, and the symmetrical center of all the dyads in the P+I pair. The last note of the series is the first note of both the R and IR forms, and the symmetrical center of all the dyads in that pair. So the interval between the first and last notes of the series is also the interval between the two axes of inversion of the array, that is, between the P+I axis and the R+IR axis.

This interval is a crucial factor in determining which chords are available in a particular array. All such chords must share the possibility of being partitioned into two dyads that are symmetrical on axes separated by this interval. To put it in slightly different terms, all of the dyads in the P+I pair will have a sum equivalent to twice the value of the first note of P, while all of the dyads in the R+IR pair will have a sum equivalent to twice the value of the last note of P, which is the first note of R and IR. The interval between those sums will be twice as large, mod 12, as the interval between the first and last notes of the series.

In the array of Example 4.15, the first pair of series is symmetrical around Eb, and each dyad in that pair describes sum 6 (twice the value of the first note, Eb). The

---

[23] The following are unavailable: (0124), (0126), (0135), (0137), (0146), (0148), (0157), (0236), (0247), and (0258).

Example 4.16   *Four-part array understood as two pairs of inversionally related series-forms*

P	E♭	E	C	D	D♭	B♭	B	F♯	G	A	A♭	F
I	E♭	D	F♯	F♭	F	A♭	G	C	B	A	B♭	D♭
sum:	6	6	6	6	6	6	6	6	6	6	6	6

R	F	G♯	A	G	G♭	C♭	B♭	C♯	D	C	F♭	E♭
IR	F	D	C♯	E♭	E	C♭	C	A	A♭	B♭	G♭	G
sum:	10	10	10	10	10	10	10	10	10	10	10	10

second pair of series are symmetrical around F, and each dyad in that pair describes sum 10 (twice the value of the last note, F). The difference between those two sums is 4 (twice the size of the interval between E♭ and F), and any array whose two sums differ by 4 (e.g. 0 and 4, 2 and 6, 4 and 8, 6 and 10, 8 and 0, 10 and 2) will permit only certain chords to occur. A different interval between first and last notes, resulting in different dyad sums, will permit a largely different group of chords to occur. In general, the chords that are available with one of the distances between dyad sums are not available with the others. The most obvious exceptions have to do with whole-tone harmonies, which are available no matter what the interval between first and last notes of the series and between the resulting dyad sums.

The interval between the first and last notes of the series is thus crucial in determining what kinds of chords will be available in a four-part array. And there are further, subtle interdependencies between the structure of a series and the chords of a four-part array. For example, if an even interval is formed between a note in the nth order position and the note in the complementary order position, n positions from the end, then a whole-tone harmony will occur in the four-part array in those two positions.

In constructing his four-part arrays, Stravinsky creates a distinctive and narrowly circumscribed harmonic world, one dependent in subtle ways on the structure of his series. His music moves through that world, and realizes those arrays compositionally, in a variety of ways. Example 4.17 contains the passage that concludes the second of the *Movements*, together with the four-part array on which it is based. It also provides the set-class identity of each of the twelve chords, together with the array and chords from *A Sermon, a Narrative, and a Prayer*, for the sake of comparison. The passage from *Movements* is nearly homophonic (anticipations or retardations occasionally displace a note slightly from its rhythmic position in the array). The P-form of the series is, for the most part, isolated in the piano while the other three forms are distributed among the remaining instruments. The series from *A Sermon, a Narrative, and a Prayer* and *Movements* begin and end on the same note. As a result, virtually all of the chord-types, and four of the actual chords, are shared between the two arrays. Because both series begin on E♭ and end on F, the first chord of both arrays is the whole-tone E♭–F, and the last chord is a four-note segment of the

Example 4.17 A four-part array realized compositionally
(a) *Movements*, II, conclusion, mm. 62–67

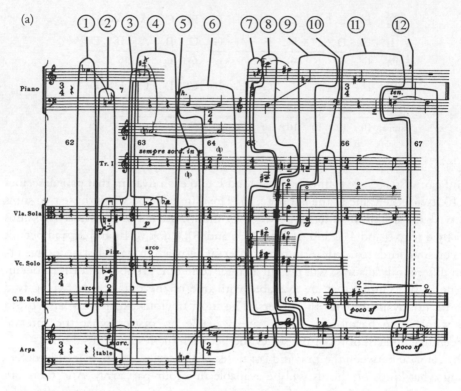

whole-tone cycle, [C♯, E♭, F, G]. Of the chord-types in the array for *A Sermon, a Narrative, and a Prayer*, only one is absent from the array from *Movements*; of the chord-types in the array for *Movements*, only two are excluded from the array for *A Sermon, a Narrative, and a Prayer*. The whole-tone bias of Stravinsky's four-part arrays is particularly evident in the array for *Movements*, where eight of the twelve chords are whole-tone subsets. Indeed, right at the center of the array and of the passage, the sixth and seventh chords together describe an entire whole-tone collection: C–D–E–F♯–G♯–A♯.

The array for *Requiem Canticles* (Series 1) also contains eight whole-tone harmonies among its twelve chords (see Example 4.18).[24] Apart from the first two and last two chords, all are whole-tone subsets. The non-whole-tone chords, however, distinguish this array from those of *Movements* and *A Sermon, a Narrative, and a Prayer*.

---

[24] In Chord 10 (the third chord of the passage), the bass note should be E♯ according to the array but is G♯ in the score. This is a familiar kind of serial error in these works, involving misreading a treble as a bass clef. In Chord 1 (the last chord of the passage), the soprano note should be A♯ according to the array, but is G♯ in the score. The first sketch for the passage shows the serially correct A♯, so this may have been a copying error at a later stage. Both errors should be corrected in performance, as should the notes in Horn I and Harp that double them.

Example 4.17 (*cont.*)
(b) four-part array with chords identified
(c) four-part array for *A Sermon, a Narrative, and a Prayer*, with chords identified

(b)

	①	②	③	④	⑤	⑥	⑦	⑧	⑨	⑩	⑪	⑫
P	E♭	E	B♭	A♭	A	D	C	B	C♯	F♯	G	F
I	E♭	D	A♭	B♭	A	E	F♯	G	F	C	B	C♯
R	F	G	F♯	C♯	B	C	D	A	A♭	B♭	E	E♭
IR	F	E♭	E	A	B	B♭	A♭	C♯	D	C	F♯	G

↑ ↑ ↑ ↑ ↑ ↑ ↑ ↑ ↑ ↑ ↑ ↑

(02) (0125) (0246) (0125) (02) (0246) (0268) (0246) (0147) (026) (0237) (0246)

(c)

	①	②	③	④	⑤	⑥	⑦	⑧	⑨	⑩	⑪	⑫
P	E♭	E	C	D	C♯	B♭	B	F♯	G	A	G♯	F
I	E♭	D	F♯	E	F	G♯	G	C	B	A	B♭	C♯
R	F	G♯	A	G	F♯	B	B♭	C♯	D	C	E	E♭
IR	F	D	C♯	E♭	E	B	C	A	G♯	B♭	F♯	G

↑ ↑ ↑ ↑ ↑ ↑ ↑ ↑ ↑ ↑ ↑ ↑

(02) (026) (0147) (0125) (0125) (013) (0125) (0147) (0147) (013) (0246) (0246)

The interval between the first and last notes of the series is a perfect fourth. As a result, Chord 1 is a perfect fourth and Chord 12 is a four-note segment of the cycle of perfect fourths. Chord 12 is thus a member of sc(0257), perhaps the most distinctive sonic fingerprint of Stravinsky's diatonic music. It arises here, however, in a purely serial manner, by virtue of the interval between the first and last notes of the series and the resulting structure of this particular four-part array.

The same is true of the array for *The Flood* (see Example 4.19).[25] As in *Requiem*

---

[25] The series-form labeled P here is actually I according to Stravinsky's own designation, as discussed earlier. Stravinsky's compositional sketches for this passage (Documents Nos. 218–0003 and Nos. 218–0014) show that he conceived the passage as an array of four series forms: P (labeled I in Example 4.19); I (labeled P in Example 4.19); R, by which he actually means the retrograde of I (labeled R in Example 4.19); and RI, by which he means the inversion of his R, which is actually the retrograde of I (labeled IR in Example 4.19). This information was generously provided by Lynne Rogers. My relabeling makes it easier to discuss this four-part array in relation to the four-part arrays in other works and, of course, whatever the labels, the musical relationships remain the same.

Example 4.18   A four-part array realized compositionally
(a) *Requiem Canticles*, Exaudi, mm. 71–76
(b) four-part array (from Series 1) with chords identified

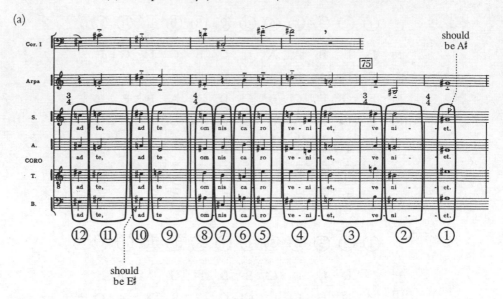

(a)

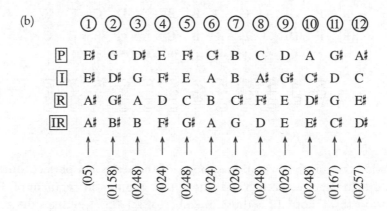

(b)

Example 4.19 A four-part array realized compositionally

(a) *The Flood*, mm. 62–67 and 80–82

(a)

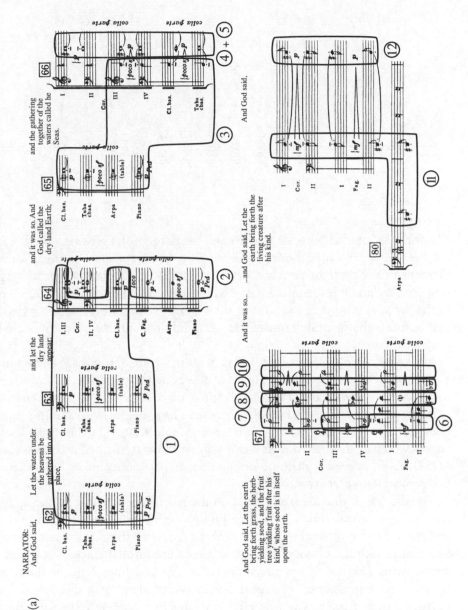

Example 4.19 (*cont.*))
(b) four-part array with chords identified

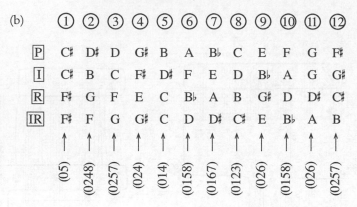

Canticles, the interval between the first and last notes of the series is a perfect fourth and, as a result, the first chord is a perfect fourth and the last chord is a four-note segment of the cycle of perfect fourths, or sc(0257). The harmonies in between, however, are much less conspicuously whole-tone in origin. Indeed, (0257) recurs in the array, as Chord 3, and (0158), the major seventh chord, occurs twice. This demonstrates the flexibility of these arrays amid their inherent bias toward whole-tone harmonies.

Just as the arrays for *Movements* and *A Sermon, a Narrative, and a Prayer* begin with a whole-tone and end with a segment of the cycle of whole-tones, and the arrays for *Requiem Canticles* and *The Flood* begin with a perfect fourth and end with a segment of the cycle of fourths, the array for *Threni* begins with a minor third and ends with a cycle of four minor thirds (see Example 4.20). The diminished-seventh chord, which in another context might suggest an octatonic orientation as surely as (0257) might suggest a diatonic orientation, is here inherent in the structure of Stravinsky's four-part array.

The discussion thus far has focused on the harmonic structure of the arrays and their compositional realizations. The linear organization of the music, its voice leading, varies but maintains certain common characteristics. As a general matter, in Stravinsky's settings of these arrays, the precompositional rows of the array, the series forms, are realized as instrumental or registral lines only in short spurts. Instead, the instrumental or registral lines weave their way through the array, moving actively from row to row, rarely sticking with a single series form for more than three or four consecutive notes.

The actual voicing of the arrays is difficult to account for in any systematic way, but generally observes three principles. First, the voice leading is usually smooth or "parsimonious."[26] As in common-practice tonal music, common tones are retained where possible and a note in one chord usually moves to the nearest available note in the next chord or, failing that, by a relatively small interval. Second, the chord spacings are usually open, with the larger intervals toward the bottom. Between registrally adjacent lines, the smallest intervals are generally and the semitone entirely avoided. Third, although they rarely follow the serial ordering for more than a few notes at a time, they nonetheless often project set-types that may be found as segmental subsets of the series. For example, referring back to Example 4.18, the first four notes in the soprano part, C–D–D♯–E, come from two different series-forms. But the set-type they describe, (0124), can also be found as a segmental subset of the series, for example as the first four notes of the P or I forms. Stravinsky thus achieves a multi-dimensional presentation of the musical content of the series within his array settings.[27]

Stravinsky's four-part arrays thus offered him a reasonably satisfactory solution to his harmony problem, particularly in the writing of chorales or homophonic progressions of chords. The harmonies are constrained in their content and linked to each other by the structure of the arrays. The melodic dimension is controlled at a deep level by the linear unfolding of the series forms and, in the actual instrumentation, by generally parsimonious voice leading that projects linear statements of set types found also as segments of the series. Stravinsky's procedure is not fully systematic, particularly in the melodic dimension, but apparently satisfied him both theoretically and musically, to judge by the frequency with which he used it.

In addition to music based on full-fledged four-part arrays discussed thus far (from *Threni, Movements, A Sermon, a Narrative, and a Prayer, The Flood,* and *Requiem Canticles*), there are numerous other passages that express the same principle of layering series forms and deriving chords as vertical slices through the array. Chronologically, the first such passage, and the clear prototype for the rest, is the passage from *Agon* shown in Example 4.21c.[28] Stravinsky's own row chart for the

---

[26] This is the principle of voice leading that Schoenberg calls the "law of the shortest way": "In the voice leading, only that [should] be done which is absolutely necessary for connecting the chords. This means each voice will move only when it must; each voice will take the smallest possible step or leap, and then, moreover, just that smallest step which will allow the other voices also to take small steps" (Arnold Schoenberg, *Theory of Harmony*, trans. Roy Carter [Berkeley: University of California Press, 1978], 39). The notion of "smoothness" or "parsimony" in voice leading has been explored and elaborated in recent theoretical literature, including Richard Cohn, "Maximally Smooth Cycles, Hexatonic Systems, and the Analysis of Late-Romantic Triadic Progressions," *Music Analysis* 15/1 (1996), 9–40; Richard Cohn, "Neo-Riemannian Operations, Parsimonious Trichords, and Their *Tonnetz* Representations," *Journal of Music Theory* 41/1 (1997), 1–66; and Lewin, "Some Ideas About Voice-Leading Between Pcsets."

[27] This multi-dimensional presentation recalls, in the melodic dimension, Schoenberg's "secondary dimension" or "associative harmony" as described by Babbitt, Haimo, and Hyde. See footnote 4, p. 143 above.

[28] The row chart and sketch in Example 4.21 are transcribed in Tucker, "Stravinsky and His Sketches." Tucker argues that the final chords of the Coda are the first example of "vertical serialism" in Stravinsky. This movement comes before he composed "Surge, aquilo," which is adduced by others as the first (see footnote 10, p. 148 above). The sketch and its implications were first discussed in *Avec Stravinsky*, 185.

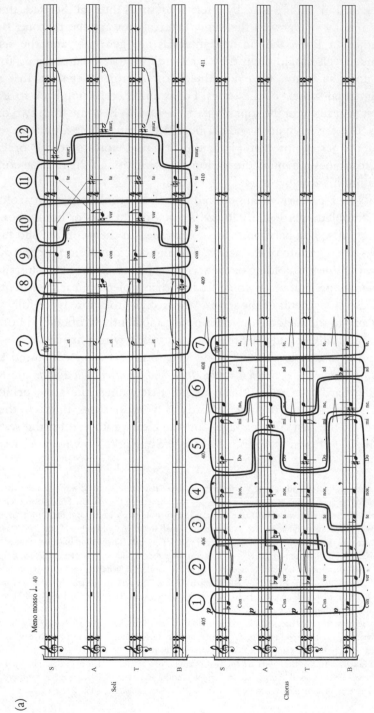

Example 4.20 A four-part array realized compositionally
(a) *Threni*, mm. 405–17

Example 4.20 (*cont.*)

(a) (*cont.*)

(b) four-part array with chords identified

(a)

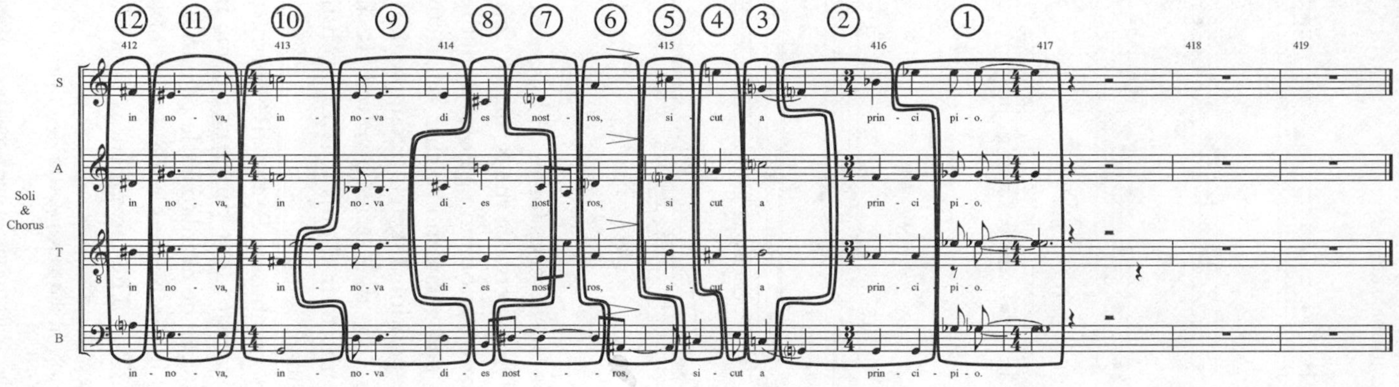

(b)

	①	②	③	④	⑤	⑥	⑦	⑧	⑨	⑩	⑪	⑫
P	D♯	G♯	G	A	C♯	A	D	B	E	C	F	F♯
I	D♯	A♯	B	G♯	F	A	E	G	D	F♯	C♯	C
R	F♯	F	C	F	E	B	D	A	A♯	G	G♯	D♯
IR	F♯	G	C♯	G♯	C♯	B♭	B, D♯	B	D	F	E	A
	← (03)	← (0235)	← (015)	← (026)	← (026)	← (015)	← (0127)	← (026)	← (026)	← (0127)	← (0347)	← (0369)

Example 4.21 A two–part array
(a) Stravinsky's row chart
(b) compositional sketch

passage (Example 4.21a) lines up the four basic series forms (P, I, R, and IR, which Stravinsky calls "R. Inv."). The vertical lines between the R and IR forms indicate Stravinsky's intention to create four chords by combining notes from the two series forms and, allowing for anticipations and retardations, that is exactly how the passage is constructed, both in the compositional sketch (Example 4.21b) and the final version (Example 4.21c). Because the two series involved, R and IR, are related by inversion around B♭, so are the four chords derived from them, again allowing for anticipations and retardations.[29]

Two-part arrays of this kind, usually combining R and IR, persist throughout Stravinsky's later music even after the standard four-part arrays come into regular use. Upon occasion, two two-part arrays can be heard to coalesce into a single four-part array – that is the strategy adopted in the Narrative movement of *A Sermon, a Narrative, and a Prayer* (see Example 4.22).[30] The movement is punctuated by the

---

[29] These two forms are often combined contrapuntally in this movement of *Agon*. The extensive invariance between these two row forms is discussed in Chapter 3.

[30] The same strategy is adopted in, and accounts for the entire structure of, the second of the *Movements*.

Example 4.21 (*cont.*)
(c) *Agon*, mm. 248–53

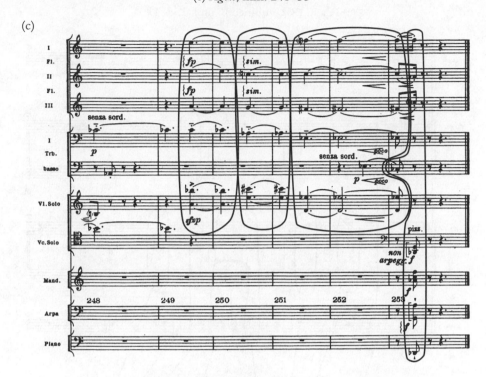

two passages shown in the example, each of which marks the end of a section
(notice the double bars at the end of each).[31] The movement as a whole ends with
reference to a four-part array that combines these two two-part arrays.

Just as a four-part array can be created as a combination of two two-part arrays,
an eight-part array can be created by combining the two halves of a four-part
array. That is what happens in the fifth of the *Movements* (see Example 4.23, which
reproduces the opening measures and the array on which they are based).[32] In the
piano, the four-part array is folded over and eight-note harmonies are created by

---

[31] In Example 4.22a, the R-form of the series is missing its ninth note, D. If this is an inadvertent omission by the
composer, it is one that is impossible to rectify.

[32] A revealing compositional sketch for the fifth of the *Movements* is reproduced as Plate 20 in *Pictures and
Documents* (New York: Simon and Schuster, 1978). It shows the four series forms written out so that the first six
chords are aligned directly above the last six with Stravinsky's written comment, "vertical B's [members of the
second hexachord] and A's [members of the first hexachord] of the 4 forms." With regard to the passage ana-
lyzed in Example 4.23, Stravinsky wrote: "No theorist could determine . . . the derivation of the three Fs
announcing the last movement simply by knowing the original order, no matter how unique the combinatorial
properties of this particular series" (*Memories and Commentaries*, 106). But now it can be told: two of the three Fs
come from the first vertical of the four-part array; the third is the first note of R, heard simultaneously in the
trumpet.

Example 4.22   Two two-part arrays in the Narrative movement of *A Sermon, a Narrative, and a Prayer*

(a) R and IR combined in mm. 138–41

(a)

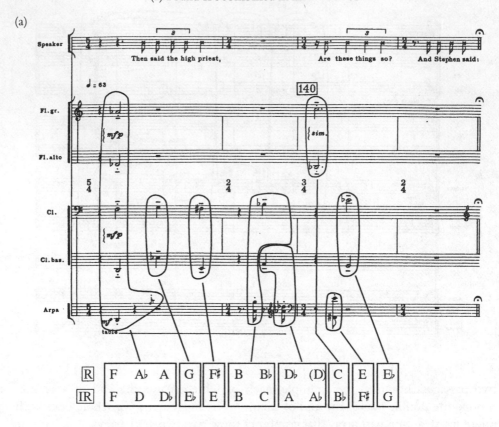

combining Verticals 1+7, 2+8, 3+9, 4+10, 5+11, and 6+12.[33] (Note again the predominance of whole-tone harmonies, in Verticals 1, 3, 5, 6, 7, 8, 10, and 12.) The arrays thus act as important and flexible compositional resources for Stravinsky in this period.

The rotational arrays and the four-part arrays (with their two-part subdivisions and eight-part elaborations) are Stravinsky's most original contributions to twelve-tone music and music theory. Both of these innovations have a common source in Stravinsky's desire to write chordal passages. For the most part, his twelve-tone

---

[33] "The *Movements* are the most advanced music from the point of view of construction of anything I have composed . . . Every aspect of the composition was guided by serial forms, the sixes, quadrilaterals, triangles, etc. The fifth movement, for instance (which cost me a gigantic effort – I wrote it twice), uses a construction of twelve verticals" (*Memories and Commentaries* [Berkeley: University of California Press], 106). The "construction of twelve verticals" is the four-part array, not, as Taruskin claims (*Stravinsky and the Russian Traditions* [Berkeley: University of California Press, 1996] 1657), a rotational array, the verticals of which play no role at all in *Movements*.

Example 4.22 (*cont.*)
(b) P and I combined in mm. 183–85

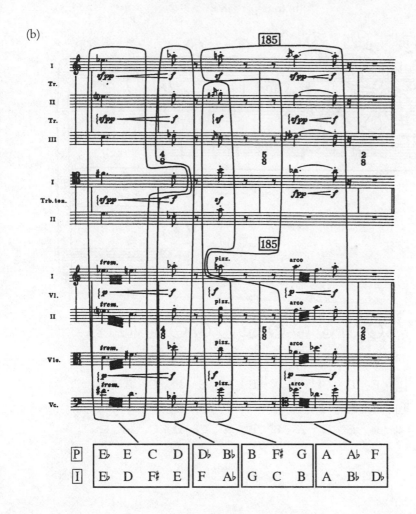

music is linear-contrapuntal in texture and the serial lines operate with a high degree of polyphonic independence. When chorale passages occur, they are almost always controlled by the rotational or four-part arrays. Conversely, Stravinsky was apparently motivated to exploit the verticals of the rotational arrays and to create the four-part arrays precisely in order to write chorales that evoke the sound of solemn, sacred hymns. Stravinsky's most striking innovations, then, the ones that are richest in theoretical interest and implication, emerged as a solution to a specific compositional problem. In composing with the verticals of the rotational and four-part arrays, Stravinsky was not so much building a system as responding pragmatically to an immediate and pressing expressive need.

Example 4.23   Creating an eight-part array by folding a four-part array in half
(a) *Movements*, V, mm. 141–44
(b) four-part array

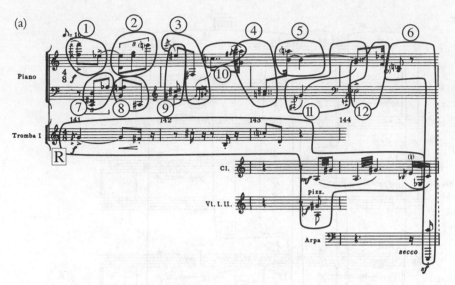

5

EXPRESSION AND MEANING

THE PROBLEM OF EXPRESSION: "MUSIC IS POWERLESS TO EXPRESS ANYTHING"

Stravinsky is known as an anti-expressive composer. His most famous utterance – "I consider that music is, by its very nature, essentially powerless to express anything at all" – would seem to be corroborated by the dry, astringent sound of so much of his music.[1] The Stravinsky literature normally describes him as an arch-structuralist, the creator of forms for their own sake. And the sense of Stravinsky's music as inexpressive is often taken as particularly true of his late works, with their elaborate serial plans. Indeed, Stravinsky himself encouraged the idea of his music as absolute, pure interval music, as part of his ongoing effort to distance himself from his Russian folkloristic roots.[2]

But Stravinsky's music is, in fact, highly expressive of dramatic situations and emotional states. After all, most of his works, including virtually all of those that are best known, are either ballets (such as *The Firebird, Petrushka, The Rite of Spring, Les Noces*), operas (such as *Oedipus Rex, The Rake's Progress*), or settings of religious texts (such as *Symphony of Psalms, Mass*). It seems obvious, for example, that the Sacrificial Dance from the *Rite of Spring* and the opening "chaos music" from *The Flood* sound different from each other, that neither sounds anything like Anne Truelove's Lullaby from *The Rake's Progress*, and that the differences in sound can be explained, to a significant degree, by the dramatic and emotional situations that Stravinsky is depicting. His music vividly represents a wide range of human emotions and experiences.

Stravinsky's comment about musical expression, then, would seem to have a narrow range of reference, one that would not exclude the possibility of symbolic representation. He himself attempted this clarification later in his life:

[1] Igor Stravinsky, *An Autobiography* (New York: Norton, 1962), 53. The *Autobiography*, like many of the written works that bear Stravinsky's name, was largely ghostwritten (see Craft, "Walter Nouvel and *Chroniques de ma vie*," in *Selected Correspondence*, vol. II, 487–502). This remark, however, is one that Stravinsky explicitly acknowledged as his own, in the course of refining it (see footnote 3, p. 184 below).

[2] This is a central contention of Richard Taruskin, *Stravinsky and the Russian Traditions* (Berkeley: University of California Press, 1996). See, in particular, pp. 1–19. This book is also a notable exception to the interpretive tradition of treating Stravinsky as an arch-formalist. See also Daniel Albright, *Stravinsky: The Music Box and the Nightingale* (New York: Gordon & Breach, 1989).

That overpublicized bit about expression (or non-expression) was simply a way of saying that music is suprapersonal and superreal and as such beyond verbal meanings and verbal descriptions. It was aimed against the notion that a piece of music is in reality a transcendental idea "expressed in terms of" music, with the *reductio ad absurdum* implication that exact sets of correlatives must exist between a composer's feelings and his notation . . . A piece of music may be "beautiful," "religious," "poetic," "sweet," or as many other expletives as listeners can be found to utter them. All right. But when someone asserts that a composer "seeks to express" an emotion for which the someone then provides a verbal description, that is to debase words *and* music.[3]

Stravinsky thus excludes not musical expressiveness generally, but rather personal self-expression. He does not consider his music a vehicle for representing his own internal emotional states: "If I went out and narrowly escaped being run over by a trolley car, I would not immediately rush for some music paper and try to make something out of the emotion I had just felt."[4] Musically, that doctrine translates into his disdain for typically late-romantic musical gestures of heightened self-expression (the soaring violins, the long appoggiaturas, the dense chromaticism). His music is relatively empty of the traditional yearnings and sighs that connote expressiveness in romantic music.

But, despite their lack of traditional signs of musical expressiveness, Stravinsky's works are replete with static symbolic representations, many of which were pointed out by the composer himself.[5] Musical symbols are built up in Stravinsky's music by an extensive network of cross-references, both to traditional musical models and to his own works. Stravinsky's music, taken as a whole, deploys a reasonably consistent gestural language, one which he uses to give expressive shape both to his dramatic or narrative works and to his instrumental works, including those of his last compositional period. Stravinsky uses certain expressive "topics" consistently in his late music to convey a variety of musical meanings.[6]

TOPICS

The expressive topics I will discuss vary in their musical content. Some involve specific pitch classes, harmonies, and pitch relationships, while others are timbral,

---

[3] *Expositions and Developments*, 101.

[4] Comment made during an interview with Paul Rosenfield in January 1925. *Musical Impressions: Selections from Paul Rosenfield's Criticism*, ed. Herbert Leibowitz (New York: Hill and Wang, 1969), 146.

[5] See, for example, his comments on the second movement of the *Symphony in Three Movements* as music for the "Apparition of the Virgin" scene from a proposed film of *The Song of Bernadette* (*Expositions and Developments*, 77) and his further observation that "each episode in the Symphony is linked in my imagination with a concrete impression, very often cinematographic in origin, of the war" (*Dialogues*, 50–52); on his dramatic setting in *The Flood* (*Expositions and Developments*, 123–27 and *Dialogues*, 72–80); on *Oedipus Rex* (*Dialogues*, 27–32); on the second movement of the *Symphony of Psalms*, which "makes the most overt use of musical symbolism in any of my music before *The Flood*" (*Dialogues*, 45).

[6] On a topical approach to musical meaning, see Leonard G. Ratner, *Classic Music: Expression, Form, and Style* (New York: Schirmer, 1980); Wye Allenbrook, *Rhythmic Gesture in Mozart: Le Nozze di Figaro and Don Giovanni* (Chicago: University of Chicago Press, 1983); Kofi Agawu, *Playing with Signs: A Semiotic Interpretation of Classic Music* (Princeton: Princeton University Press, 1991); and Robert Hatten, *Musical Meaning in Beethoven: Markedness, Correlation, and Interpretation* (Bloomington: University of Indiana Press, 1994).

textural, or gestural. These topics can occur in various combinations, thereby creating rich networks of meaning. Some draw on widely shared, traditional musical associations, and would be held in common between Stravinsky and much of his audience. Others operate only within Stravinsky's *oeuvre*, and derive their symbolic value from their inter-opus reference, in the manner of a private symbolic language.[7] I will understand a topic as any musical figure (pitch center, harmony, melodic gesture, texture, etc.) used consistently as a musical symbol of some dramatic situation or emotional state. There are many other inter-opus references in Stravinsky's music with an expressive impact that is either too narrow or too diffuse for them to function as an expressive topic. Some of these are limited in scope and sharply defined in expressive value, like the fateful alternation of minor or major thirds, often in timpani, in *Oedipus Rex*, *Symphony in Three Movements* (first movement), *Canticum Sacrum* ("Euntes in mundum"), *Agon* (Pas-de-Quatre and Interludes), and *Requiem Canticles* (Interlude). Others are so pervasive as to lose any clear or consistent expressive impact, like the seeming clash of major and minor, or the use of the (0235) tetrachord. But many are like those discussed here, sufficiently widespread to be of interest but sharply focused enough to retain a clear symbolic weight.

Expressive topics are among the principal sources of continuity across Stravinsky's diverse *oeuvre*. Stravinsky's serial turn marks a profound shift in the style and structure of his music. Very few of his traditional musical fingerprints, including his signature harmonies, melodies, rhythms, and scales, remain intact or even recognizable in the last of the late works. What does remain, however, is a commitment to certain ways of representing the world, of making musical meaning.

Stravinsky's late music has often been devalued by comparison with his earlier music. It has been dismissed as a product of compositional dotage, the result of sycophantic currying of favor with the younger generation of twelve-tone composers. In this view, Stravinsky abandoned his greatest achievements in order to seem, to himself and others, *au courant* with the latest developments, resulting in works that are sterile and artificial.[8] I will try to show, on the contrary, that Stravinsky's late works deploy a new and evolving musical language in the service of immediate expressive goals. In the previous chapters, I have shown that the late works are structurally rich. In this chapter, I will show that they are also among the most powerfully and movingly expressive that he ever wrote.

I will begin by describing ten expressive topics that play an important role in the

---

[7] My inclusion of musical gestures that are part of a semi-private symbolic language represents a significant departure from the more familiar sense of the term "topic" as used by Ratner and Allenbrook, who emphasize its public, communal nature.

[8] The detractors include the preeminent Stravinsky scholar of our time, Richard Taruskin: "[After the Second World War] Stravinsky, as we know, lapsed quickly back into modernist respectability and social indifference. In the 50's, he suffered a Schoenberg crisis as profound and transforming as Bartók's Stravinsky crisis had been in the 20's. Few, though, would claim that he weathered his crisis as successfully as Bartók had done, or that his capitulation to historical determinism was less damaging a 'compromise' than Bartók's reconciliation with the public" (Richard Taruskin, "Bartók and Stravinsky: An Odd Couple at Last Reunited?," *The New York Times*, 25 October 1998). I discuss these matters in Chapter 1 of this book and, with particular reference to the impact on Stravinsky of Babbitt and Boulez, in "Babbitt and Stravinsky Under the Serial 'Regime,'" *Perspectives of New Music* 35/2 (1999), 17–32.

Table 5.1

Topic	Musical features	Expressive associations	Examples
E to D	Motion from E-centered music (inflected as phrygian or minor), with descending melodic motions and phrygian tetrachords, to D-centered music (inflected as major), with ascending melodic motions and major tetrachords	Motion from grief and lamentation to acceptance or transcendence of death	Prototype: *Orpheus*, first and last scenes Late works: *Cantata*, Prelude; *In Memoriam Dylan Thomas*, Prelude and Postlude
A	Centricity on A; an A–E frame for melodic and harmonic activity; inversion on I_E^A; clash of A-major/minor and C/C♯; harmonies A–B–E, A–D–E, and A–B–D–E	A garden of delight; love's kingdom; a transcendent realm beyond the vicissitudes of daily life	Prototype: *The Rake's Progress*, Act I, Scene 1 Late works: *Cantata*, Ricercar I; *Septet*, I; *Canticum Sacrum*, "Surge, aquilo"; *Movements*, IV; *Variations*
F	Centricity on F; the perfect fifth F–C as a framing interval; harmonies F–B♭–C or F–B–C	Death, funerary, dirge, mourning	Prototype: *Symphonies of Wind Instruments* Late works: *Agon*; *Introitus*; *Epitaphium*; *Requiem Canticles*, Prelude and Postlude
Bells	Evocation of the sound of church bells through instrumentation	Solemn, ritualistic, ecstatic, hieratic	Prototype: *Les Noces* Late works: Three Shakespeare Songs, "Full fadom five"; *Sermon, Narrative, Prayer*, last movement; *Requiem Canticles*, Postlude
Chorale	Homophonic hymns, chorales, "chordal dirges"	Sacred, devotional	Prototype: *Symphonies of Winds* Late works: virtually all
Canon	Strict, imitative counterpoint of two or more lines	The learned style, either as satire of academic pedantry or ritualistic evocation of Renaissance or Baroque masters	Prototype: Symphony of Psalms, II Late works: *Sermon, Narrative, Prayer*; *Cantata*; *Canticum Sacrum*; *Agon*; *Double Canon*; *Threni*
Diatonic versus Chromatic	Contrast of diatonic (major, minor, modal) with chromatic (octatonic, serial, twelve-tone)	human vs. fantastic; reality vs. dream; death vs. life; awake vs. asleep; bright vs. dark	Prototypes: *Firebird*, *The Rake's Progress* Late works: *Three Shakespeare Songs*, "Musick to heare" and "Full fadom five"; *Agon*; *Flood*
Stutter	Melodic alternation of two notes one or two semitones apart; oscillation of two harmonies	Somber muteness in the face of death	Prototype: *Oedipus Rex* Late works: *Elegy for J. F. K*; *Introitus*; *Requiem Canticles*, Exaudi

Table 5.1 (*cont.*)

Topic	Musical features	Expressive associations	Examples
Silence	Rest in all parts (other than as a simple demarcation of a formal boundary) of at least two beats in duration	Pausing before the abyss; rapt contemplation of eternal mysteries	Prototype: *Les Noces* Late works: *Cantata*, "Westron Wind"; *Abraham and Isaac*; *Variations*; *Requiem Canticles*, Interlude and Postlude
Coda	Conclusion of work in which rhythm slows amid fragmentation of principal melodic ideas	Ecstatic transcendence; opening out into the infinite; a time beyond time	Prototypes: *Les Noces*, *Symphony in C*, *The Fairy's Kiss* Late works: *Septet*, I; *Agon*; *Requiem Canticles*, Postlude

late music. In the process, I touch on virtually all of the late works and offer a suggestion of their expressive range and power. With that topical framework in place, I will then offer interpretive readings of two complete works: the first movement of the Septet, one of Stravinsky's first works to incorporate serial procedures, and the Postlude of *Requiem Canticles*, an idiomatic twelve-tone composition and Stravinsky's last major work. Table 5.1 summarizes the ten topics.

FROM GRIEF (E) TO TRANSCENDENCE OF DEATH (D)

Stravinsky often uses a tonal motion from E to D to symbolize a grief that yields to an acceptance or transcendence of death.[9] The E-music is often phrygian-inflected, thus borrowing the traditional lamenting associations of that mode, and often involves descending melodic motions. The D-music is often major in inflection, borrowing the traditional joyous association of that mode, and often involves ascending melodic motions.

Example 5.1 reprints the opening measures of the first scene and the opening and concluding measures of the last scene from *Orpheus*, one of Stravinsky's last neoclassical compositions. As the first scene begins, according to the stage directions, "Orpheus weeps for Eurydice. He stands motionless, with his back to the audience."[10] Orpheus's lyre is represented by the orchestral harp, which adjoins two

[9] Traditional associations with E minor include "gently lamenting" (Friedrich Rochlitz, *Für Freunde der Tonkunst*, 1824) and "a confined life, the inconstancy of things, the lament of sympathy, but without any trace of longing desire" (Ferdinand Hand, *Ästhetik der Tonkunst*, 1837). Traditional associations with D major include "courage, splendor, majesty, and noisy joy" (G. F. Ebhardt, *Die höhern Lehrzweige der Tonsetzkunst*, 1830) and "ample, grand, and noble" (William Porter, *The Musical Cyclopedia*, 1834). Citations drawn from Rita Steblin, *A History of Key Characteristics in the Eighteenth and Early Nineteenth Centuries* (Rochester, NY: University of Rochester Press, 1996).

[10] Stravinsky offered a more complete description of the scenario in a talk broadcast on WQXR, New York, November 1, 1949, reprinted in *Pictures and Documents*, 380–81: "I begin at the moment when Orpheus weeps

phrygian tetrachords (E–D–C–B and A–G–F–E) to create an entire phrygian scale. The music is strongly centered on E, and the melodic motions are generally descending. The final scene, "Orpheus' Apotheosis," in which Apollo "wrests the lyre from Orpheus and raises his song heavenwards," begins as the first did, but after four measures shifts to ascending motions within a D-centered dorian scale. By the end of the final scene, the F♮ has been replaced by F♯, to create a quasi-D major ending (the presence of C♮ in the final chord and of B♭ and F♮ in the melodies suggests a continued tug in this music toward D minor). The large-scale motion in the ballet from its E phrygian opening to its D dorian and eventually D major ending is an evocative musical representation first of Orpheus' grief upon the death of Eurydice and, later, of an ecstatic transcendence of both of their deaths.

The first scene of the *Cantata* is organized along similar lines (see Example 5.2). The text speaks of death and salvation, beginning with an evocation of a dark night of despair and ending with a soul received by Christ. The seven-measure introduction is described by Stravinsky in his program note as "in the Phrygian mode."[11] Like the opening measures of *Orpheus*, it is exclusively diatonic, centered on E, and features a descending phrygian tetrachord, E–D–C–B. An even more striking parallel to *Orpheus* is found in the harmonic progression, which involves an identical progression of tetrachords related by inversion.[12] In both cases, [E, G, A, B] moves to [C, D, E, G] by the inversion that maps E and G onto each other, then moves back the same way.

The scene ends with what Stravinsky calls a "cadence to D major." There is actually an E added to the D major triad, creating another form of the same tetrachord-type heard in the opening. Nonetheless, the passage as a whole gives a strong sense of moving from darkness to light, from death to salvation, as it moves from E phrygian to D major. The similarity of the two passages confirms the symbolic impact of this large-scale motion.[13]

The same progression with the same symbolic value occurs also in Stravinsky's serial music, although with necessary modifications to fit the new musical context.

Footnote 10 (*cont.*)

for Eurydice, his beloved wife, who has died of a serpent bite. His friends bring him gifts and offer him expressions of sympathy, but he is overwhelmed with grief, he is inconsolable. He . . . plays upon his lyre, and his sorrowful song attracts the Angel of Death, who pities him." At the end of the ballet, "Orpheus is no more, but his song lives. Apollo appears radiant in sunlight, the god raises the lyre of Orpheus, lifting his deathless song to the eternal sky."

[11] Stravinsky, "Program Note for *Cantata*," reprinted in Eric Walter White, *Stravinsky: The Composer and His Works* (Berkeley: University of California Press, 1966), 429.

[12] In Example 5.2a, I have placed a few passing notes, incidental to the progression, in parentheses. In Example 5.1a, the harmonic progression excludes the notes played by the harp.

[13] Something similar happens in Act II, Scene 2 of *The Rake's Progress*, but with a wickedly ironic twist. Tom Rakewell has just informed Anne Truelove that he has forsaken her in order to marry a bearded lady, Baba the Turk. Tom and Anne lament the death of their love, and express their grief in E minor. After a distraught Anne departs, Baba sings her triumph in D major. As in *Orpheus* and the *Cantata*, we see a progression from death and grief to triumph, from darkness to light, represented musically by the same tonal motion from E (now minor rather than phrygian, but still making prominent use of the descending tetrachord E–D–C–B) to D major, but now with obviously satiric intent.

Example 5.1   Moving from E to D in *Orpheus*
(a) first four measures of the first scene
(b) first nine measures of the last scene
(c) final three measures of the last scene

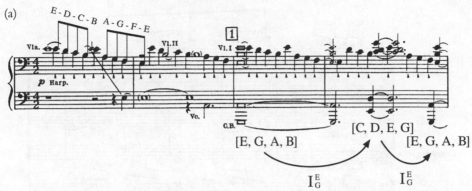

Example 5.2   Moving from E to D in *Cantata*
(a) Prelude, mm. 1–7
(b) Prelude, conclusion, mm. 20–24

(a)

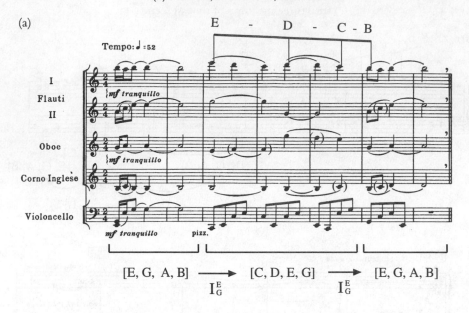

"in the Phrygian mode"

(b)

[D, E, F♯, A]

"cadence to D-major"

Example 5.3   Projected cadence on E in Stravinsky's initial compositional sketch for the opening measures of *In Memoriam Dylan Thomas*, Prelude

In Memoriam Dylan Thomas is Stravinsky's first completely serial work. It consists of a setting of Thomas's poem "Do not go gentle" for baritone and string quartet, flanked by an instrumental Prelude and Postlude for string quartet and trombone quartet. This is Thomas's fierce poem of lamentation on the death of his father. Stravinsky was moved to set the poem as an expression of his own grief at Thomas's sudden death, which cut short a planned operatic collaboration.[14]

Example 5.3 shows Stravinsky's first compositional sketch for what would become the first phrase of the Prelude.[15] In the bass, Stravinsky presents a five-note idea, E–F–F♯–E♭–D, followed by its retrograde.[16] The bass line thus begins and ends on E. The two upper voices consist only of approaches to E from a semitone above or below. Stravinsky apparently wanted a cadence on E and planned to figure out later which series forms would end appropriately, with either D♯–E or F–E. The central idea, then, is a serial passage that centers and cadences on E.

In the final published version of the passage, the bass again begins and ends on E, and the planned cadence on E is elaborated into a cadence on an E major triad (notated as F♭ major) (see Example 5.4a). When the same music returns in the Postlude, it is assigned to the string quartet and transposed down a step to end on D major (see Example 5.4b). As in the works previously discussed, this motion, emphasized by an exact transposition of repeated material, symbolizes an acceptance of death, or possibly a triumph over death. The expressive meaning of the poetic text is thus reinforced in the Prelude and Postlude in purely instrumental terms.

---

14 "In May 1953 Boston University proposed to commission me to write an opera with Dylan. . . . 'His' opera was to be about the rediscovery of our planet following an atomic misadventure. There would be a recreation of language, only the new one would have no abstractions; there would be only people, objects, and words. He promised to avoid poetic indulgences: 'No conceits, I'll knock them all on the head'. . . . He agreed to come to me in Hollywood as soon as he could. Returning there I had a room built for him, an extension from our dining room, as we have no guest room. . .I wrote him October 25 in New York and asked him for word of his arrival plans in Hollywood. I expected a telegram from him announcing the hour of his airplane. On November 9 the telegram came. It said he was dead. All I could do was cry" (*Conversations*, 86–88).

15 Document No. 109–0694 in the Stravinsky Archive at the Paul Sacher Foundation.

16 The five-note idea in the sketch is related by retrograde-inversion to what later emerged as the series for the piece: E–E♭–C–C♯–D. Both the five-note idea in Example 5.3 and the final version of the series begin on E and end on D. The same musical motion that leads from first note to last within the series is composed-out over a large musical span in the relationship between the Prelude and the Postlude.

Example 5.4 Moving from E to D in *In Memoriam Dylan Thomas*
(a) Prelude, mm. 1–6, with cadence on E major
(b) Postlude, mm. 11–16, with cadence on D major

Both E and D, as pitch centers, have a significant independent life in Stravinsky's music. The first movement of *Symphony of Psalms*, for example, is largely confined around an E minor triad, with either phrygian or octatonic inflections, as an expression of its grief-laden text. But the release, the brightening, when it comes, is to G, not to D. In similar fashion, D often maintains its symbolic value, independent of any relationship with E. In *Oedipus Rex*, for example, D is strongly associated with revelation of painful truths – it is Mellers's "key of light."[17]

But it is in their juxtaposition, in the directed motion from E to D, that their symbolic value takes on its greatest potency. There is obviously nothing intrinsically death-like about E or luminous about D. They take on their meanings, separately and in conjunction, through associations with earlier music and, more significantly, through their consistent usage in Stravinsky's own music.

A AS LOVE'S GARDEN

Like E and D, A as a pitch center also has a consistent symbolic role in Stravinsky's music: it denotes a realm outside the daily, where love reigns.[18] Its musical manifestations, beyond a harmonic focus on A, often include an A–E frame for melodic and harmonic activity, a sense of inversion on I^A_E, apparent clashes of A major and A minor (with particular emphasis on a clash of C with C$\sharp$), the inversionally related harmonies A–B–E and A–D–E, and the inversionally symmetrical harmony A–B–D–E.

The first scene of *The Rake's Progress* combines all of these elements (see Example 5.5).[19] Throughout the opera, A represents the tranquility of a country garden, a realm apart from the flux and dangers of normal daily life. In the first scene of the opera, it is Anne's realm, where "love alone reigns." In the final scene of the opera, A (now inflected to minor) represents the madhouse, another realm apart from the daily, where Tom finally reunites with Anne and then dies.

The amorous associations of A go back at least to the second movement of the *Octet*. The melodic theme of that movement is strongly centered on A, and features a persistent clash of C and C$\sharp$. It has a sinuous, warm, untroubled character. In describing the biographical context for this music, Craft writes, "The love affair [between Igor and Vera] did not inspire a *Tristan und Isolde*. . . .But Stravinsky's next

---

[17] Wilfrid Mellers, "Stravinsky's Oedipus as 20th-Century Hero," in *Stravinsky: A New Appraisal of His Work*, ed. Paul Henry Lang (New York: Norton, 1963), 34–46.

[18] Traditional associations of A major include "declarations of innocent love, satisfaction with one's state of affairs, hope of seeing one's beloved again when parting, youthful cheerfulness and trust in God" (Gustave Schilling, *Universal-Lexicon der Tonkunst*, 1835–36) and "confidence and hope, of the heart gladdened by love, and unconstrained cheerfulness" (Ferdinand Hand, *Ästhetik der Tonkunst*, 1837). Citations drawn from Steblin, *A History of Key Characteristics in the Eighteenth and Early Nineteenth Centuries*.

[19] For a discussion of this opening, and of the central role of the C–C$\sharp$ motive throughout the opera, see my "The Progress of a Motive in Stravinsky's *The Rake's Progress*," *The Journal of Musicology* 9/2 (1991), 165–185. A major is Mozart's key of love, most obviously in *Così fan tutte*, and, according to Stravinsky, "the *Rake* was deeply involved in *Così*" (*Memories and Commentaries*, 158).

Example 5.5   A-centricity in *The Rake's Progress*, Act I, Scene 1, mm. 1–14

creation, the *Octet*, written with the throes behind him, is one of his happiest. The lineaments of gratified desire are audible in every phrase."[20]

In a somewhat more religious context, the *Cantata* contains a passage described by Stravinsky as "based on a tonal-modal A" (see Example 5.6).[21] The text describes a place beyond death where the soul might sing eternally – a religious equivalent of Anne's garden. The perfect fifth A–E functions as a cadential harmony three times, until supplanted by G at the final "Amen," in a cadence that Stravinsky describes as having a "Plagal flavor."[22]

The same cadential fifth, and the same focus on A, characterizes the concluding section of "Surge, aquilo" (from *Canticum Sacrum*), Stravinsky's first twelve-tone movement (see Example 5.7). The series for this movement ends C–B–A, a feature which enables the persistent focus on A amid the twelve-tone operations.[23] The text, from the "Song of Songs," is erotically charged, and concerns a garden into which the lovers enter to eat and drink. The textual imagery links this aria to the

[20] *Glimpses of a Life*, xv.

[21] Stravinsky, "Program Note for *Cantata*," reprinted in White, *Stravinsky: The Composer and His Works*, 429.

[22] Ibid, 430. See Chapter 3 for discussion of the perfect fifth as a cadential marker in Stravinsky's serial music.

[23] The last twelve notes in the vocal part traverse the P-form of the series, A♭–G–F–D–G♭–E–E♭–D♭–B♭–C–B–A, and incomplete statements of the R-form begin in mm. 80 and 83. The series for the Coda in *Agon* is very similar (see Chapter 3 for discussion), but its musical realization offers little support to any sense of A-centricity.

opening of *The Rake's Progress*, a link that is reinforced by their shared musical focus on A.

It may seem odd to mention *Movements* and *Variations* in any discussion of musical expression, much less one that is focused on gardens of earthly or heavenly delights. These are, after all, among the most abstract and formally elaborate of Stravinsky's instrumental works. Nonetheless, portions of both works share a focus on A and related musical issues and thus belong in an expressive family with the passages from *The Rake's Progress*, *Cantata*, and *Canticum Sacrum*, discussed above.

Example 5.8 reprints the Interlude that precedes and sets the scene for the fourth of the *Movements*.[24] The serial source of the passage is the IR-form of the series: F–Eb–E–A–B–Bb–Ab–Db–D–C–F♯–G. The passage begins with a chord consisting of its first four notes and ends with a chord consisting of its last five notes. Between those two punctuation points, there is a vivid musical evocation of Anne's garden. The perfect fifth, A–E, is sustained for most of the passage, creating a musical frame for what follows. In measure 93, it is juxtaposed with another perfect fifth C♯–G♯ (actually stated as a perfect fourth), to create a larger symmetrical harmony, A–C♯–E–G♯, a major seventh chord on A. The sustained C♯ is immediately and insistently challenged by C♮. In all of these senses – the focus on A, on the perfect fifth A-E, the symmetrical balance, the clash of C♯ and C♮ – this passage breathes the musical atmosphere of the country garden.

The same atmosphere pervades the entire fourth movement, which follows immediately. The fourth is serially the simplest of the five movements, based as it is on complete, untransposed statements of the four basic forms of the series: the prime (P), the inversion starting on the same first note (I), the retrograde (R), and the inversion of the retrograde starting on the same first note (IR). In the opening phrase, a statement of IR in the orchestra gives rise to a striking sustained chord, built up, as in the preceding interlude, from a combination of A–E and C♯–G♯ (see Example 5.9).[25] The high-register string harmonics create an ethereal, otherworldly effect, one that reinforces the symbolic weight of the chord itself, with its focus on A and its internal symmetry. It might be stretching a point to suggest that the passage sounds pastoral or amorous, but it certainly evokes a world set apart from the flux of daily life.

As the movement continues, this sustained harmony (A–E/C♯–G♯) is supplanted by another one, similarly constructed and orchestrated (D–A/F♯–C♯ in mm. 110–17), then returns as the movement comes to its conclusion (mm. 123–32).[26] The three chords can be thought of as major seventh chords on A, D, and A,

---

[24] "[The Interludes] are introductions rather than codas; the conductor should pause *before* them" (*Themes and Episodes*, 25).

[25] Note that the violas and cellos are playing in treble clef.

[26] Isomorphic partitioning of the inversionally related series forms produces these inversionally related chords. Serially, the chords are notes 3, 4, 7, and 8 of the IR-form, the R-form, and, again, the IR-form. The sustained harmonies in the Sermon movement of *A Sermon, a Narrative, and a Prayer* result from a similar procedure of creating chords by sustaining selected notes of a series. But, in the Sermon, the partitioning is not isomorphic and, as a result, the chords are of many different types.

Example 5.6   A-centricity with cadences on A–E in *Cantata*, conclusion of Ricercar I

Example 5.6 (*cont.*)

[A, E]   "plagal flavor"

hinting at a plagal cadence and recalling the static oscillation of harmonies in the first scene of *The Rake's Progress*. Stravinsky refers to this progression as one of the few moments in the work that resist the prevailing "tendency toward anti-tonality."[27] The sense of symmetrical balance, both within and between the chords, works together with their prominent perfect fifths, particularly A–E in the first and third chords, and their hint of a plagal cadence on A major, to confirm the kinship of this passage with those of *The Rake's Progress*, the *Cantata*, and "Surge, aquilo," discussed above. In purely instrumental terms, then, and in a strictly twelve-tone context, Stravinsky has recreated the atmosphere of an unearthly paradise, one detached from the vagaries of daily life.

The same complex of musical ideas penetrates still more deeply into the structure of *Variations*, but is paradoxically less evident on the musical surface. As discussed in Chapter 2, in writing his twelve-tone music, Stravinsky did not normally begin by writing a series. Instead, he generally wrote a concrete tune, specific as to register, rhythm, and often instrumentation as well. Then he massaged the tune until it contained one iteration of each of the twelve tones, and treated that succession of tones as a series. The generative melody for *Variations* is shown in Example 5.10.[28] The

---

[27] *Memories and Commentaries*, 107.

[28] The melody is provided in *A Stravinsky Scrapbook*, ed. Robert Craft (London: Thames & Hudson, 1983), 130, with Craft's explanation that "Stravinsky wrote this copy of the series of his *Variations* in flight between Chicago and New York, April 14, 1965." The melody appears also in Claudio Spies, "Some Notes on Stravinsky's *Variations*," *Perspectives of New Music* 4/1 (1965); reprinted in *Perspectives on Schoenberg and Stravinsky*, ed. Benjamin Boretz and Edward Cone (Princeton: Princeton University Press, 1968), 214. Stravinsky gives a

Example 5.7 A-centricity and a final cadence on A–E in *Canticum Sacrum*, "Surge, aquilo," conclusion

Example 5.8   A-centricity in *Movements*, mm. 92–95, Interlude between the third and
fourth movements

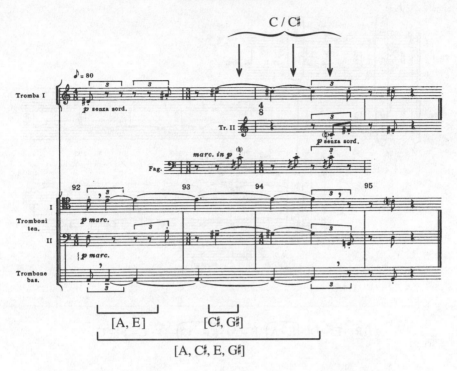

melody begins with the first five notes of an A minor scale. A and E are the registral
extremes within which B and D balance each other symmetrically. Clearly a sense
of A-orientation, together with some of the familiar associated symmetries and
harmonies, forms part of Stravinsky's initial conception. (In the sixth through ninth
notes, the same sort of arrangement is suggested, only now oriented toward A♭, a
semitone lower.)

A special interest in A can be traced also into the rotational arrays derived from
the series. Stravinsky was never interested in abstract theorizing about music and
gave no published account of his twelve-tone approach. He did, however, provide a
single, brief fragmentary explanation of his rotational arrays and the chords derived
from them (see Example 5.11).[29] Stravinsky begins his explanation by copying out

Footnote 28 (*cont.*)
   version of the same melody in whole notes in his program note for *Variations*, reprinted in *Themes and Episodes*,
   60. The first four notes of the series, [A, B, C, D], recall both the bassoon solo at the beginning of *The Rite of
   Spring* and the opening trumpet fanfare of *Agon*. Neither of these is notably an A-centered work, however, and
   I am not proposing any topical kinship between them and *Variations*.
[29] The sketch shown in Example 5.11 is reprinted in *A Stravinsky Scrapbook*, ed. Craft, 120 and in Taruskin,
   Stravinsky and the Russian Traditions, 1655. Craft explains that, although the demonstration involves the hexachord
   from the series for *Variations*, it was intended for, and later deleted from, a program note for *Abraham and Isaac*.

Example 5.9   A-centricity in *Movements*, IV, mm. 96–109

the array generated from the first hexachord of the series for *Variations*. His principal concern is to explain the structure of the array columns or verticals, particularly the third vertical. He places this in a box and provides a summary of its contents. He then appends an interesting technical explanation of the origin of this chord in the rotations and transpositions, but the technical aspects are of less interest in the present context than the content of the chord itself: A–C–C♯–E.[30] This is a chord rooted on A, framed by the perfect fifth A–E, and embedding a clash of C and C♯; in short, one which embodies many of the musical elements of Anne's garden, just as the serial melody does. This is the chord that Stravinsky chose for his unique demonstration of his serial methods – obviously he was acutely aware of its place among his materials for this work.

There is a sense, then, that in its deepest precompositional impulses, both melodic and harmonic, *Variations* is formed from a familiar complex of musical ges-

---

[30] Stravinsky's explanation, with the original spelling and grammar, reads: "Some stressed octaves and fifths and doubled intervals in some of the chords which could be found in this score shouldn't contradict the serial (~~and not harmonical~~) basis of the composition; the origin of it lies not in an horisontal contrapunctical accord of different voices but in a vertical similtaneous clang (sounding?) of several notes belonging to a certain number of forms played together." Quoted in Taruskin, *Stravinsky and the Russian Traditions*, 1655.

Example 5.10   Generative melody for *Variations*, with an initial focus on A

A   A♭
A - E   A♭ - E♭
A - B - E / A - D - E   A♭ - B♭ - E♭ / A♭ - D♭ - E♭
A - B - D - E   A♭ - B♭ - D♭ - E♭
A - B - C - D - E

tures that center around the note A. In the actual music, however, the sense of focus on A is fleeting at best. *Variations* is probably the least steeped of any of Stravinsky's late works in the structural or expressive habits of his earlier music. Events unfold with astonishing rapidity in this work, and moments of relative repose are rare.

One may catch a brief glimpse of the garden, however, in Variation VI (see Example 5.12). In this variation, delicately spaced chords, taken from the verticals of the array shown in Example 5.11, are interspersed with a chattering trio of trombones, taken from the rows of two different arrays.[31] The first and third chords of the progression represent the third chord of the array, the A major/minor chord that Stravinsky identified and discussed. Stravinsky has arranged the chord with the perfect fifth A–E at the bottom, providing a sense of rootedness, and emphasized it by repetition – it is the only chord to occur more than once in the passage. It is thus linked to the A-centered world of the precompositional plans for this work. A sense of focus on A, and on the perfect fifth A–E, is maintained in the final chord of the passage, and one hears at least an echo of a C/C♯ clash in the highest sounding voice. In addition, there is an inevitable sense of inversional balance in any progression involving the verticals of Stravinsky's rotational arrays, as discussed in Chapter 4.

In a subtle, attenuated way, the variation as a whole thus evokes the world beyond time of the other A-related passages discussed here. The sixth variation lies right at the midpoint of the eleven variations that comprise the work. Here, by virtue of the rhythm, duration, spacing, and content of the chords, we achieve a momentary sense of repose and stasis compared with the ceaseless flux of the rest of the work. The only comparable moment elsewhere in the piece is in the final chords, which are organized on a similar basis and presented in a similar way. Right at the center of this extraordinarily dense, busy work, then, we are permitted for a moment to reenter Anne's garden.

---

[31] For a thorough serial analysis of *Variations*, see Paul Phillips, "The Enigma of Variations: A Study of Stravinsky's Final Work for Orchestra," *Music Analysis* 3/1 (1984), 69–89. There is an apparent mistake in the second chord of the progression. The A♯ in Piano and Horn III should be F♯, according to the array. In reading the array, Stravinsky evidently misread the bottom line as being in bass clef. In the present discussion, I leave it uncorrected, but it should almost certainly be corrected in performance.

Example 5.11 Stravinsky's explanation of the verticals of his rotational arrays, using the first hexachord of *Variations* as his example (the third vertical is an A-major/minor chord)

F AS EMBLEM OF DEATH

The association of the funerary with a harmonic complex on F (including a focus on F as a pitch center, the perfect fifth F–C as a framing interval, and the harmonies F–Bb–C or F–B–C) is one with deep roots in Stravinsky's music. The *Symphonies of Wind Instruments*, for example, concludes with an extended funereal chorale, intended originally and first published independently as a memorial for Claude

Debussy.[32] Snatches of the chorale are inserted into the first part of the published *Symphonies*, and the first such insertion is shown in Example 5.13. The chorale texture represents a distinct expressive topic and I will return to it, and to this passage, later. It suffices now to observe that the passage is strongly centered on F as a point of departure and arrival in both outer voices, and that the F is thus associated with the dirge-like atmosphere.[33]

In the music of the last period, with its succession of requiems and memorial works, F plays a prominent symbolic role, one that is most fully realized in conjunction with two other topics – chorale textures and bell-like timbres – to be discussed later. *Introitus*, a requiem in memory of T. S. Eliot, begins with the three chords shown in Example 5.14a along with Stravinsky's own serial analysis.[34] The instrumentation, harp and piano supported by tam-tams, strongly recalls other bell-like passages and the texture is that of a chordal dirge. Its somber character is enhanced by the extreme low register. Stravinsky has made mistakes in realizing his serial plan for the second and third chords, and I have corrected these in Example 5.14b.[35] The final chord of the progression should be [F, A, B♭, C]. This chord is centered on F, and contains both an F major triad, [F, A, C], and another familiar trichordal component of the F-topic, [F, B♭, C].[36]

Another funeral piece that shares a focus on F is the *Epitaphium* (written to the memory of Prince Max Egon zu Fürstenberg). Like the other short works of the period (*Double Canon, Anthem, Elegy for J. F. K.*), *Epitaphium* dispenses with the rotational arrays that shape the major works. Indeed, its serial structure is extremely simple, as Stravinsky explains: "There are four short antiphonal strophes for the harp, and four for the wind duet [flute and clarinet], and each strophe is a complete

---

[32] For information on the genesis of *Symphonies of Wind Instruments*, see "'Hymns of Praise' for Debussy: Stravinsky's *Symphonies of Winds*," in *Glimpses of a Life*, 370–82. According to Craft, the very opening of the piece was written first, before the chorale, and Stravinsky referred to both as "hymns of praise." See also Stephen Walsh, "Stravinsky's Symphonies: Accident or Design," in *Analytical Strategies and Musical Interpretation: Essays on Nineteenth- and Twentieth-Century Music*, ed. Craig Ayrey and Mark Everist (Cambridge: Cambridge University Press, 1996), 35–71. Taruskin argues that the work is modeled on the Russian Orthodox office of the dead (*Stravinsky and the Russian Traditions*, 1488–93). The autograph score and short score draft are reproduced in facsimile as *Igor Strawinsky: Symphonies d'Instruments à Vent: Faksimileausgabe des Particells und der Partitur der Erstfassung* (1920), ed. André Baltensperger and Felix Meyer (Winterthur: Paul Sacher Stiftung/Amadeus, 1991).

[33] Another striking association of F with the funerary involves the Prelude to the Graveyard scene in *The Rake's Progress*. There, the contrapuntal lines meander and intertwine in an atmosphere of dark foreboding, then converge and conclude on an F major triad.

[34] The relevant compositional sketch is reproduced in *Strawinsky: Sein Nachlass, sein Bild*, ed. Hans Jörg Jans and Christian Geelhaar (Basel: Kunstmuseum, 1984), 179.

[35] These mistakes, which involve misreading a treble for a bass clef, are discussed in my "Stravinsky's Serial Mistakes," *The Journal of Musicology* 17/2 (1999). When this three-chord progression recurs with some additional notes in mm. 32–33, Stravinsky corrects his mistakes.

[36] The final chord of *Introitus* is a tetrachord of the same type, but not centered on F: [C♯, D♯, E, G♯]. A comparison with the final chord of *Requiem Canticles*, [B♭, C, C♯, F], is instructive. The two chords share a bass note F, a perfect fifth F–C, and the trichord F–B♭–C. As tetrachords, they are also related by inversion around F. They are thus bound together not only by their shared set-class membership, but also by their mutual, and mutually reinforcing, focus on F.

Example 5.12   Verticals from the array in Example 5.11, including the A major/minor
chord, in *Variations*, mm. 73–85

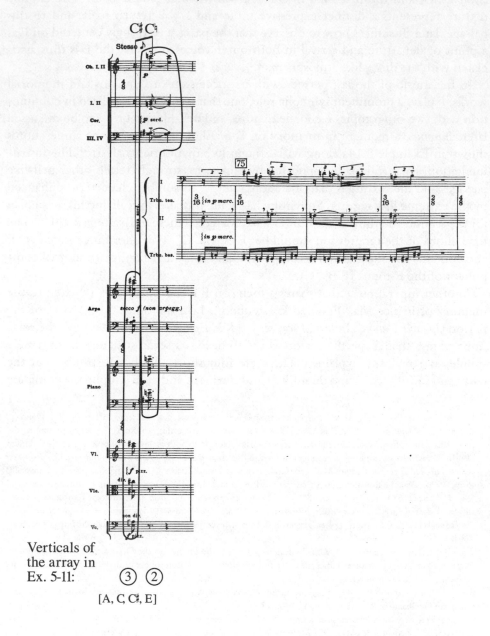

Verticals of
the array in
Ex. 5-11:

[A, C, C♯, E]

Example 5.12 (*cont.*)

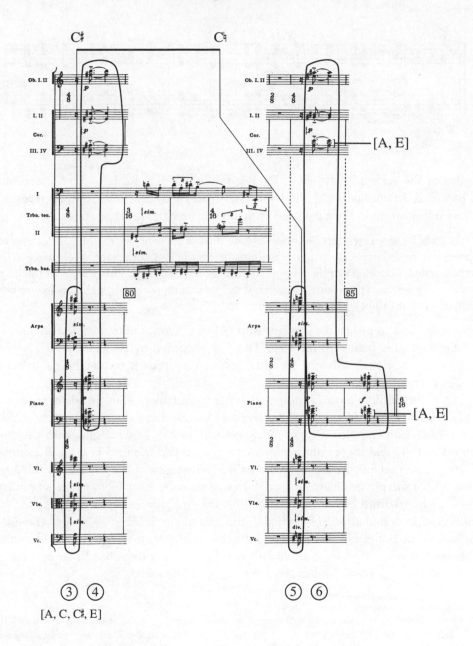

Example 5.13   F-centered chorale in *Symphonies of Wind Instruments*, mm. 4–8

order of the series – harp: O, I, R, RI; winds: O, RI, R, I."[37] As discussed in Chapter 2, Stravinsky wrote the wind duet first, then went back and interspersed short interjections in the harp in an effort to enhance the funereal atmosphere:

> Only after I had written this little twelve-note duet did I conceive the idea of a series of funeral responses between bass and treble instruments and, as I wanted the whole piece to be very muffled, I decided that the bass instrument should be a harp. The first bar of the harp part was, however, written last. As I worked the music out, it became a kind of hymn, like Purcell's *Funeral Music for Queen Mary*.[38]

Example 5.15 reprints the last measure of the work. Like *Requiem Canticles*, *Epitaphium* ends with F in the bass. The F is preceded by B♭ and C. This might suggest a traditional cadential formula; at the very least it recalls the prominent F–B♭–C trichords of *Requiem Canticles*, and *Introitus*.

Agon, Stravinsky's abstract, non-representational ballet, is linked to these explicitly funerary works by a similar harmonic focus. Example 5.16 compares the beginnings and endings of *Agon* and *Requiem Canticles*. *Agon* begins with the trichord F–B–C and moves quickly to a cadence on the trichord F–G–C (Example 5.16a). The perfect fifth F–C, with a strong orientation toward F, is thus filled in first with a sharply dissonant B, then with a more consonant G, to create a familiar (027). The trichord F–G–C is sustained for the final six measures of *Agon*, with a sustained D added shortly before the end (Example 5.16b).[39] *Requiem Canticles* behaves in strikingly similar fashion. It begins on the same trichord, F–B–C, with the same strong orientation toward F, and ends with a tetrachord that embeds a form of (027), F–B♭–C, and adds C♯ (Examples 5.16c and d).[40]

---

[37] *Memories and Commentaries*, 106.   [38] Ibid.

[39] There is disagreement in the analytical literature regarding the centricity of the *Agon* Pas-de-Quatre, which begins and concludes the ballet. Some analysts, persuaded by the obvious focus of the trumpet melody, consider C the centric tone (see, for example, Carl Wiens, "Igor Stravinsky and 'Agon'" [Ph.D. dissertation, University of Michigan, 1997]). Others, persuaded more by the bass line which so often offers support for the melody a perfect fifth below, consider F the centric tone (see, for example, Anthony Payne, "Stravinsky's Chords [II]," *Tempo* 77 [1966], 6: "The opening 'Pas-de-Quatre' finds the composer content to use an F modality with sharpened fourth and occasional flattened supertonic"). In my view, C is the principal melodic tone, but serves to confirm F as the principal harmonic tone. F and C support each other in an F-centered harmony.

[40] The resemblance between the openings has been noticed before. See Charles Wuorinen and Jeffrey Kresky, "On the Significance of Stravinsky's Last Works," in *Confronting Stravinsky*, ed. Jann Pasler (Berkeley: University of

Example 5.14 Cadential arrival on F in *Introitus*
(a) mm. 1–2
(b) with mistakes corrected

The kinship is striking, and suggests an aspect of *Agon* that might not otherwise be evident. *Agon* begins with four male dancers standing with their backs to the audience. At the end of the ballet, when the opening music has been recapitulated and the final cadence is approaching, the female dancers exit and the male dancers resume their initial posture. The music suggests that this posture declares a world apart from the lively world of the rest of the dance, first a world before creation, and then a world after the end of this world. *Agon* begins and ends, then, with a kind of radically condensed requiem. It is framed by a death-suffused vision of the kind that permeates all of *Requiem Canticles*.

The relationship between the musical symbols discussed thus far (motion from E to D and harmonic complexes centered on A and F) and the dramatic states they may be taken to represent (grief and acceptance, transcendent love, death) is in no sense causal. The music is not grief-stricken because it is centered on E, luminous because centered on D, amorous because centered on A, or funereal because centered on F. Rather, Stravinsky orients the music toward those centers when he

California Press, 1986), 264. This type of harmony, sc(016), often spaced as a major seventh with a perfect fourth or tritone above its lowest note, is identified by Taruskin as "the Rite chord" because of its persistent use in that work (see *Stravinsky and the Russian Traditions*, 939–47). See also Pieter van den Toorn, *The Music of Igor Stravinsky* (New Haven: Yale University Press, 1983), for accounts of the sonority in *The Rite of Spring* and other works.

Example 5.15   Arrival on F in the final measure of *Epitaphium*

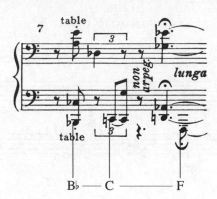

wants to represent a certain dramatic situation. These centers are among the rules, the arbitrary givens, the self-imposed limitations that provide Stravinsky with a starting point and a framework for composition. In that sense, they are analogous to serial procedures – seemingly restrictive limitations that, paradoxically, enable the compositional process.

Along with serial procedures, Stravinsky apparently accepted the intrinsic value of pitch among the artistically valid constraints: "It is very important to me to remember the pitch of the music at its first appearance: if I transpose it for some reason I am in danger of losing the freshness of first contact and I will have difficulty in recapturing its attractiveness."[41] For Stravinsky, then, specific pitches might absorb a consistent expressive charge. In conceiving a melody or a passage as oriented toward D, E, A, or F, Stravinsky commits himself to the expressive impact that, for him, they conventionally embody.

BELLS

The evocation of bells, particularly funerary bells, can be traced back to Stravinsky's earliest works, and occurs with particular frequency in his latest ones, as Craft points out in his review of Boris Asaf'yev's *A Book About Stravinsky*:

The bell-like sounds that become part of the substance of *Noces* are already present in the texture of *The Nightingale*, in harp and string harmonics, in the timbres of piano and celesta, not to mention the actual bells in the Emperor's court at the beginning of Act II and the funeral gong in Act III. Asaf'yev, who knew that Stravinsky would have heard the great bell of the Nikolsky Sobor in his cradle, could not have been surprised by the continuing evocation of bells in the later music – in the second of the *Shakespeare Songs*, in the setting of Thomas Dekker's *Prayer*, in the *Introitus*, and in *Requiem Canticles*. In a talk at the Cleveland Institute of Music in 1968, Victor Babin recalled a visit to Stravinsky in his Hollywood

----
[41] *Conversations*, 17.

Example 5.16 Two F-centered works
(a) *Agon*, opening
(b) *Agon*, final cadence

Example 5.16 (*cont.*)
(c) *Requiem Canticles*, Prelude, opening; (d) *Requiem Canticles*, Postlude, final cadence

(c)

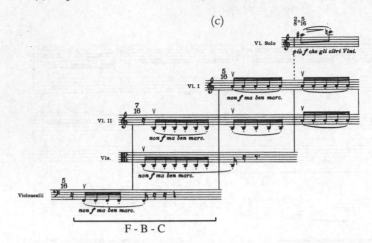

F - B - C

(d)

F - B♭ - C (+C♯)

home during which the composer "showed me his *In Memorian Dylan Thomas* . . . explaining to me how the four trombones sounded like funeral bells . . ."[42]

"Full fadom five," the second of the *Three Shakespeare Songs*, is the only one of the late works that makes explicit textual reference to bells (see Example 5.17).[43] The bells here are funeral bells, rung by sea nymphs in honor of a character from Shakespeare's *The Tempest* who has apparently drowned, and they are evoked musically by both timbral and intervallic means. The unusual declamation in the voice, with its emphasis on the final nasal in "ding" and "dong" and the pizzicato in the viola both contribute to the overall effect. The effect is reinforced by the prominence given to the interval of the perfect fifth, and to harmonies that consist of two perfect fifths – members of sc(027). The work ends with a progression of two such harmonies, related by the inversion that exchanges F and B♭. Another such harmony, [D♭, E♭, A♭], begins the final passage, and still another, [B♭, C, F], is arpeggiated in the voice. The open, ringing quality of this harmony captures the bell-like sound here, although it should be acknowledged that the same harmony is extraordinarily prevalent in Stravinsky's music, often at cadences, and usually with no bell-like associations whatsoever.

If one were to identify a pitch center for this passage and this song as a whole, it would almost certainly be E♭, but the F is also extremely prominent at the end, both sustained in the flute, the highest sounding part, and as a center of inversional symmetry in the voice, flanked by the C below and the B♭ above. This focus on F, and the prominent use of this harmony, F–B♭–C, links this piece with the funerary F-pieces discussed above. The conclusion of "Full fadom five" draws its expressive impact from its simultaneous reference to the F-topic and the bells-topic.

In the setting of Thomas Dekker's Prayer, the last movement of *A Sermon, a Narrative and a Prayer*, bells are evoked by a melody played in unison by the contrabass (alternating pizzicato and arco), harp, and piano, with each note accompanied by a stroke in one of the three tam-tams. This bell-melody runs through virtually the entire movement, with occasional interruptions – its final measures are reprinted in Example 5.18. Like many of Stravinsky's melodies written around the same time, this one traces a path through a rotational array, in this case the array built from the first hexachord of the I-form of the series (see annotations in Example 5.18). The melody as a whole moves through the rows of the array, concluding with rows IV and I, as shown on the example. Each row of the array begins with E♭ (circled on the example) and there are many other common tones among the rows of the array, as well as frequent repetitions of notes in the actual music.

---

[42] "Stravinsky and Asaf'yev," in *Glimpses of a Life*, 258–59, 268–69. The role of bells as an expressive topic in Stravinsky's late music is addressed by Glenn Watkins, *Pyramids at the Louvre* (Cambridge, Mass.: Harvard University Press, 1994), 215–28; Louis Andriessen and Elmer Schönberger, *The Apollonian Clockwork: On Stravinsky*, trans. Jeff Hamburg (Oxford: Oxford University Press, 1989); and Jeffrey Perry, "A 'Requiem for the Requiem': On Stravinsky's *Requiem Canticles*," *College Music Symposium* 33/34 (1993/94), 237–57.

[43] The opening of the song anticipates the explicit reference to bells in the final lines of the text. Craft refers to the introductory measure as a "motive of bells" (*Avec Stravinsky*, 149).

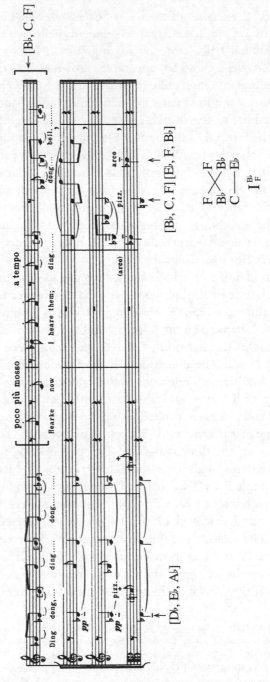

Example 5.17 Bells ringing in *Three Shakespeare Songs,* "Full fadom five," last four measures

Example 5.18 A bell-like melody in *A Sermon, a Narrative, and a Prayer*, mm. 253–end (contrabass, harp, piano, and tam-tams only)

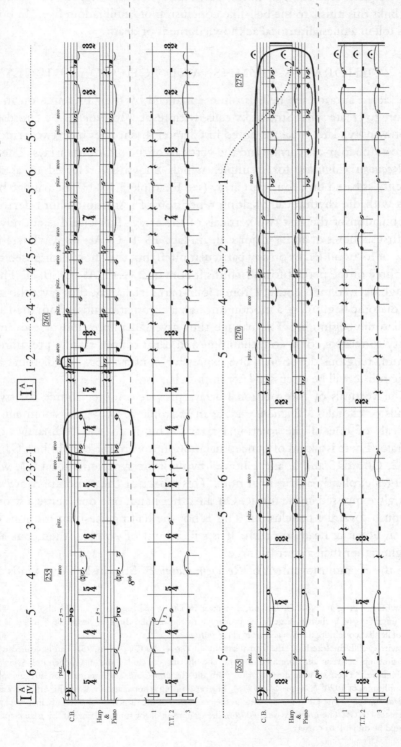

The frequent repetition of notes, particularly the E♭, suggests the tolling of bells and links this music to the bell-like conclusion of "Full fadom five." In both works, bells toll in a quasi-liturgical acknowledgment of death.

CHORALES, HYMNS, AND "CHORDAL DIRGES"

The sacred aura of the bells is often enhanced by their presentation in a chorale texture to create what Stravinsky calls, with respect to *Introitus*, "a chordal dirge."[44] In Stravinsky's late music, as noted in Chapter 4, chorales have two principal serial sources: the four-part arrays and the verticals of the rotational arrays. The Interlude of *Requiem Canticles*, for example, which Stravinsky referred to as a "formal lament," is based on a four-part array (see Example 5.19).[45] The passage begins and ends with the rhythmically halting repetition of a six-note chord derived from a combination of the first two verticals of the array. This chord is entirely diatonic, the first six notes of an E♭ major scale, in fact: E♭–F–G–A♭–B♭–C. There is no clear sense of focus on E♭, or on any particular pitch, but the chord is disposed to emphasize three of the perfect fourths/fifths it contains: G–C, A♭–E♭, B♭–F. The passage, though derived in its entirety from a four-part serial array, thus gives the impression of a diatonic beginning, a motion through a chromatic midsection, then a return to its diatonic beginning. The passage thus gives an impression of movement from clarity to relative confusion, then renewed clarification, amid a prevailing sense of solemn, religious devotion. (The expressive contrast between diatonic and chromatic music will be discussed later in this chapter.)

The verticals of the rotational arrays provide another source for twelve-tone hymns or chorales. *Variations* ends as in Example 5.20, with a statement of the six verticals of one of the rotational arrays. This is an extraordinarily compressed chorale. There is a kind of conceptual motion toward the concluding G♯: Chords 6 and 2, Chords 5 and 3, and Chord 4 by itself are symmetrical on G♯, which then emerges explicitly as the final note. This aspect of the structure, however, is not strongly expressed in the music. On the other hand, one does sense a strong, vigorous push toward a conclusion. This is not the halting, hesitant motions of a dirge but an ecstatic, headlong rush. It is still a kind of chorale, then, but a hymn of delight rather than a chordal dirge.

In the Exaudi movement of *Requiem Canticles*, Stravinsky's two kinds of twelve-

---

44 Stravinsky, "Program Note for *Introitus*," reprinted in *Themes and Episodes*, 63: "The choral chant is punctuated by fragments of a chordal dirge." The prototype of the chordal dirge in Stravinsky's music is the extended chorale that concludes the *Symphonies of Wind Instruments*.

45 Stravinsky calls the Interlude "the formal lament" in *Themes and Conclusions*, 98. Craft has called attention to the relationship between this Interlude and the chorale that concludes and interpenetrates *Symphonies of Wind Instruments*: "The two-note dirge-rhythm from the *Requiem Canticles*'s Interlude had already appeared in the Symphonies of 1920" (*Glimpses of a Life*, 5). The relationship is noted also by Taruskin, *Stravinsky and the Russian Traditions*, 1650. The G♮ in the alto flute in the realization of the fifth vertical is serially incorrect and should be corrected to G♯. The note D is omitted from the realization of the ninth vertical. If this is an error, it is one that would be difficult to correct.

Example 5.19   A "chordal dirge" in *Requiem Canticles*, Interlude, mm. 136–46
(a) annotated score

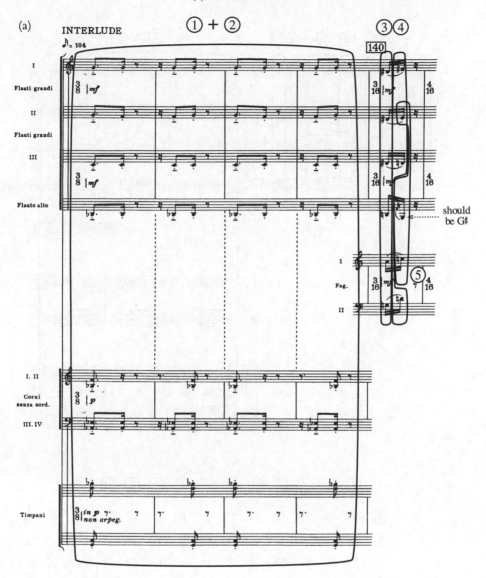

Example 5.19 (*cont.*)
(a) (*cont.*)
(b) four–part array

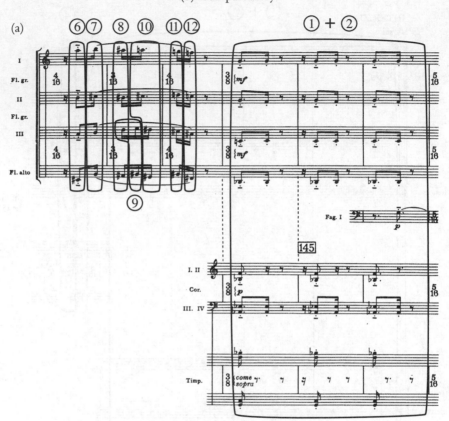

Example 5.20   A highly compressed chorale in *Variations*, last five measures
(a) annotated score
(b) rotational array (based on the second hexachord of the P–ordering)

(a)

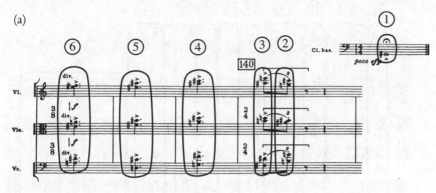

(b)

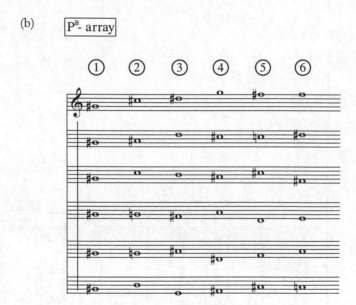

Example 5.21 Chorales with distinct serial derivations in *Requiem Canticles*, Exaudi
(a) mm. 71–80

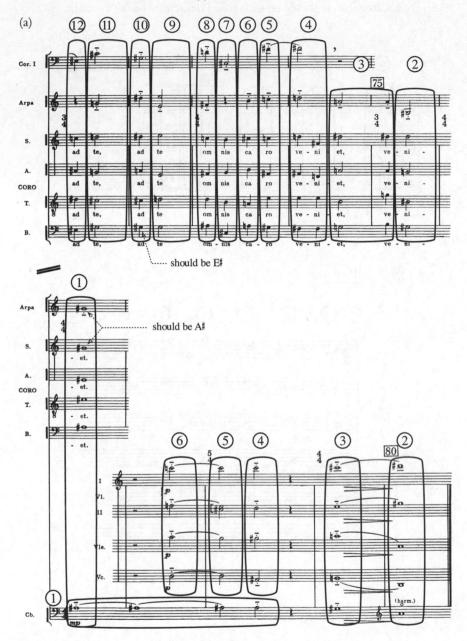

Example 5.21 (*cont.*)
(b) four–part array
(c) rotational array

(b) ① ② ③ ④ ⑤ ⑥ ⑦ ⑧ ⑨ ⑩ ⑪ ⑫

P	E♯	G	D♯	E	F♯	C♯	B	C	D	A	G♯	A♯
R	A♯	G♯	A	D	C	B	C♯	F♯	E	D♯	G	E♯
I	E♯	D♯	G	F♯	E	A	B	A♯	G♯	C♯	D	C
IR	A♯	B♯	B	F♯	G♯	A	G	D	E	F	C♯	D♯

(c) R^A- array

① ② ③ ④ ⑤ ⑥

A♯	G♯	A	D	C	B
A♯	B	E	D	C♯	C
A♯	D♯	C♯	C	B	A
A♯	G♯	G	F♯	E	F
A♯	A	G♯	F♯	G	C
A♯	A	G	G♯	C♯	B

tone chorales, based on the four-part arrays or the verticals of the rotational arrays, are heard in immediate succession (see Example 5.21).[46] The choral parts, doubled in Horn I and Harp, describe the twelve chords from the four-part array, while the instrumental conclusion describes the six verticals from the rotational array. The chord in measure 76 consists of an overlap between the two, with the shared A♯ as a kind of pivot. Although the two passages have a different kind of serial structure, they nonetheless share the same hushed, devotional atmosphere.

In the late music, chorales are always attributable to the verticals of either the rotational or the four-part arrays. Conversely, Stravinsky designed those arrays with the intention of using them to write twelve-tone chorales. He was not interested in their originality or power as twelve-tone constructs, although they possess both in abundance, but rather, as discussed in Chapter 4, used them to answer a particular expressive need for a music that solemnly evokes a scene of religious devotion.

[46] In the bass part in m. 72, the first note should be E♯ according to the array, not G♯ as in the score (the serially-incorrect G♯ is doubled by Horn I). This is almost certainly the result of misreading the lowest row of an array as bass rather than treble clef. In the soprano part in m. 76, A♯ is indicated by the array, not G♯ as in the score (the serially incorrect G♯ is doubled by Harp). Both errors should be corrected in performance, and I assume their correction in this discussion.

CANON

Canons – strictly imitative counterpoint – occur infrequently in Stravinsky's music prior to the compositional crisis of 1952, but very often thereafter. They seem to have represented, for him, a promising point of intersection between a historically informed interest in traditional counterpoint and Webernian serialism.[47] Indeed, canons are so widespread in Stravinsky's late music that it is difficult to make tenable claims about their expressive impact. In some cases, they seem to function as an emblem of an over-intellectualized pedantry, the "learned style" carried to a self-mocking extreme.

This is certainly the case in the passage from *A Sermon, A Narrative, and A Prayer* in which the Jews dispute with St. Stephen (see Example 5.22).[48] The passage is organized as a double canon. The leader of the first canon is Bassoon I, which cycles methodically down through the R^B-array and then back up again.[49] Its follower is Bassoon II, which cycles down through the R^B-array beginning in m. 122. The leader of the second canon is Oboe I, shifting to Oboe II in m. 121 and the follower is Oboe II, shifting to Oboe I in the same place. This second canonic line cycles through the R^A-array. The motions through the arrays are entirely systematic and every note is accounted for.[50] The perfectly systematic array structure and its realization as a double canon are evidently intended to depict the contentious Jews in their refusal to accept Stephen's teaching.[51]

More commonly, canons in Stravinsky's late music have a somber, ritualistic quality, as in *Cantata*, *Canticum Sacrum*, *Threni*, and the *Double Canon for String Quartet* ("Raoul Dufy in Memoriam").[52] Canons can also have a playful, light-hearted quality, as Stravinsky revels in his compositional craft. That is true of many of the canons in *Agon* and in *Greeting Prelude* (Stravinsky's arrangement of "Happy

[47] This is the central contention of Glenn Watkins, "The Canon and Stravinsky's Late Style," in *Confronting Stravinsky*, ed. Pasler, 217–46.

[48] Canons have a similar expressive impact in the aria "Since it is not by merit" from *The Rake's Progress*, with its satire on the pedantry of "grave doctors" (i.e. scholars). Also, in *In Memoriam Dylan Thomas*, when the text refers to "grave men" (i.e. scholars, again), the texture becomes overtly canonic, including by augmentation. Of course, the entire piece is imitative and often canonic, but in this passage canon is foregrounded and marked as an expressive topic.

[49] Rows may be presented either in normal or in retrograde order – the analytical labels in Example 5.22 make no distinction.

[50] There are a few slight imperfections in the realization of the arrays, and these are probably best understood as serial mistakes. The B♮ in Oboe II in m. 123 should be B♭, and the wrong note is repeated in the canonic imitation in Oboe I in m. 126. (It is interesting to note that the correct B♭ is present when the same row of the array is stated in Oboe I in m. 120 and 123.) Similarly, the incorrect G♯ in Oboe II in m. 126 is confirmed by the canonic imitation in Oboe I in m. 129, but heard correctly as F♯ in mm. 119 and 122. These mistakes should probably be corrected in performance.

[51] This passage obviously raises the question of Stravinsky's alleged anti-semitism, which has been vigorously debated between Craft and Taruskin (see Chapter 1, footnote 12). The text was chosen by Craft, but the musical setting was obviously Stravinsky's alone.

[52] Perry, "A 'Requiem for the Requiem,'" argues that "In so much of Stravinsky's oeuvre, [canon- or fugue-like imitation] seems to serve as a kind of signpost which states, 'Ritual in Progress.'" He adduces the second movement of the *Symphony of Psalms* as an example.

Birthday to You"). It is this diversity of affective impact that makes it difficult to generalize about the expressive value of canons.

Once Stravinsky came to rely on his rotational arrays, he scarcely ever again employs an explicit canon. That is apparently because, as discussed in Chapter 3, the arrays themselves embody a kind of six-voice canon. Each row of the array describes the same succession of intervals as the row above it and below it, but beginning one note later or earlier. In that sense, canons have been sublimated into the arrays, so deeply, in fact, as to be virtually inaudible.

DIATONIC AND CHROMATIC

The contrast of diatonic and chromatic elements as an expressive device has its roots in Stravinsky's earliest music, and in the music of his Russian forebears. It is a means, in Taruskin's words, of "differentiating the human and fantastic worlds by contrast between diatonic and chromatic harmony, the chromatic/fantastic being of the third-related kind (whole-tone or octatonic) to play off against the fifth relations of the human music."[53] In the *Firebird*, for example, this dichotomy is maintained in the contrast between the fantastic world of Kaschey and the Firebird and the human world of Ivan and the Princesses. In *The Rake's Progress*, some forty years later, the same dichotomy is used to contrast the dark, painful, reality of Tom Rakewell's "progress" with the bright illusions of his dreams and his madness.[54] Of course the interaction between diatonic and chromatic (often octatonic) elements is a central feature of Stravinsky's first- and second-period music, one that is scarcely reducible to simple mapping of diatonic/chromatic onto human/fantastic. Nonetheless it remains a significant dramatic resource in the later period as well. Its symbolic resonance generally associates diatonic elements with simplicity, nostalgic dreams, a time before life begins and after it ends, a cessation of striving and seeking, a bright, undifferentiated blankness, and associates chromatic/serial elements with complexity, intricate reality, yearning and striving, a dark and richly differentiated life.

Agon was written over a period of several years during which Stravinsky's style was evolving rapidly. As a result, it is his most heterogeneous work. Its opening scene is essentially diatonic, but it quickly becomes more chromatic, then intermittently serial, and finally twelve-tone serial. It comes as a stunning shock, then,

---

[53] Taruskin, *Stravinsky and the Russian Traditions*, 275. Taruskin explores the diatonic–octatonic relationship in great detail, as does van den Toorn, *The Music of Igor Stravinsky*. That relationship is one component in the interpretation of Stravinsky's music offered in Albright, *Stravinsky: The Music Box and the Nightingale*: "This, I think, is what Stravinsky's music is 'about': the deep equivalence of the natural and the artificial. At the center of his dramatic imagination is the desire to juxtapose in a single work two competing systems – one of which seems natural, tasteful, approved alike by man and God, the other of which seems artificial, abhorrent, devilish – and to subvert these distinctions as best he can" (4).

[54] Chandler Carter, "Stravinsky's 'Special Sense': The Rhetorical Use of Tonality in The Rake's Progress," *Music Theory Spectrum* 19/1 (1997), 55–80. See also Chandler Carter, "The Rake's (and Stravinsky's) Progress," *The American Journal of Semiotics* 13/1–4 (1996), 183–225.

Example 5.22   A double canon satirizing the "learned style" in *A Sermon, a Narrative, and a Prayer*, mm. 113–29

Example 5.22 (cont.)

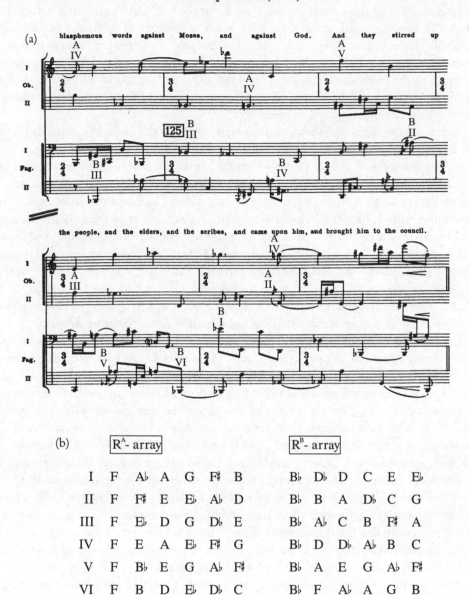

when at the end of the ballet, the twelve-tone discourse is suddenly interrupted by a recapitulation of the opening music (see Example 5.23). A twelve-tone structure gradually dissolves and fragments. As it does so, elements of the opening are recalled. Then, in a sharp shock of clarification, the opening music returns. Stravinsky has created subtle links between the two musics – the concluding notes of some of the twelve-tone series or fragments thereof are found within the chord in m. 553 that signals the return of the opening music – but the contrast between them is nonetheless striking and abrupt.[55]

I have already suggested the death-infected nature of the last scene, with its focus on F and its dramatic ending as the dancers turn their backs to the audience. Like life, the ballet ends as it begins, with a bright blankness. The sudden shift from the serial Four Trios to the diatonic Coda in Example 5.23 thus takes on symbolic weight. It seems to connote a movement from a dark, intricate dream of life to an awakening into death. As in *The Rake's Progress*, the moment of final clarification is also the moment of death – Tom achieves a transcendent vision of love and dies. His progress was a "foolish dream" in which he "hunted shadows, disdaining [Anne's] true love." As Nick Shadow remarks early in Tom's progress, "Sweet dreams, my master. / Dreams may lie, but dream. / For when you wake, you die" (Act I, Scene 2). In similar fashion, the recapitulation of the opening music in *Agon* is an awakening, a moment of clarification, which is also a symbolic death.

In "Full fadom five," one of the *Three Shakespeare Songs*, the serial emerges from the diatonic like coral and pearls from the formless ocean. As described in Chapter 2, this sense of emergence characterizes both Stravinsky's compositional process in writing the song and the musical unfolding in time of the song itself (see Example 2.3). Stravinsky's first sketch for the song was a simple E♭ minor scale, a diatonic source on which he planned to impose a serial shape. His second sketch was the melody for the first line of the text: "Full fadom five thy Father lies." This melody is written primarily with perfect fourths and fifths, suggesting the cyclic origins of the diatonic collection and retaining a sense of formlessness, of material awaiting its eventual shape. The third sketch is the melody for the next four lines of text. Here Stravinsky settles on the definitive shape of his E♭ minor scale, now a seven-note series subject to the usual transformations. The definitive serial idea thus emerges from the primordial diatonic collection, imagined first as a simple minor scale, then as a relatively undifferentiated cycle of fourths or fifths.

The use of a diatonic collection, with its cyclic, perfect-fifth-based structure, as an emblem of the formless or oceanic similarly characterizes the beginning of *The Flood*. Stravinsky describes the first eight measures of this work as his "Representation of Chaos":

---

[55] For a persuasive analytical account of the links between the serial and diatonic music, see Susannah Tucker, "Stravinsky and His Sketches: The Composing of *Agon* and Other Serial Works of the 1950s" (D.Phil. dissertation, Oxford University, 1992), 232–42.

Example 5.23 Twelve-tone music yields suddenly to the return of the diatonic music of the opening in *Agon*, mm. 539–67

Example 5.23 (*cont.*)

Example 5.23 (*cont.*)

My "Representation of Chaos" is not so different from Haydn's. But what does "Chaos" mean? "Things without forms"? "The negation of reality"? This is phraseomania – and suggests something beyond the limits of my poor imagination. How, please, does one represent chaos in music? I took certain elements, intervals, and chords made up of fourths. My "material of Chaos" is limited, however, and I couldn't make my chaos last very long. At the beginning of the Te Deum [which begins in measure 9], I begin my serial construction. Thus "chaos" may also be thought of as the antithesis of "serial."[56]

Stravinsky's representation of chaos begins with two twelve–note chords (the first page of his short score is reproduced as Example 5.24).[57] Above the score, Stravinsky has provided a derivation of each chord from a particular registration of the circle of fifths. To generate the first chord, Stravinsky writes a series of notes that begins on C1, then alternates ascending compound perfect fourths with descending perfect fifths: C1–F2–B♭1–E♭3–A♭2–C♯4–F♯3–B4–E4–A5–D5–G6. The chord simply arranges those notes in a single vertical stack. To generate the second chord, Stravinsky writes a series of notes that begins on C6, then alternates descending compound perfect fourths with ascending perfect fifths. The two generating series are thus mirror images of each other (or would be if Stravinsky had not violated the pattern by writing compound ascending perfect fifths from A to E and from D♭ to G♯). This slightly flawed second series of notes is arranged as a vertical stack to create the second of the chords.[58] Both chords thus have their origin in the primordial circle of fifths. The series for the work, and the music based on it, emerge from these chords like the created world from the formless void that preceded it. Of course, there is nothing chaotic or formless about these chords. Their symbolic value derives not from their internal structure but from their relationship with what follows. The real, created world is one of chromatic flux and movement. The world before time and when time has again ceased is static, symmetrical, and, in a deep sense, diatonic.

MELODIC-RHYTHMIC STUTTER

Stravinsky's melodic lines frequently involve the alternation of two pitches either a semitone or a whole-tone apart. Stravinsky himself described this as "two reiterated notes [which] are a melodic–rhythmic stutter characteristic of my speech from *Les Noces* to the *Concerto in D*, and earlier and later as well – a lifelong affliction, in fact."[59] This melodic gesture is so widespread that it is difficult to generalize about

---

[56] *Expositions and Developments*, 124–25. With regard to the brevity of this representation of chaos, it is interesting to note that in the premiere of this work, on television, mm. 1–8 were played twice!

[57] The relevant page of manuscript is reproduced in *Strawinsky: sein Nachlass, sein Bild*, 172.

[58] There is an apparent misprint in the published score: in m. 3, the top 2nd violin part should be E, not D, to conform to the intention embodied in the sketch.

[59] Stravinsky and Craft, *Themes and Episodes*, 58. Stravinsky makes this observation with reference to the alternation of the notes D and E in the vocal line of *Elegy for J. F. K.*, shown in Example 5.25. Van den Toorn, *The Music of Igor Stravinsky*, relates the "melodic–rhythmic stutter" to Stravinsky's persistent predilection for musical oscillations of all kinds: "The 'two reiterated notes' are ultimately a form of back-and-forth oscillation; and in this

Example 5.24   Twelve-note chords derived from stacks of fourths and fifths in
Stravinsky's short score for *The Flood*, opening measures

its affective impact. It is often associated with grief, or with a kind of somber mute-
ness in the face of death, but its specific meaning is always shaped by the local
musical context.

Stravinsky's own illustration of the stutter is the melodic alternation of D and E
in the vocal line of *Elegy for J. F. K.* to set the words, "The Heavens are silent"
(see Example 5.25).[60] Serially, the passage simultaneously unfolds P
(G♯–D–E–F♯–C–B–F–G–A–A♯–C♯–D♯, beginning in the voice, moving through
the chord in m. 15, and concluding in the alto clarinet) and R

respect they may indeed be found reaching into every crevice of melodic, rhythmic, formal, or pitch-relational
matter" (440). Norbert Jers, *Igor Strawinskys späte Zwölftonwerke (1958–1966)* (Regensburg: Gustav Bosse Verlag,
1976), 167–69, contains a useful list and discussion of melodic stutters in Stravinsky's late music.
[60] The poetic text is by W. H. Auden.

Example 5.25 A melodic stutter amid retrograde and inversional symmetry
(a) *Elegy for J. F. K.,* mm. 9–17
(b) serial structure

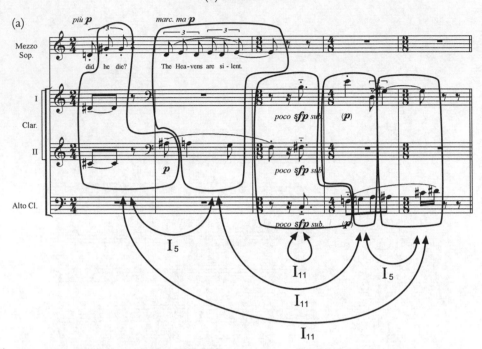

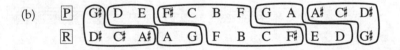

(D♯–C♯–A♯–A–G–F–B–C–F♯–E–D–G♯, beginning in the two clarinets, sharing the chord in measure 15, and concluding in the first clarinet). The passage as a whole thus is organized retrograde-symmetrically, enclosing the melodic stutter within a self-contained structural block.

The melodic D–E oscillation lies atop a progression of five harmonies. The retrograde-symmetry of the serial structure is apparent in the relations among the harmonies: the first and last harmonies have the same content, as do the second and fourth chords. But Stravinsky's musical articulation of these particular chords adds also an element of inversional symmetry that contributes to the passage's self-enclosure. All five chords are inversionally symmetrical at I_{11}, a relationship not directly related to the serial structure but independently created by the composer. I_{11} maps the first chord onto itself and thus onto the last chord, the second chord onto itself and thus onto the second-to-last chord, and the third chord onto itself.

The inversional symmetry of the progression as a whole and each of the chords that comprise it reinforces a feeling of self-enclosure.

Within this enclosed structure, the music conveys a sense of harmonic oscillation that mirrors the melodic stutter. The first chord slides smoothly to the second at I_5, with one of its whole steps, C♯–D♯, slipping up a semitone to D–E, and the other, G♯–A♯, slipping down a semitone to G–A. At the end of the passage, the whole-tones slip back into their original position as the fourth chord moves to the fifth. This harmonic oscillation, coming amid the strongly articulated retrograde and inversional symmetries, expressively colors the melodic stutter, imparting to it a sense of inescapable circularity, of forced acquiescence in an incomprehensible fate. Stravinsky's melodic stutters often share this or a similar expressive impact.

SILENCE

Stravinsky's disjunctive style of writing often makes use of silence to intensify the boundaries between sections, to create a sense of discontinuity. Most commonly, silences are used to articulate distinct blocks or sections and, as such, their structural and formal role seems to override any particular expressive impact. But occasionally a relatively long silence, of two or more beats at the prevailing tempo, will intrude within a block or section, and when it does, it gets marked with expressive meaning.

In an obvious, literal sense, sudden long silences simply convey a sense of cessation – what was active and alive is now still. But they can also suggest a pause before the abyss in a kind of rapt contemplation of eternal mysteries (see Example 5.26). In the passage from the *Cantata* (Example 5.26a), the voices end hopefully at Rehearsal No. 16 on a kind of C major. B♮ enriches the harmony and E♮ substitutes for E♭ in what sounds like a bright, Picardy-third ending to a predominantly C minor movement.[61] After a pause of two beats, however, the instruments conclude with a melancholy, minor-mode rebuttal, punctuated by pauses. The silences signal a shift from light to darkness. In the passage from *Abraham and Isaac* (Example 5.26b), God has just told Abraham to sacrifice Isaac. The silence in m. 46 suggests Abraham's mute, horrified contemplation of God's implacable and incomprehensible command.

CODA

Many of Stravinsky's late works (including *Threni, A Sermon, a Narrative, and a Prayer, Variations,* and *Introitus*) end with slow, solemn chorales. In a few late works, however, he returns to an expressive topic that was more characteristic of earlier

---

[61] I am imagining that C is retained as a harmonic root from the music before Rehearsal No. 15. Of course the actual harmony in the three measures before Rehearsal No. 16 is E minor, suggesting a mingling of C major and E minor that is familiar from the first movement of the *Symphony in C*. My thanks to Lynne Rogers for this observation.

Example 5.26   Expressive silence
(a) *Cantata*, "Westron wind," last ten measures

Example 5.26 (*cont.*)
(b) *Abraham and Isaac*, mm. 41–47

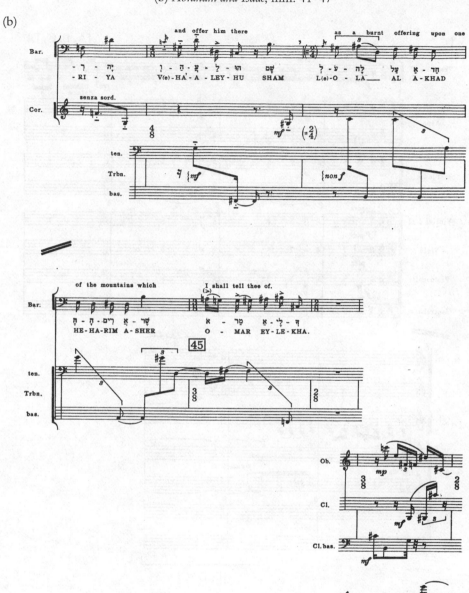

Example 5.27 An expressive coda in *Agon*
(a) opening, mm. 1–7

Example 5.27 (*cont.*)
(b) the same music fragmented and elongated in the
conclusion of the Pas-de-Quatre, mm. 56–60

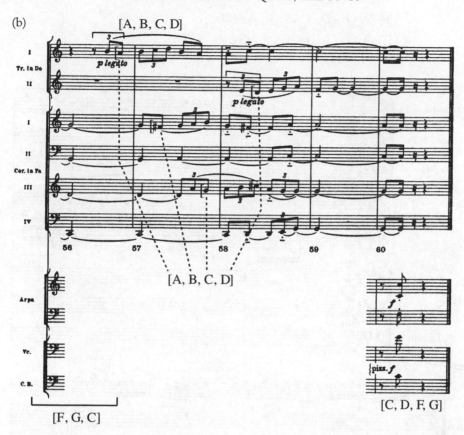

ones, namely the coda. In a Stravinskian coda, time seems almost to stop. Rhythmic activity suddenly slows almost to the point of cessation. A principal motive from earlier in the piece is repeated in a radically augmented and fragmented form. In the rapturous conclusions of *Les Noces*, *Symphony in C*, *Symphony of Psalms*, and *The Fairy's Kiss*, we gain a glimpse of the infinite, of a time beyond time.[62]

Codas of this kind, when they do occur in the late music, tend to be relatively compressed, as in *Agon* (see Example 5.27). In the Pas-de-Quatre that begins the ballet, the opening motive, consisting of [A, B, C, D], is heard in a rhythmically active fanfare and ends on a sustained chord, [F, G, C] (Example 5.27a). In the coda

---

[62] With reference to the Postlude to the *Requiem Canticles*, discussed later in this chapter, Pierre Suvchinsky comments: "The Postlude is one of those endings, like that of *Les Noces*, which do not end, or end in infinity. And this is where Stravinsky adds a dimension to Western music, beyond the classical composers. Think, for comparison, of the ending of a Beethoven or Brahms symphony, which simply thumps more loudly with each repeat" (quoted in *Chronicle*, 329).

Example 5.28   Diatonic and A–centered: Septet, first movement, mm. 1–7

Example 5.28 (*cont.*)

to the movement, which also returns as the conclusion of the entire ballet, the motive is heard again with a sustained articulation and in rhythmic augmentation. It is presented in counterpoint with modified transpositions of itself which, taken together, spell out an enlarged version. The coda begins with the sustained chord [F, G, C] and ends with the same chord, now with D added (Example 5.27b). On a very small scale, then, this coda captures a sense of motivic recall and culmination amid sudden slowing of rhythmic motion. Here, as in all of Stravinsky's codas, the sudden cessation of motion in time and space creates a sense of opening out into the infinite, a glimpse of a transcendent realm.

SEPTET, FIRST MOVEMENT

The first movement of the Septet engages many of the expressive topics discussed thus far. As a result, it can be understood virtually in its entirety in dramatic, expressive terms. It begins with the fanfare shown in Example 5.28. The passage is based, in part, on a six-note series, A–E–D–C–B–A, with C♯ occasionally either substituted for the C♮ or added at the end. The series is short and diatonic, both typical of Stravinsky's series at this time. It is heard only in its original, untransposed form and in its inversion beginning on A, which preserves the same first three notes. The

Example 5.29 A diatonic, A-centered coda: Septet, first movement, final seven
measures

effect of the contrapuntal intertwining of P- and I-forms in various rhythmic values
and at various rhythmic distances is a kind of diatonic wash, harmonically not well
defined, but clearly centered on A.

The movement concludes with an A-centered coda, in which the series is heard
in a slow-moving canon with itself (see Example 5.29). At the same time, the cello
plays a portion of the series in inversion: (A)–D–E–F–G, with F♮ and G♮ substituting for F♯ and G♯.[63] The movement is thus framed by A-centered moments, very
much in the manner of *The Rake's Progress*. As in that work, there is a strong suggestion of departure from and return to a place apart from the flux and stress of the
quotidian. The sense of transcendence is particularly pronounced in the Septet
coda, which is also entirely diatonic – white notes only for its first five measures,
then with F♯ and C♯ for the final two. In this way, Stravinsky suggests a return to the
primordial time before time of *The Flood* and "Full fadom five."

The Septet coda also creates a sense of cessation of motion by sharply slowing the

---

[63] This canonic design, including the inversion in the cello, is apparent in Stravinsky's compositional sketch for this
passage, transcribed in Christoph Neidhofer, "An Approach to Interrelating Counterpoint and Serialism in the
Music of Igor Stravinsky, Focusing on the Principal Diatonic Works of his Transitional Period" (Ph.D. dissertation, Harvard University, 1999), Example 6.27.

rate of rhythmic and contrapuntal activity and by allowing the principal motive to fragment and dissolve amid slow-moving harmonies. It thus strongly recalls the rapturous, transcendent conclusions of works like *Les Noces*, *Symphony in C*, and *The Fairy's Kiss*. In all of these works, primary motivic material is recalled as though from a great distance, from a world beyond this one.

Before the A-centered world can be regained, however, this movement undergoes a significant tonal journey, the principal stages of which are traced in Example 5.30. After the A-centered opening fanfare, the music shifts first to E minor (Rehearsal No. 1), then to D major (Rehearsal No. 3). That motion, A–E–D, composes-out the first three notes of the series.[64] In expressive terms, the music engages a progression from E minor to D major so frequently evoked in Stravinsky's music as an emblem of death and the acceptance of death. After emerging on D, the music enters a developmental thicket of canons, culminating in an intensive stretto (Rehearsal No. 8) in which each voice enters a perfect fifth higher than the previous. The canons are abruptly terminated by loud chords with C♯ in the bass (before Rehearsal No. 9). These chords effectively interrupt the musical journey in both tonal and expressive terms. Tonally, over the large span, the music has traversed the first four notes of the series, with the interruptive C♯ substituting for C♮. Expressively, the journey has led to a dense, contrapuntal forest from which there is no obvious exit. At this point, the journey is interrupted, and recommenced from the beginning.

The second half of the movement is a modified recapitulation of the first. The A-centered fanfare returns just as in the opening (Rehearsal No. 9), and is followed as before by E minor music (Rehearsal No. 10).[65] But after only a single measure, the E minor music is abruptly transposed down a whole-tone to D, and the music that follows is thus heard a whole-tone lower than in the first half of the piece.[66] This transposition enables a complete composing-out of the series by pushing the music a step farther along the serial path. The second half of the movement now traces a path from A (Rehearsal No. 9), through E (Rehearsal No. 10), D (one measure after Rehearsal No. 10), C (Rehearsal No. 12 – this is the music that was heard in D in the first half of the piece), B (Rehearsal No. 13), to a concluding return to A (Rehearsal No. 14, the coda). Before the B is reached, there is a sudden silence, a gap in the discourse that separates the earlier stages of the journey from its conclusion. Then, as the B is attained, the music pauses on a brief, contemplative stutter, signaling an acceptance of the imminent completion of the journey. When the journey is completed, with the opening music transformed into a rapturous

[64] This much of the musical journey is discussed in Chapter 3. Craft identifies the large-scale succession as "in A," then "the minor dominant," then the "subdominant." He does not relate this succession to the series, but does confirm my identification of the relevant tonal centers. See "Analyses par Robert Craft," in *Avec Stravinsky*, 143–44.

[65] At this point, Stravinsky writes a key signature of three naturals, canceling the three sharps of the previous A major. This is the last key signature in all of his music.

[66] This kind of "transposed repetition" as a generator of form is discussed in Chapter 3 and in my "A Strategy of Large-Scale Organization in the Late Music of Stravinsky," *Integral* 11 (1999), 1–36.

Example 5.30   Topical stages in a musical journey: Septet, first movement

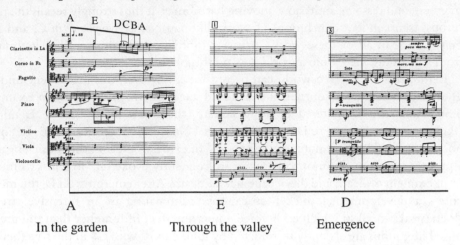

A   E   D

In the garden   Through the valley   Emergence

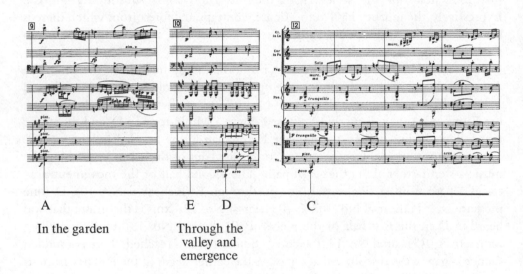

A   E   D   C

In the garden   Through the
                     valley and
                     emergence

Example 5.30 (*cont.*)

A thicket of canons   Journey interrupted

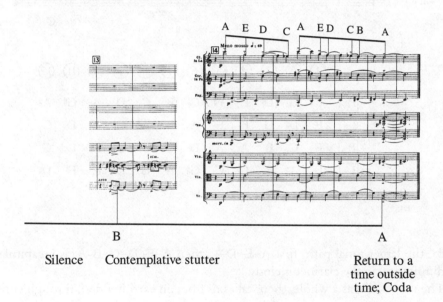

Silence   Contemplative stutter   Return to a
                                                   time outside
                                                   time; Coda

Example 5.31 An F-centered chorale with tolling bells: *Requiem Canticles*, Postlude, mm. 289–92

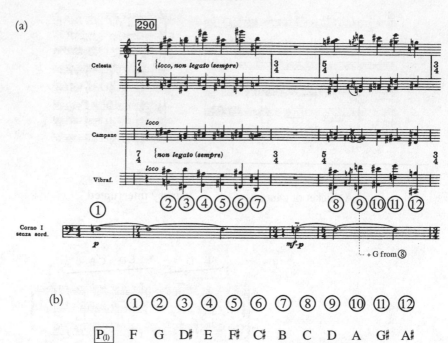

coda, the larger tonal path, first A–E–D–C then A–E–D–C–B–A, is recapitulated in diminution in the clarinet melody.[67]

The movement as a whole, then, takes us from an earthly Eden, through contact with death and an acceptance of death, eventually regaining our starting point, but now with a sense of ecstatic transcendence. It can be thought of as a compressed re-enactment of Tom Rakewell's "progress" from the country garden to the transcendent vision achieved in the madhouse. And, from a different point of view, it may also be taken as a musical reflection of Stravinsky's own musical progress, from the safe, cloistered environment of his neoclassicism, through a disorienting crisis, to a new musical language, one that both embodies and transcends what came before: a perilous voyage and a safe arrival that is both a return and a transcendence.

---

[67] In addition to whatever expressive meanings one might attach to this progression, it certainly contributes to a sense that Stravinsky is interested in purposeful, large-scale motions that cut across the sectional boundaries.

REQUIEM CANTICLES, POSTLUDE

The final movement, the Postlude, of the *Requiem Canticles* is among Stravinsky's most moving and effective works. Its power derives in part from its biographical circumstances – it concludes his last major piece, a requiem that he evidently intended as his own.[68] It is also immensely effective in musical terms, drawing on many expressive topics and using them in mutually reinforcing ways.[69]

The movement consists of two distinct and separately evolving musical strands. The first involves three twelve-chord chorales, scored for celeste, campane (tubular bells), and vibraphone. The second involves five widely spaced chords presented before, between, and after the chorales. These chords, scored for flutes, piano, harp, and French horn, have been referred to as "chords of death."[70] The two strands are separated by silences, the longest and most profoundly expressive he ever wrote.

Each of the chorales is based on a four-part array – Example 5.31 contains the first of them. Instead of four different forms of a single series, as in Stravinsky's standard four-part array, this array consists of the P and I forms of the two different series used in *Requiem Canticles*.[71] The chords differ accordingly – now each of the chords is symmetrical around F, which is the unique pitch-class of the first chord. Centricity on F, implicit in the internal structure of each of the chords, is confirmed by many other aspects of the music, and strongly evokes that death-charged topic. The instrumentation of the chords, for celeste, campane, and vibraphone,

---

[68] Only the slight, lovely *The Owl and the Pussycat* comes later. The personal nature of the *Requiem Canticles* is confirmed by Vera Stravinsky's comment to Craft: "*He* and *we* knew he was writing it for himself" (quoted in *Chronicle*, 376–77). The work was also designed as a memorial to friends recently deceased: "The sketch book of the *Requiem Canticles* is also a necrology of friends who died during its composition. The composer once referred to these pasted-in obituaries as a 'practical commentary.' Each movement seems to relate to an individual death, and though Stravinsky denies that it really does, the framing of his musical thoughts by the graves of friends (that touching cross for Giacometti) exposes an almost unbearably personal glimpse of his mind" (*Bravo, Stravinsky*, 48; reprinted in *Chronicle*, 309).

[69] For other, related interpretations of the expressive meaning of the Requiem Postlude, see Perry, "A 'Requiem for the Requiem,'" 237–257; and Andriessen and Schönberger, *The Apollonian Clockwork: On Stravinsky*.

[70] The term "chord of death" comes from Craft, in his description of a performance of the *Requiem Canticles* at Stravinsky's own funeral. He describes the structure of the Postlude as "the chord of Death, followed by silence, the tolling of bells, and again silence, all thrice repeated, then the three final chords of Death alone" (*Chronicle*, 415).

[71] Taruskin describes the unusual four-part arrays in the Postlude and the more standard one in the Interlude of *Requiem Canticles* in "The Traditions Revisited: Stravinsky's Requiem Canticles as Russian Music," in *Music Theory and the Exploration of the Past*, ed. Christopher Hatch and David W. Bernstein (Chicago: University of Chicago Press, 1993), 525–50; and *Stravinsky and the Russian Traditions*, 1648–74. See also Karen Lesley Grylls, "The Aggregate Re-ordered: A Paradigm for Stravinsky's 'Requiem Canticles'" (Ph.D. dissertation, University of Washington, 1993) and Jeffrey Kresky, "A Study in Analysis" (Ph.D. dissertation, Princeton University, 1974). Series 1, F–G–D♯–E–F♯–C♯–B–C–D–A–G♯–A♯, is used in the Exaudi, Rex Tremendae, and Lacrimosa movements. Series 2, F–C–B–A–A♯–D–C♯ D♯–G♯–F♯–E–G, is used in the Prelude, Dies Irae, Tuba Mirum, and Libera Me movements. The two series are used together in the Interlude and Postlude. The relationship between the two series is explored in Taruskin, "The Traditions Revisited" and *Stravinsky and the Russian Traditions*; and Claudio Spies, "Some Notes on Stravinsky's Requiem Settings," *Perspectives of New Music* 5/2 (1967), 98–123; reprinted in *Perspectives on Schoenberg and Stravinsky*, ed. Benjamin Boretz and Edward Cone (Princeton: Princeton University Press, 1968), 223–50.

Example 5.32 Moving toward an F-centered diatonicism
in the *Requiem Canticles*, Postlude
(a) harmonic summary of the five "Chords of Death"

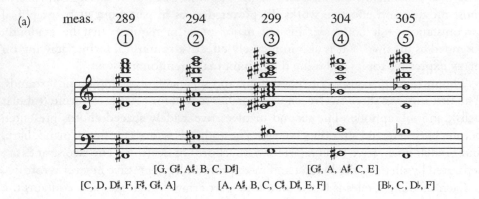

imparts an unmistakable bell-like aura to the chorale. In this way, Stravinsky vividly conjoins these three musical symbols of the solemn and the sacred – F-centricity, chorale, and bells – into what was, for him, the ultimate chordal dirge.

The "chords of death" are derived from the rotational arrays, Stravinsky's other source of twelve-tone chorale harmonies. To create the "chords of death," Stravinsky used the rotational arrays in a way that is unique to this piece. It is remarkable that in the last movement of his last major work, Stravinsky was still innovating, still looking for new twelve-tone combinations and, more specifically, for new ways of writing twelve-tone chords.

Stravinsky combines verticals from six different rotational arrays to create chords that range in size from four to eight notes (see Example 5.32).[72] Chord 1 combines the final verticals of the R^B- and IR^B-arrays of Series 1. The structure of these arrays guarantees that these two verticals are related to each other by inversion. As a result, Chord 1 can be understood as a combination of two inversionally related forms of sc(01367), or could have been understood in that way had Stravinsky not omitted the B. In similar fashion, Chord 2 combines the last verticals from the P^B- and I^B-arrays of Series 2. Were it not for the omission of D, this chord could be understood as a combination of two inversionally related forms of sc(01348). Chord 3 combines the last vertical of P^A (with B conjoined) with the last vertical of I^B (with F substituting for F♯). This vertical, with the same substitution, comprises Chord 5 in its entirety. Chord 4 would have been of the same type as Chord 5 if it had not adjoined a G♯, and if Chord 5 had not substituted F for F♯. As it is, however, Chord 4 is structurally more similar to Chord 2 than to Chord 5.

---

[72] My serial analysis is based on Stravinsky's compositional sketches, which are reprinted and discussed in Grylls, "The Aggregate Re-ordered: A Paradigm for Stravinsky's 'Requiem Canticles,'" 90–95. The serial derivation proposed in Taruskin, "The Traditions Revisited" and *Stravinsky and the Russian Traditions*, is inauthentic. Craft's explanation (in *A Stravinsky Scrapbook*, 132; reprinted in *Selected Correspondence*, vol. II, 471), derided by Taruskin as "unaccountably inaccurate and irrelevant," is partly correct.

Example 5.32 (cont.)
(b) serial derivation in the verticals of selected rotational arrays

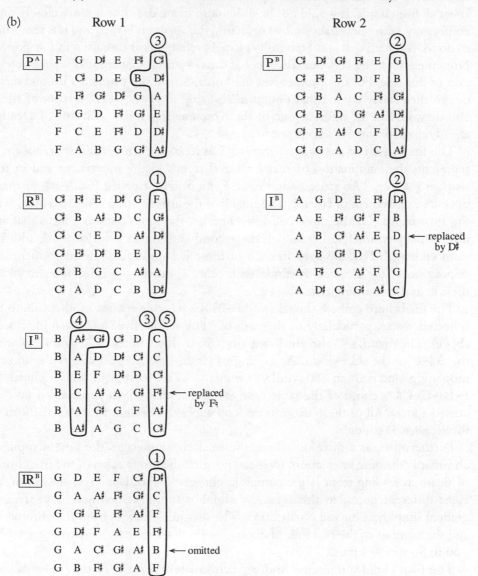

Stravinsky's apparent intention was to create chords with certain kinds of internal symmetries and mutual relationships. But the deviations from the apparent plan affect all five chords. It would not be difficult to bring the chords more closely into conformity with the serial plan by correcting the apparent errors, and it is tempting to do so. After all, that was Stravinsky's usual preference, as discussed in Chapter 2. Nonetheless it is the very pervasiveness of the deviations that argues for their retention in this case. For this progression of chords, Stravinsky planned a unique serial design then freely altered that design in realizing it. A "correct" version of these chords would be of interest, but in their present form, the "Chords of Death" already make persuasive and expressive sense.

The final chord of the progression has F as its bass. That definitive arrival on F represents the culmination of many musical trends in the movement and in the work as a whole.[73] An arpeggiation of an F minor triad (spelled F–G♯–B♯–F) spans the entire movement in Horn I. The final F of the arpeggiation is the bass-note F of the final chord. Of the three bell-like chorales, the first contains chords that are inversionally symmetrical around F, the second ends on an F major triad, and the third ends with F in the bass. In each of these ways, the final chord confirms an association of the *Requiem* Postlude with other F-inflected works, and thus with their shared immersion in death.

The final chord embeds the trichord F–B♭–C, which provides another link to F-inflected works, particularly to the ends of "Full fadom five" and *Agon* (discussed above). The dyad B♭–C also recalls the first two melodic notes of *Requiem Canticles*, the A♯–C in the solo violin. According to Craft, this pair of notes is a common mourning interval in Stravinsky's music.[74] The complete final chord is F–B♭–C–C♯, a chord of the same type as the one that concludes *Introitus* (as discussed above). All of these associations lend expressive weight to the final chord of the *Requiem* Postlude.

Furthermore, as a diatonic subset, the final chord engages the potent topic of chromatic/diatonic interaction. One can imagine the progression of the five chords of death as leading from large, complex, chromatic chords of five, six, seven, or eight different notes, to this relatively simple diatonic conclusion, a process of gradual simplification and clarification. The diatonic emerges from the chromatic, and the contrast of the two links the *Requiem* Postlude to that rich expressive tradition in Stravinsky's music.

The final chord summarizes and crystallizes latent features of the previous four (see Example 5.33). Example 5.33a traces occurrences of triads and segments of the

[73] See Kresky, "A Study in Analysis."

[74] "On April 17 [1968], he began to compose an extra instrumental prelude to the *Requiem Canticles*, for a performance of the work in memory of Dr. Martin Luther King. He started with the first two notes of the violin solo in the Canticles, the interval that appears in so much of his mourning music and the same notes that he played on the piano when he touched the instrument for the first time after his illness. The prelude was abandoned when he saw that it could not be completed in time for the May 2 performance date" (*Chronicle*, 346). A♯–C appears frequently in *Requiem Canticles* and *Elegy for J. F. K.* It is also a recurring segment in the serial charts for *Abraham and Isaac*, but not used as a melodic stutter or an obvious emblem of mourning in that work. It is unclear which other works Craft may have had in mind.

Example 5.33 Diatonic emergence in *Requiem Canticles*, Postlude, "Chords of Death"
(a) triads and segments of the 5- or 7-cycles as registral segments
(b) the fifth chord embedded in the third and, in inversion, in the second
(c) registral segments that consist of a triad-plus-one-note

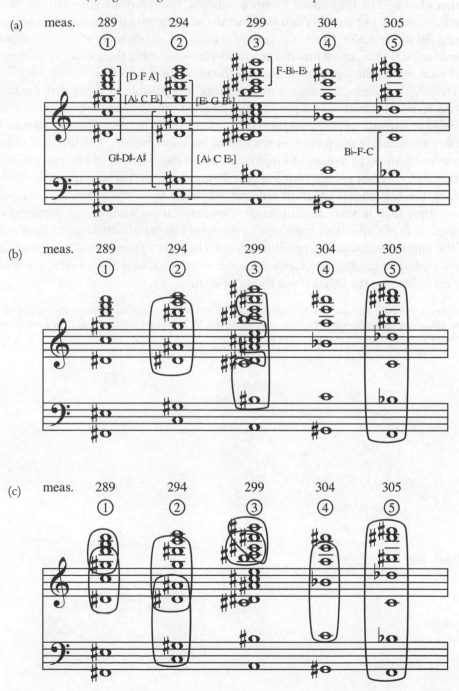

circle of fourths or fifths occurring as registral segments through the five chords.
The final chord, which can be understood as a combination of a triad, Bb–Db–F,
with a segment of the circle of fourths or fifths, F–Bb–C, thus has its origins in the
earlier chords. The final chord occurs as a literal, though nonsegmental, subset of
the third chord and an inversion of it occurs as a segmental subset of the second
chord (Example 5.33b). If the final chord is understood not merely as a representative of sc(0237) but, more broadly, as a triad–plus–one–note, then many echoes may
be found among the segmental subsets of the previous chords (Example 5.33c).[75]

Despite these links, however, I do not think it is possible to argue that the final
chord is the culmination of a purposeful, directed, predictable motion. Rather, in
its relative sparsity, its conspicuous triadic, circle-of-fifths, and diatonic aspects, it
creates a reasonably sharp contrast with what has come before. The links are there,
but overshadowed by a sense of simplification and clarification, of emerging from a
darkly rich chromatic night into a bright diatonic day. In that way, the progression
among the five chords of death reflects and draws upon the chromatic/diatonic
opposition that is such an important expressive topic throughout Stravinsky's
oeuvre. It draws upon that topic also in the symbolic weight attached to each pole
of the chromatic/diatonic opposition. As in *The Rake's Progress* and *Agon*, the diatonic ending of the *Requiem Canticles* comes as an awakening from a rich, complex
dream of life into the bright, hard reality of death.

[75] Kresky, "A Study in Analysis," identifies sc(0237) and sc(0137) as what he calls an "X-shape" and demonstrates
its role in shaping this five-chord progression. In Example 5.33, I broaden his definition of X-shape to include
any set-class that contains a major or minor triad as a subset.

LIST OF STRAVINSKY'S LATE WORKS

(with dates of composition)

1951–52	*Cantata*
1952–53	Septet
1954	*Three Songs from William Shakespeare*
1954	*In Memoriam Dylan Thomas*
1955	*Canticum Sacrum*
1953–57	*Agon*
1957–58	*Threni*
1958–59	*Movements*
1959	*Epitaphium*
1959	*Double Canon*
1960–61	*A Sermon, a Narrative, and a Prayer*
1961–62	*The Flood*
1962	*Anthem*
1962–63	*Abraham and Isaac*
1963–64	*Variations*
1964	*Elegy for J. F. K.*
1964	*Fanfare for a New Theater*
1965	*Introitus*
1965–66	*Requiem Canticles*
1966	*The Owl and the Pussycat*

BIBLIOGRAPHY

Agawu, Kofi, "Stravinsky's Mass and Stravinsky Analysis," *Music Theory Spectrum* 11/2 (1989), 139–63.

Albright, Daniel, *Stravinsky: The Music Box and the Nightingale* (New York: Gordon & Breach, 1989).

Alm, Irene, "Stravinsky, Balanchine, and *Agon*: An Analysis Based on the Collaborative Process," *Journal of Musicology* 7/2 (1989), 254–69.

Andriessen, Louis and Schönberger, Elmer, *The Apollonian Clockwork: On Stravinsky*, trans. Jeff Hamburg (Oxford: Oxford University Press, 1989).

Antokoletz, Elliott, "Interval Cycles in Stravinsky's Early Ballets," *Journal of the American Musicological Society* 39 (1986), 578–614.

Babbitt, Milton, "Some Aspects of Twelve-Tone Composition," *The Score and I.M.A. Magazine* 12 (1955), 53–61.

"Remarks on the Recent Stravinsky," *Perspectives of New Music* 2/2 (1964), 35–55; reprinted in *Perspectives on Schoenberg and Stravinsky*, ed. Benjamin Boretz and Edward Cone (Princeton: Princeton University Press, 1968; reprint edn. New York: Norton, 1972), 165–85.

"Since Schoenberg," *Perspectives of New Music* 12 (1973), 3–28.

"Order, Symmetry, and Centricity in Late Stravinsky," in *Confronting Stravinsky*, ed. Jann Pasler (Berkeley: University of California Press, 1986), 247–61.

"Stravinsky's Verticals and Schoenberg's Diagonals: A Twist of Fate," in *Stravinsky Retrospectives*, ed. Elham Haimo and Paul Johnson (Lincoln, Nebr.: University of Nebraska Press, 1987).

Words About Music, ed. Stephen Dembski and Joseph N. Straus (Madison: University of Wisconsin Press, 1987).

Bailey, Kathryn, "The Craft/Stravinsky Conversation Books: Bibliography and Commentary," *Studies in Music (Ontario)* 3 (1978), 48–71.

The Twelve-Note Music of Anton Webern (Cambridge: Cambridge University Press, 1991).

Berger, Arthur, "Problems of Pitch Organization in Stravinsky," *Perspectives of New Music* 2/1 (1963), 11–42; reprinted in *Perspectives on Schoenberg and Stravinsky*, ed. Benjamin Boretz and Edward Cone (Princeton: Princeton University Press, 1968), 123–55.

Boulez, Pierre, *Boulez on Music Today*, trans. S. Bradshaw and R. R. Bennett (London: Faber & Faber, 1971).

Pierre Boulez: Conversations with Célestin Deliège, no translator named (London: Eulenburg Books, 1976).

"Stravinsky: Style or Idea? In Praise of Amnesia," in *Orientations: Collected Writing of Pierre Boulez*, ed. Jean-Jacques Nattiez, trans. Martin Cooper (London: Faber and Faber, 1986), 349–59.

"The Stravinsky–Webern Conjunction," in *Orientations: Collected Writing of Pierre Boulez*, ed. Jean-Jacques Nattiez, trans. Martin Cooper (London: Faber and Faber, 1986), 364–69; originally published as "La Conjunction Stravinsky/Webern," sleeve note for the recording by Boulez, Vega C30 A 120.

"Stravinsky Remains," in *Stocktakings from an Apprenticeship*, ed. Paule Thevenin, trans. Stephen Walsh (Oxford: Clarendon Press, 1991), 55–110.

"Trajectories – Ravel, Stravinsky, Schoenberg," in *Stocktakings from an Apprenticeship*, ed. Paule Thevenin, trans. Stephen Walsh (Oxford: Clarendon Press, 1991), 188–205.

Boykan, Martin, "Neoclassicism and Late Stravinsky," *Perspectives of New Music* 1/2 (1963), 155–69.

Brindle, Reginald Smith, *Serial Composition* (Oxford: Oxford University Press, 1966).

Brody, Martin, "'Music for the Masses': Milton Babbitt's Cold War Music Theory," *Musical Quarterly* 77 (1993), 161–92.

Burkhart, Charles, "Stravinsky's Revolving Canon," *Music Review* 29/3 (1968), 161–64.

Carter, Chandler, "The Rake's (and Stravinsky's) Progress," *The American Journal of Semiotics* 13/1–4 (1996), 183–225.

"Stravinsky's 'Special Sense': The Rhetorical Use of Tonality in *The Rake's Progress*," *Music Theory Spectrum* 19/1 (1997), 55–80.

Clifton, Thomas, "Types of Symmetrical Relations in Stravinsky's 'A Sermon, a Narrative, and a Prayer,'" *Perspectives of New Music* 9/1 (1970), 96–112.

Cohn, Richard, "Bartók's Octatonic Strategies: A Motivic Approach," *Journal of the American Musicological Society* 44 (1991), 262–300.

"Maximally Smooth Cycles, Hexatonic Systems, and the Analysis of Late-Romantic Triadic Progressions," *Music Analysis* 15/1 (1996), 9–40.

"Neo-Riemannian Operations, Parsimonious Trichords, and Their *Tonnetz* Representations," *Journal of Music Theory* 41/1 (1997), 1–66.

Cone, Edward, "Stravinsky: The Progress of a Method," *Perspectives of New Music* 1/1 (1962), 18–26; reprinted in *Perspectives on Schoenberg and Stravinsky*, ed. Benjamin Boretz and Edward T. Cone (Princeton: Princeton University Press, 1968), 156–64.

"The Uses of Convention: Stravinsky and his Models," *Musical Quarterly* 48/3 (1962), 287–99; reprinted in *Stravinsky: A New Appraisal of his Work*, ed. Paul Henry Lang (New York: Norton, 1963).

"Editorial Responsibility and Schoenberg's Troublesome 'Misprints,'" *Perspectives of New Music* 11/1 (1972), 65–75.

Craft, Robert, "Anton Webern," *The Score* 13 (1955), 9–22.

"Reihenkompositionen: Vom 'Septett' zum 'Agon,'" *Musik der Zeit* 12 (1955), 43–54.

"A Personal Preface," *The Score* 20 (1957), 7–13.

Avec Stravinsky (Monaco: Editions du Rocher, 1958).

Bravo Stravinsky, photographs by Arnold Newman, text by Robert Craft (Cleveland: World Publishing Corp, 1967).

Stravinsky: Chronicle of a Friendship 1948–1971 (New York: Knopf, 1972; revised and expanded edn. Nashville: Vanderbilt University Press, 1994).

Prejudices in Disguise (New York: Alfred A. Knopf, 1974).

"Boulez in the Lemon and Limelight," in *Prejudices in Disguise*, 207–13.

"Stravinsky Pre-Centenary," *Perspectives of New Music* 19/1–2 (1980–81), 464–77.

"On a Misunderstood Collaboration: Assisting Stravinsky," *The Atlantic Monthly* (December 1982), 68; reprinted as "Influence or Assistance?" in *Present Perspectives: Critical Writings* (New York: Alfred A. Knopf, 1984), 246–64; reprinted again in *Stravinsky: Glimpses of a Life* (New York: St. Martin's Press, 1992), 33–51.

"Stravinsky: Letters to Pierre Boulez," *The Musical Times* 123 (1982), 396–402; revised and expanded in *Selected Correspondence*, vol. II, 347–63.

"Roland-Manuel and *La Poétique Musicale*," in Craft, ed., *Selected Correspondence*, vol. II, 503–17.

"Walter Nouvel and *Chroniques de ma vie*," in Craft, ed., *Selected Correspondence*, vol. II, 487–502.

"Conversations with Stravinsky," in *Present Perspectives: Critical Writings* (New York: Alfred A. Knopf, 1984), 265–75; reprinted in *Stravinsky: Glimpses of a Life* (New York: St. Martin's Press, 1992), 61–70.

"Pluralistic Stravinsky," in *Present Perspectives: Critical Writings* (New York: Alfred A. Knopf, 1984), 293–312.

"Stravinsky: A Centenary View," in *Present Perspectives: Critical Writings* (New York: Alfred A. Knopf, 1984), 215–31.

Dearest Babushkin: Selected Letters and Diaries of Vera and Igor Stravinsky (New York: Thames & Hudson, 1985).

"Jews and Geniuses," *New York Review of Books*, 16 February 1989, 35–37; reprinted in *Small Craft Advisories* (New York: Thames & Hudson, 1989), 274–81.

Small Craft Advisories (New York: Thames & Hudson, 1989).

Stravinsky: Glimpses of a Life (New York: St. Martin's Press, 1992).

"The Relevance and Problems of Biography," in *Stravinsky: Glimpses of a Life* (New York: St. Martin's Press, 1992), 276–90.

Craft, Robert, ed. *A Stravinsky Scrapbook* (London: Thames & Hudson, 1983).

Stravinsky: Selected Correspondence, 3 vols. (New York: Alfred A. Knopf, 1982–85).

Craft, Robert and Stravinsky, Vera, *Stravinsky in Pictures and Documents* (New York: Simon and Schuster, 1978).

Cross, Jonathan, *The Stravinsky Legacy* (Cambridge: Cambridge University Press, 1998).

Danuser, H., ed., *Igor Strawinsky: Trois pièces pour quatuor à cordes: Skizzen, Fassungen, Dokumente, Essays* (Winterthur: Amadeus, 1994).

Del Mar, Norman, *Orchestral Variations* (London: Eulenburg, 1981).

Druskin, Mikhail, *Igor Stravinsky: His Personality, Works, and Views*, trans. Martin Cooper (Cambridge: Cambridge University Press, 1983).

Dubiel, Joseph, "Three Essays on Milton Babbitt," Part 1: *Perspectives of New Music* 28/2 (1990), 216–61; Part 2: *Perspectives of New Music* 29/1 (1991), 90–123, Part 3: *Perspectives of New Music* 30/1 (1992), 82–131.

Eimert, Herbert, *Lehrbuch der Zwölftontechnik* (Wiesbaden: Breitkopf & Härtel, 1954).

"Die Drei Shakespeare-Lieder (1953)," *Musik der Zeit* 12 (1955), 35–38.

Forte, Allen, *The Harmonic Organization of The Rite of Spring* (New Haven: Yale University Press, 1978).

"Harmonic Syntax and Voice Leading in Stravinsky's Early Music," in *Confronting Stravinsky*, ed. Jann Pasler (Berkeley: University of California Press, 1986).

The Atonal Music of Anton Webern (New Haven: Yale University Press, 1998).

Gable, David, "Boulez's Two Cultures: The Post-War European Synthesis and Tradition," *Journal of the American Musicological Society* 43/3 (1990), 426–56.

Gauldin, Robert and Benson, Warren, "Structure and Numerology in Stravinsky's *In Memoriam Dylan Thomas*," *Perspectives of New Music* 23/2 (1985), 166–85.

Gerhard, Roberto, "Twelve-Note Technique in Stravinsky," *The Score* 20 (1957), 38–43.

"Die Reihentechnik des Diatonikers," *Musik der Zeit* 1 (1958), 18–22.

Graybill, Roger, "Intervallic Transformation and Closure in the Music of Stravinsky," *Theory and Practice* 14/15 (1989/90), 13–34.

Grylls, Karen Lesley, "The Aggregate Re-ordered: A Paradigm for Stravinsky's 'Requiem Canticles'" (Ph.D. dissertation, University of Washington, 1993).

Haimo, Ethan, "Editing Schoenberg's Twelve-Tone Music," *Journal of the Arnold Schoenberg Institute* 8/2 (1984), 141–57.

Schoenberg's Serial Odyssey: The Evolution of His Twelve-Tone Method, 1914–1928 (London: Oxford University Press, 1990).

Haimo, Ethan and Johnson, Paul, "Isomorphic Partitioning and Schoenberg's Fourth String Quartet," *Journal of Music Theory* 28/1 (1984), 47–72.

Hasty, Christopher, "On the Problem of Succession and Continuity in Twentieth-Century Music," *Music Theory Spectrum* 8 (1986), 58–74.

"Phrase Formation in Post-Tonal Music," *Journal of Music Theory* 28/2 (1984), 167–90.

"Composition and Context in Twelve-Note Music of Anton Webern," *Music Analysis* 7/3 (1988), 281–312.

Heinemann, Stephen, "Pitch-Class Set Multiplication in Boulez's *Le Marteau sans maître*" (D.M.A. diss., University of Washington, 1993).

"Pitch-Class Set Multiplication in Theory and Practice," *Music Theory Spectrum* 20/1 (1998), 72–96.

Hogan, Catherine, "Threni: Stravinsky's Debt to Krenek," *Tempo* 141 (1982), 22–29.

Hoogerwerf, F. W., "Tonal and Referential Aspects of the Set in Stravinsky's Septet," *Journal of Musicological Research* 4 (1982), 69–84.

Horgan, Paul, *Encounters with Stravinsky* (New York: Farrar, Straus, Giroux, 1972).

Horlacher, Gretchen, "The Rhythms of Reiteration: Formal Development in Stravinsky's Ostinati," *Music Theory Spectrum* 14/2 (1992), 171–87.

Hyde, Martha, "The Roots of Form in Schoenberg's Sketches," *Journal of Music Theory* 24 (1980), 1–36.

Schoenberg's Twelve-Tone Harmony: The Suite Op. 29 and the Compositional Sketches (Ann Arbor: UMI Research Press, 1982).

"Musical Form and the Development of Schoenberg's Twelve-Tone Method," *Journal of Music Theory* 29 (1985), 85–143.

"Neoclassic and Anachronistic Impulses in Twentieth-Century Music," *Music Theory Spectrum* 18/2 (1996), 200–35.

Imbrie, Andrew, "One Measure of Eternity," *Perspectives of New Music* 9/2–10/1 (1971), 51–57.

Jers, Norbert, *Igor Strawinskys späte Zwölftonwerke (1958–1966)* (Regensburg: Gustav Bosse Verlag, 1976).

Johns, Donald, "An Early Serial Idea of Stravinsky," *Music Review* 23/4 (1962), 305–13.

Johnson, Paul, "Cross-Collectional Techniques of Structure in Stravinsky's Centric Music," in *Stravinsky Retrospectives*, ed. Ethan Haimo and Paul Johnson (Lincoln, Nebr.: University of Nebraska Press, 1987).

Joseph, Charles, "Structural Coherence in Stravinsky's *Piano-Rag Music*," *Music Theory Spectrum* 4 (1982), 76–91.

Keller, Hans, "'In Memoriam Dylan Thomas': Stravinsky's Schoenbergian Technique," *Tempo* 35 (1955), 13–20.

Keller, Hans and Cosman, Milein, *Stravinsky Seen and Heard* (London: Toccata Press, 1982; reprint edn. New York: Da Capo Press, 1986).

Kielian-Gilbert, Marianne, "Relationships of Symmetrical Pitch-Class Sets and Stravinsky's Metaphor of Polarity," *Perspectives of New Music* 21/1–2 (1982–83), 209–40.

"The Rhythms of Form: Correspondence and Analogy in Stravinsky's Designs," *Music Theory Spectrum* 9 (1987), 42.

Koblyakov, Lev, *Pierre Boulez: A World of Harmony* (London and New York: Harwood Academic Publishers, 1990).

Kohl, Jerome, "Exposition in Stravinsky's Orchestral Variations," *Perspectives of New Music* 18/1–2 (1979–80), 391–405.

Kramer, Jonathan, "Moment Form in Twentieth-Century Music," *Musical Quarterly* 64 (1978), 177–94.

"New Temporalities in Music," *Critical Inquiry* 7 (1981), 539–56.

"Discontinuity and Proportion in the Music of Stravinsky," in *Confronting Stravinsky*, ed. Jann Pasler (Berkeley: University of California Press, 1986), 174–94.

The Time of Music: New Meanings, New Temporalities, New Listening Strategies (New York: Schirmer Books, 1998).

Krenek, Ernst, *Studies in Counterpoint Based on the Twelve-Tone Technique* (New York: G. Schirmer, 1940).

"New Developments of the Twelve-Tone Technique," *The Music Review* 4 (1943), 81–97.

"Contribution to Appendix 1," in Josef Rufer, *Composition with Twelve Notes Related Only to One Another*, trans. Humphrey Searle (New York: Macmillan, 1954), 188–91.

"Extents and Limits of Serial Techniques," *Musical Quarterly* 46 (1960), 210–32; reprinted in *Problems of Modern Music*, ed. Paul Henry Lang (New York: Norton, 1960), 72–94.

"Some Current Terms," *Perspectives of New Music* 4 (1966), 81–84.

"A Composer's Memorial," *Perspectives of New Music* 9–10 (1971), 7–9.

Kresky, Jeffrey, "A Study in Analysis" (Ph.D. dissertation, Princeton University, 1974).

Leibowitz, Herbert, ed., *Musical Impressions: Selections from Paul Rosenfeld's Criticism* (New York: Hill and Wang, 1969), 146.

Leibowitz, René, *Schoenberg and His School: The Contemporary Stage of the Language of Music*, trans. Dika Newlin (New York: Philosophical Library, 1949).

Lewin, David, "A Study of Hexachord Levels in Schoenberg's Violin Fantasy," *Perspectives of New Music* 6/1 (1967), 18–32.

"*Moses und Aron*: Some General Remarks, and Analytic Notes for Act I, Scene 1," *Perspectives of New Music* 6/1 (1967), 1–17.

"Inversional Balance as an Organizing Force in Schoenberg's Music and Thought," *Perspectives of New Music* 6/2 (1968), 1–21.

Generalized Musical Intervals and Transformations (New Haven: Yale University Press, 1987).

"Some Ideas about Voice-Leading Between Pcsets," *Journal of Music Theory* 42/1 (1998), 15–72.

Libman, Lillian, *And Music at the Close: Stravinsky's Last Years* (New York: Norton, 1972).

Lourié, Arthur, "Neo-Gothic and Neo-Classic," *Modern Music* 5 (1928), 3–8.

Mason, Colin, "Stravinsky's Newest Works," *Tempo* 53–54 (1960), 2–10.

"Serial Procedures in the Ricercar II of Stravinsky's Cantata," *Tempo* 61–62 (1962), 6–9.

Mead, Andrew, "Webern, Tradition, and 'Composing with Twelve Tones,'" *Music Theory Spectrum* 15/2 (1993), 173–204.

The Music of Milton Babbitt (Princeton: Princeton University Press, 1994).

Mellers, Wilfrid, "Stravinsky's Oedipus as 20th-Century Hero," in *Stravinsky: A New Appraisal of His Work*, ed. Paul Henry Lang (New York: Norton, 1963), 34–46.

Messing, Scott, *Neoclassicism in Music: From the Genesis of the Concept Through the Schoenberg/Stravinsky Polemic* (Ann Arbor: UMI Research Press, 1988).

Mori, Akane, "Proportional Construction in Relation to Formal Process in the Early Serial Music of Igor Stravinsky" (Ph.D. dissertation, Yale University, 1989).

"Proportional Exchange in Stravinsky's Early Serial Music," *Journal of Music Theory* 41/2 (1997), 227–60.

Morris, Robert, "Generalizing Rotational Arrays," *Journal of Music Theory* 32/1 (1988), 75–132.

"New Directions in the Theory and Analysis of Musical Contour," *Music Theory Spectrum* 15/2 (1993), 205–28.

Morton, Lawrence, "Current Chronicle," *Musical Quarterly* 40/4 (1954), 573–75.

"Stravinsky at Home," in *Confronting Stravinsky*, ed. Jann Pasler (Berkeley: University of California Press, 1986), 332–48.

Moss, Lawrence, "The Princeton Seminar in Advanced Musical Studies," *The Score* 26 (1960), 67–69.

Müller, Alfred, "Igor Stravinsky: Movements for Piano and Orchestra," *Melos* 46/2 (1984), 112–42.

Nabokov, Nicholas, *Old Friends and New Music* (London: Hamish Hamilton, 1951).

Neff, Severine, "Schoenberg and Goethe: Organicism and Analysis," in *Music Theory and the Exploration of the Past*, ed. Christopher Hatch and David W. Bernstein (Chicago: University of Chicago Press, 1993).

Neidhofer, Christoph, "Analysearbeit im Fach Komposition/Musiktheorie über die Movements for Piano and Orchestra von Igor Strawinsky" (Master's thesis, Musik-Akademie der Stadt Basel, 1991).

"An Approach to Interrelating Counterpoint and Serialism in the Music of Igor Stravinsky, Focusing on the Principal Diatonic Works of his Transitional Period" (Ph.D. dissertation, Harvard University, 1999).

O'Donnell, Shaugn, "Transformational Voice Leading in Atonal Music" (Ph.D. dissertation, City University of New York, 1997).

Payne, Anthony, "Stravinsky's *The Flood*," *Tempo* 70 (1964), 2–8.

"Two New Stravinsky Works (*Abraham and Isaac* and *Elegy for J. F. K.*)," *Tempo* 73 (1965), 12–15.

"Stravinsky's Chords (I)," *Tempo* 76 (1966), 6–12 and "Stravinsky's Chords (II)," *Tempo* 77 (1966), 2–9.

"Stravinsky's *Requiem Canticles*," *Tempo* 81 (1967), 10–19.

Perle, George, "Evolution of the Tone Row: The Twelve-Tone Modal System," *Music Review* 2 (1941), 273–87.

"The Harmonic Problem in Twelve-Tone Music," *The Music Review* 15 (1954), 257–67.

Serial Composition and Atonality (5th edn. Berkeley: University of California Press, 1981).

"Composing with Symmetries," in *The Listening Composer* (Berkeley: University of California Press, 1990), 123–70.

Perry, Jeffrey, "A 'Requiem for the Requiem': On Stravinsky's *Requiem Canticles*," *College Music Symposium* 33/34 (1993/94), 237–57.

Peyser, Joan, "Stravinsky–Craft, Inc.," *American Scholar* 52 (1983), 513–18.

Phillips, Paul, "The Enigma of Variations: A Study of Stravinsky's Final Work for Orchestra," *Music Analysis* 3/1 (1984), 69–89.

Pousseur, Henri, "Stravinsky by Way of Webern," *Perspectives of New Music* 10/2 (1972), 13–51 and 11/1 (1972), 112–45.

Ramuz, C. F., *Souvenirs sur Igor Stravinsky* (Lausanne: Mermod, 1946).

Rehding, Alexander, "Towards A 'Logic of Discontinuity' in Stravinsky's *Symphonies of Wind Instruments*: Hasty, Kramer and Straus Reconsidered," *Music Analysis* 17/1 (1998), 39–65.

Rogers, John, "Some Properties of Non-duplicating Rotational Arrays," *Perspectives of New Music* 7/1 (1968), 80–102.

Rogers, Lynne, "Dissociation in Stravinsky's Russian and Neoclassical Music," *International Journal of Musicology* 1 (1992), 201–28.

"Stravinsky's Break with Contrapuntal Tradition: A Sketch Study," *The Journal of Musicology* 13/4 (1995), 476–507.

"Rethinking Form: Stravinsky's Eleventh-Hour Revision of the Third Movement of His Violin Concerto," *The Journal of Musicology* 17/2 (1999), 272–303.

"Stravinsky's Serial Counterpoint and the Voice of God," paper presented to the Society for Music Theory, Atlanta, 1999.

Rust, Douglas, "Stravinsky's Twelve-Tone Loom: Composition and Precomposition in *Movements*," *Music Theory Spectrum* 16/1 (1994), 62–76.

Salzman, Eric, "Current Chronicle: Princeton," *Musical Quarterly* 53 (1967), 80–86.

Schoenberg, Arnold, *Theory of Harmony*, trans. Roy Carter (Berkeley: University of California Press, 1978).

Searle, Humphrey, "Webern's Last Works," *The Monthly Musical Record* 76 (1946), 231–37.

Smyth, David, "Stravinsky at the Threshold: A Sketch Leaf for *Canticum Sacrum*," *Mitteilungen der Paul Sacher Stiftung* 10 (1997), 21–26.

"Stravinsky's Second Crisis: Reading the Early Serial Sketches," Paper presented to the conference of the Society for Music Theory, Phoenix, 1997.

"Stravinsky as Serialist: the Sketches for *Threni*," unpublished paper.

Somfai, Laszlo, "Sprache, Wort und Phonem im vokalen Spätwerk Strawinskys," in *Über Musik und Sprache*, ed. Rudolf Stephan (Mainz: Schott, 1974), 34–44.

Souvtchinsky, Pierre, "Thoughts on Stravinsky's *Requiem Canticles*," *Tempo* 86 (1968), 6–7.

Spies, Claudio, "Some Notes on Stravinsky's *Abraham and Isaac*," *Perspectives of New Music* 3/2 (1965), 104–26; reprinted in *Perspectives on Schoenberg and Stravinsky*, ed. Benjamin Boretz and Edward Cone (Princeton: Princeton University Press, 1968), 186–209.

"Some Notes on Stravinsky's *Variations*," *Perspectives of New Music* 4/1 (1965), 62–74; reprinted in *Perspectives on Schoenberg and Stravinsky*, ed. Benjamin Boretz and Edward Cone (Princeton: Princeton University Press, 1968), 210–22.

"Some Notes on Stravinsky's Requiem Settings," *Perspectives of New Music* 5/2 (1967), 98–123; reprinted in *Perspectives on Schoenberg and Stravinsky*, ed. Benjamin Boretz and Edward Cone (Princeton: Princeton University Press, 1968), 223–50.

"Impressions after an Exhibition," *Tempo* 102 (1972), 2–9.

Stein, Erwin, "Stravinsky's Septet (1953): An Analysis," *Tempo* 31 (1954), 7–10.

"Igor Stravinsky: *Canticum Sacrum Ad Honorem Sancti Marci Nominis*," *Tempo* 40 (1956), 3–5.

Stein, Leonard, "Schoenberg and 'Kleine Modernsky,'" in *Confronting Stravinsky*, ed. Jann Pasler (Berkeley: University of California Press, 1986), 310–24.

Straus, Joseph, "A Principle of Voice Leading in the Music of Stravinsky," *Music Theory Spectrum* 4 (1982), 106–24.

"Stravinsky's Tonal Axis," *Journal of Music Theory* 26/2 (1982), 61–290.

"Recompositions by Schoenberg, Stravinsky, and Webern," *Musical Quarterly* 72 (1986), 301–28.

"The Problem of Coherence in Stravinsky's Serenade in A," *Theory and Practice* 12 (1987), 3–10.

"The Progress of a Motive in Stravinsky's The Rake's Progress," *Journal of Musicology* 9/2 (1991), 165–85.

"Two 'Mistakes' in Stravinsky's *Introitus*," *Mitteilungen der Paul Sacher Stiftung* 4 (1991), 34–36.

"A Theory of Voice Leading for Atonal Music," in *Music Theory in Concept and Practice*, ed. James Baker, David Beach, and Jonathan Bernard (Rochester: University of Rochester Press, 1997), 237–74.

"A Strategy of Large-Scale Organization in the Late Music of Stravinsky," *Integral* 11 (1999), 1–36.

"Babbitt and Stravinsky under the Serial 'Regime,'" *Perspectives of New Music* 35/2 (1999), 17–32.

"Stravinsky's 'Construction of Twelve Verticals': An Aspect of Harmony in the Late Music," *Music Theory Spectrum* 21/1 (1999), 43–73.

"Stravinsky's Serial 'Mistakes,'" *The Journal of Musicology* 17/2 (1999), 231–71.

"The Myth of Serial 'Tyranny' in the 1950's and 1960's," *The Musical Quarterly* 83/3 (1999), 301–43.

Introduction to Post-Tonal Theory, 2nd edn. (Upper Saddle River, NJ: Prentice-Hall, 2000).

Stravinsky, Igor, *An Autobiography* (New York: Norton, 1962); originally published as *Chroniques de ma vie* (Paris: Denoel & Steele, 1935–36).

Poetics of Music in the Form of Six Lessons, trans. Arthur Knodel and Ingolf Dahl (Cambridge, Mass.: Harvard University Press, 1970).

Stravinsky, Igor and Craft, Robert, "Answers to 34 Questions: An Interview with Igor Stravinsky," *Encounter* 9/7 (1957), 3–14.

Conversations with Igor Stravinsky (New York: Doubleday, 1959; reprint edn. Berkeley: University of California Press, 1980).

Memories and Commentaries (New York: Doubleday, 1960; reprint edn. Berkeley: University of California Press, 1981).

Expositions and Developments (New York: Doubleday, 1962; reprint edn. Berkeley: University of California Press, 1981).

Dialogues and A Diary (New York: Doubleday, 1963).

Themes and Episodes (New York: Alfred A. Knopf, 1966).

Retrospectives and Conclusions (New York: Alfred A. Knopf, 1969).

Dialogues (London: Faber and Faber, 1982; Berkeley: University of California Press, 1982).

Themes and Conclusions (Berkeley: University of California Press, 1982).

Strawinsky: sein Nachlass, sein Bild, ed. Hans Jörg Jans and Christian Geelhaar (Basel: Kunstmuseum, 1984).

Stuart, Philip, *Igor Stravinsky – The Composer in the Recording Studio: A Comprehensive Discography* (New York: Greenwood, 1991).

Takaoka, Akira, "Stravinsky's Twelve-Tone Music: Some Principles of Atonal Pitch Organization" (Ph.D. dissertation, Columbia University, 1999).

Taruskin, Richard, "Chernomor to Kaschei: Harmonic Sorcery; or, Stravinsky's 'Angle,'" *Journal of the American Musicological Society* 38 (1985), 72–142.

"*Chez Petrouchka*: Harmony and Tonality *chez* Stravinsky," *19th-Century Music* 10 (1987), 265–86.

"Stravinsky's 'Rejoicing Discovery' and What it Meant: In Defense of His Notorious Text Setting," in *Stravinsky Retrospectives*, ed. Ethan Haimo and Paul Johnson (Lincoln, Nebr.: University of Nebraska Press, 1987), 162–99.

"Back to Whom? Neoclassicism as Ideology," *19th-Century Music* 16 (1993), 286–302.

"The Traditions Revisited: Stravinsky's Requiem Canticles as Russian Music," *Music Theory and the Exploration of the Past*, ed. Christopher Hatch and David W. Bernstein (Chicago: University of Chicago Press, 1993), 525–50.

Stravinsky and the Russian Traditions (Berkeley: University of California Press, 1996).

Defining Russia Musically: Historical and Hermeneutical Essays (Princeton: Princeton University Press, 1997).

Taruskin, Richard and Craft, Robert, "Jews and Geniuses: An Exchange," *New York Review of Books*, June 15, 1989, 57–58.

Tucker, Susannah, "Stravinsky and His Sketches: The Composing of *Agon* and Other Serial Works of the 1950s" (D. Phil. dissertation, Oxford University, 1992).

van den Toorn, Pieter, "Some Characteristics of Stravinsky's Diatonic Music," *Perspectives of New Music* 14/1 (1975), 104–38 and 15/2 (1977), 58–96.

The Music of Igor Stravinsky (New Haven: Yale University Press, 1983).

"Octatonic Pitch Structure in Stravinsky," in *Confronting Stravinsky*, ed. Jann Pasler (Berkeley: University of California Press, 1986), 130–56.

Stravinsky and the Rite of Spring: The Beginnings of a Musical Language (Berkeley: University of California Press, 1987).

"Stravinsky Re-Barred," *Music Analysis* 7/2 (1988), 165–96.

"Neoclassicism Revised," *Music, Politics, and the Academy* (Berkeley: University of California Press, 1995), 143–78.

"Neoclassicism and Its Definitions," in *Music Theory in Concept and Practice*, ed. James Baker, David Beach, and Jonathan Bernard (Rochester: University of Rochester Press, 1997), 131–56.

Walden, William, "Stravinsky's Movements for Piano and Orchestra: The Relationship of Formal Structure, Serial Technique, and Orchestration," *Journal of the Canadian Association of University Schools of Music* 9/1 (1979), 73–95.

Walsh, Stephen, *The Music of Stravinsky* (London: Routledge, 1988).

"Stravinsky's Symphonies: Accident or Design?" in *Analytical Strategies and Musical Interpretation: Essays on Nineteenth- and Twentieth-Century Music*, ed. Craig Ayrey and Mark Everist (Cambridge: Cambridge University Press, 1996), 35–71.

Stravinsky, A Creative Spring: Russia and France, 1882–1934 (New York: Alfred A. Knopf, 1999).

Ward-Steinman, David, "Serial Techniques in the Recent Music of Igor Stravinsky" (Ph.D. dissertation, University of Illinois, 1961).

Watkins, Glenn, "The Canon and Stravinsky's Late Style," in *Confronting Stravinsky*, ed. Jann Pasler (Berkeley: University of California Press, 1986), 217–46.

Pyramids at the Louvre (Cambridge, Mass.: Harvard University Press, 1994).

White, Eric Walter, *Stravinsky: The Composer and His Works* (Berkeley: University of California Press, 1966; revised edn. London: Faber and Faber, 1979).

Whittall, Arnold, "Thematicism in Stravinsky's *Abraham and Isaac*," *Tempo* 89 (1969), 12–16.

"Music Analysis as Human Science? *Le Sacre du Printemps* in Theory and Practice," *Music Analysis* 1 (1982), 33–53.

"The Theorist's Sense of History: Concepts of Contemporaneity in Composition and Analysis," *Proceedings of the Royal Musical Association* 112/1 (1986–87), 1–20.

"Review-Survey: Some Recent Writings on Stravinsky," *Music Analysis* 8 (1989), 169–76.

Wiens, Carl, "Igor Stravinsky and 'Agon'" (Ph.D. dissertation, University of Michigan, 1997).

Wolterink, Charles, "Harmonic Structure and Organization in the Early Serial Works of Igor Stravinsky, 1952–57" (Ph.D. dissertation, Stanford, 1979).

Wuorinen, Charles, *Simple Composition* (New York: Longman, 1979).

Wuorinen, Charles and Kresky, Jeffrey, "On the Significance of Stravinsky's Last Works," in *Confronting Stravinsky*, ed. Jann Pasler (Berkeley: University of California Press, 1986), 262–70.

INDEX

A as love's garden, 186, 193–202
associative harmony, 141–43, 175

Babbitt, Milton, 35–38, 74
bells, 52, 186, 203, 208–14, 244
Bloom, Harold, 11
Boulez, Pierre, 33–35

cadential sonorities, 119, 121–24, 143–45, 191,
    194, 210
canon, 22, 39, 99, 106, 115, 152–58, 186,
    219–21, 238–39
centricity (see also tonal focus), 38, 70, 243
chorales, 19, 137–39, 148, 164–65, 186, 203,
    214–19, 231, 243–44
codas, 139, 187, 231–37, 238–42
common-tone linkage, 59–60, 67–70, 94n., 107
"composing with intervals," 91, 141
contrapuntal approach to composition, 48, 54,
    61, 113–20, 141
Craft, Robert, 3, 6–8
cutting and pasting passages, 43, 51, 61–63, 70

diatonicism, 15–18, 23, 32, 143, 157, 224–28,
    238
diatonic vs. chromatic, 186, 214, 221–28,
    246–48

E to D, 186–93, 239

F as emblem of death, 186, 202–08, 243–46
four-part arrays, 36, 165–81, 214–19, 243

hexachordal combinatoriality, 20–21, 119

interval cycle, 99, 131, 168–74, 224–28, 246–48
inversional balance, 22, 49–52, 53, 90–91, 92,
    94, 95–99, 107–17, 145, 152–58, 163,

165–68, 188, 193–97, 214, 228, 231, 238,
    243
inversional pairing of rows (two-part array), 59,
    95–99, 119, 165, 178
isomorphic partitioning, 195n.

Krenek, Ernst, 26–33
    Studies in Counterpoint, 26
    rotational arrays, 28–32

linear combination, 103–13

major-minor clash (in A), 193, 195, 200–01

near-transposition, 163

octatonicism, 39, 94

perfect fifth as framing interval, 193, 195, 202,
    206
piano, role in composition, 42–43, 48–49

retrograde symmetry, 92–95, 111, 134–37, 157,
    229–30
RI-chain, 92–95, 107
Rorem, Ned, 33
rotational array (see also verticals), 26–32,
    64–70, 75, 103–07, 149–64, 210, 219,
    244–46

Schoenberg, Arnold, 8–21, 113
    animosity, 8–10
    influence on Stravinsky, 10–11
    Stravinsky's first exposure to, 2–3, 6–7
    WORKS
    Septet-Suite, Op. 29, 11–13
    Wind Quintet, 11, 17
segmental invariance, 94n., 95–102, 115–17

259

self-analysis, 48, 54–61, 67, 71–75, 111, 134, 203
self-borrowing, 86
serial errors, 71–80, 158–64, 165n., 170, 201, 203, 214n., 219n., 246
serial omission, 143n., 179n., 214n.
silence, 187, 231, 238, 243
Spies, Claudio, 35–36, 75–77
Stravinsky, Igor
love of rules, 44–47, 208
pre-serial oeuvre, 38–40, 185
studio, 42–43
stutter, 86–90, 99, 145, 186, 228–31, 238
WORKS
Abraham and Isaac, 86n., 87–90, 90n., 104, 106–07, 130, 145, 152–53, 158, 166, 231, 246n.
Agon, 24–25, 63n., 86n., 90n., 93–95, 107, 117, 131–34, 137n., 143–45, 150, 166, 175–78, 185, 194, 206–07, 220, 221–24, 235–37, 246–48
Anthem, 87, 90n., 141–43
Cantata, 11–15, 23, 54–58, 111–13, 188, 194, 219, 231
Canticum Sacrum, 21n., 58–60, 86n., 87, 90n., 90–91, 93n., 99, 119, 124, 134–37, 148, 185, 194, 219
Double Canon, 83–86, 219
Elegy for J. F. K., 52n., 92, 96n., 103n., 113, 228–29, 246n.
Epitaphium, 61–63, 86n., 99–102, 130–31, 203–06
The Fairy's Kiss, 139n., 235
Fanfare for a New Theater, 90n., 91, 117
Firebird, 221
The Flood, 86n., 90n., 95–99, 103n., 104, 134, 137, 149–50, 152, 152–58, 166, 171–74, 224–28, 238
Greeting Prelude, 220
In Memoriam Dylan Thomas, 58, 74, 94n., 95, 111, 137, 145, 191, 219n.
Introitus, 45–46, 54, 90n., 96n., 115, 139, 153, 158–64, 203–06, 214, 246
Les Noces, 139n., 235
Movements, 28–32, 35–36, 65–70, 86n., 90n., 103n., 124–30, 137, 166, 169–70, 178n., 179–80, 195–97
Octet, 193–94

Oedipus Rex, 185, 193
Orpheus, 63, 187–88
The Owl and the Pussycat, 86n., 90n.
The Rake's Progress, 2–3, 188n., 193, 203, 219n., 221–24, 248
Requiem Canticles, 52n., 70–71, 75–77, 87n., 90n., 104, 107, 139, 145, 152–53, 166, 170–71, 175, 185, 206, 214, 214–19, 235n., 243–48
Septet: I, 87n., 121–22, 131, 137, 237–42; II, 17–18, 86n., 92–93, 150, 166; III, 86n., 134, 137
A Sermon, a Narrative, and a Prayer, 86, 90n., 103–04, 139, 150, 153, 165–70, 178–79, 210–14, 219
Symphonies of Wind Instruments, 63n., 202–03, 214
Symphony in C, 139n., 231n., 235
Symphony in Three Movements, 185
Symphony of Psalms, 193, 219n., 235
Three Songs From William Shakespeare: "Musick to heare," 94n., 122–24; "Full fadom five," 52–54, 86n., 95, 115, 210, 224, 238, 246
Threni, 28, 34, 86n., 124n., 134n., 166, 174, 219
Variations, 87n., 104, 137, 153, 197–201, 214

Taruskin, Richard, 36–37, 39, 183, 185, 221
text setting, 45–47, 107
thematic character of row, 15, 60
tonal focus, 13, 18, 193–97, 202–06, 238–46
"tonic area" of rows, 10–13, 17
total serialism, 33
twist motive, 90–92, 95, 115, 124

van den Toorn, Pieter, 39
verticalization of series segments, 148–52
verticals (from rotational arrays), 65, 75–76, 137, 152–64, 199–200, 214–19
voice-leading, 145, 150, 158, 163, 174–75, 210

Webern, Anton, 21–26
influence on Stravinsky, 22, 60
Stravinsky's first exposure to, 2–3, 6–7
WORKS
Quartet, Op. 22, 22–23
Variations for Orchestra, Op. 30, 23–25
wedge (linear shape), 49, 53, 91, 95, 115